LITERATURE, SCIENCE, AND
A NEW HUMANITIES

Cognitive Studies in Literature
and Performance

Literature, Science, and a New Humanities
Jonathan Gottschall

Literature, Science, and a New Humanities

Jonathan Gottschall

palgrave
macmillan

First published in 2008 by
PALGRAVE MACMILLAN®
in the US—a division of St. Martin's Press LLC,
175 Fifth Avenue, New York, NY 10010.

Where this book is distributed in the UK, Europe and the rest of the world,
this is by Palgrave Macmillan, a division of Macmillan Publishers Limited,
registered in England, company number 785998, of Houndmills,
Basingstoke, Hampshire RG21 6XS.

Palgrave Macmillan is the global academic imprint of the above companies
and has companies and representatives throughout the world.

Palgrave® and Macmillan® are registered trademarks in the United States,
the United Kingdom, Europe and other countries.

ISBN-13: 978–0–230–60903–7 paperback
ISBN-10: 0–230–60903–1 paperback
ISBN-13: 978–0–230–60901–3 hardcover
ISBN-10: 0–230–60901–5 hardcover

Library of Congress Cataloging-in-Publication Data

Gottschall, Jonathan.
    Literature, science, and a new humanities / Jonathan Gottschall.
        p. cm.—(Cognitive studies in literature and performance)
        ISBN 0–230–60901–5—0–230–60903–1
            1. Literature and science. 2. Literature—Study and teaching (Higher)
    3. Literature—History and criticism—Theory, etc. I. Title.

PN55.G68 2008
801'.95—dc22   2008007261

A catalogue record of the book is available from the British Library.

Design by Newgen Imaging Systems (P) Ltd., Chennai, India.

First edition: October 2008

10 9 8 7 6 5 4 3 2 1

To Tiffani, Abigail, Annabel and to Jon, Marcia,
Deidre, Richard, Robert, David

I'm sufficiently liberal, I should assume, toward the claims of science, but with a man like Gottlieb—I'm prepared to believe that he knows all about material forces, but what astounds me is that such a man can be blind to the vital force that creates all the others. He says that knowledge is worthless unless it is proven by rows of figures. Well, when one of you scientific sharks can take the genius of a Ben Jonson and measure it with a yardstick, then I'll admit we literary chaps, with our doubtless absurd belief in beauty, loyalty and the world o' dreams, are off on the wrong track!

(English Professor Dr. Brumfit describing the bacteriologist, Dr. Gottleib, in Sinclair Lewis's *Arrowsmith*)

Contents

CONTENTS

Tables

Preface

It's not such a good time to be a literary scholar.

In April 2003 the brightest stars in the literary studies firmament were beaming on the campus of the University of Chicago (see Mitchell 2004). The editorial board of the premier journal of criticism and theory, *Critical Inquiry,* had convened in a packed hall to debate the uncertain future of the journal and the broader humanities. There sat the reader response theorist and all-around gadfly Stanley Fish, there was the Harvard postcolonialist Homi Bhaba, there was the arch-deconstructionist Hillis Miller, and there loomed Frederick Jameson, American patriarch of Marxist literary theory.

They had come together to strategize about the future of the journal and about a larger crisis in the humanities—a sickening sense that the whole enterprise is in slow, sure, and perhaps inexorable decline. Almost all of the worthies agreed that the humanities were in crisis or, at the least, mired in a thick malaise, but there was no agreement on prescriptions for change.

In this and other discussions of the crisis in the humanities, the yardstick of success was provided, explicitly or implicitly, by the sciences. If the humanities have plummeted in prestige, funding, and public interest, the drop seems all the more vertiginous given the soaring stock of the sciences. But while the ruddy good health of the sciences was contrasted to the anemia of the humanities, no attendee asked these obvious questions, "What exactly are the sciences doing so right that we are doing so wrong?" And, "Can we emulate it?"

Literature, Science, and a New Humanities poses precisely these questions and it purposes to give answers. I argue that the current aimlessness and low morale in many provinces of the humanities (but especially in the field of literary studies where I focus my arguments) derive primarily from one inescapable truth: In contrast to the gradual, halting, yet undeniable progress of scientific knowledge, literary scholars rarely produce knowledge that can withstand the critiques of the next generation. Literary study is not, in the main, a progressive discipline where the space of possible explanation is gradually narrowed. But it can be. We can accumulate progressively more reliable and durable knowledge—but only if we move closer to the sciences.

This solution may nauseate some of my colleagues. What am I saying? That we should succumb to a groveling science-envy? That we should abandon humanistic values and turn literature into a branch of the sciences? That we should dash down our dusty tomes and make haste to the lab coat store? No, no, and no. I'm only pointing out that the sciences are doing many things better than we are, and that we can gain from studying their successes without degrading any of the things that make literature special. And I'm claiming one thing more. The alternative is to let literature study keep spinning off into a corner of irrelevance to die.

This book is a call for upheaval; for new theory, method, and ethos; for paradigm shift.

Acknowledgments

The case studies of Part II are end results of an extraordinary teaching and research opportunity I experienced at St. Lawrence University (Canton, NY). I was an instructor in a general education program that introduced undergraduates to the processes of academic research. Within the broad goals of the program, teachers were given much freedom to devise interesting and unconventional offerings. The courses I taught from 2001 to 2005 were organized around the theme of *Generating Knowledge*. Here is a snippet of course description:

> This seminar is about the process by which scholars and scientists generate new knowledge—from the first recognition of a problem that needs to be solved all the way up to the publication of an explanation for the problem. Seminar participants will experience an "on the job" education in this process as they play their parts in large-scale, empirical research projects in literature and psychology. As members of research teams we will define our topics, research them, gather data about them, analyze the data, and write up our conclusions. The ambitious goal of this seminar is nothing less than to generate new knowledge and to formally disseminate this knowledge both at an academic conference and in publishable articles.

These courses were experiments in a hypertrophied version of the "participatory" pedagogical model, in which students in a "decentered" classroom learn through active discussion and other collaborative activities rather than through traditional means like lectures and note taking. It is well appreciated that much original scientific research is produced through intense collaboration between professors and their students, graduate and undergraduate. But we may forget that this is as much a successful pedagogical model as it is a successful research model: scientists believe that students learn most and best about science by actually *doing* it. The research seminars that would ultimately produce the papers of Part II were designed to explore if, and how, this model might be applied in humanities "labs."

I'm proud of my students and of our results. They include more than twenty coauthored papers and presentations in the journals and conferences of several disciplines (see Works Cited for a partial listing). Moreover, I believe that the students learned more by *doing* this work—about the narrow literatures of specific research areas, about broad theory and method in the humanities and sciences, about the frustration and exhilaration of knowledge generation—than they could likely have absorbed in a traditionally structured course.

The Saint Lawrence seminars received unstinting support from Dean Grant Cornwell and, especially, Assistant Dean Steven Horwitz. Steve was a stalwart supporter of our projects from the start, and both administrators ensured that we had access to all necessary resources (financial, institutional, technological). I am grateful to other faculty members at St. Lawrence, especially Robin Lock (Statistics) and Alan Searleman (Psychology), both of whom provided consultation on statistical matters. Like these professors, John Johnson (Penn State University) generously lent us the benefit of specialized statistical expertise.

Dana Anderson, Brian Boyd, Joseph Carroll, Frederick Crews, Marcia Gottschall, Jon Gottschall, David Michelson, Bruce McConachie, Marcus Nordlund, Steven Pinker, and Blakey Vermeule read drafts of this book. I am grateful for their patience and for their sound practical advice. I owe the greatest debt of all to my dozens of undergraduate collaborators at St. Lawrence University. Without their diligent efforts there would simply be no book.

Their names are Elizabeth Allison, Kacey Anderson, Rachel Berkey, Liana Boop, Lance Branch, Chad Burbank, Jasper Burch, Chelsea Byrnes, Peter Cahill, Christine Callanan, Keith Carpentier, Nicole Casamento, Mitch Cawson, Daniel DeLorme, Jason DeRosa, Carly Drown, Mackenzie Ewing, Matthew Fleischner, John Forrette, Jared Fostveit, Amy Gardiner, Natalie Gladd, Melissa Glotzbecker, Erica Guralnick, Allison Hartnett, Elisabeth Henry, Eloise Hilarides, Julia Jones, Kimberly Kernan, Kaia Klockeman, Chelsea Lemke, Sarah MacFarland, Tyler Magnan, Kristen Manganini, Johanna Martin, John Masland, Sara Merrihew, Tanya Milan-Robertson, Jessica Mott, Maia Moyer, Kate Muse, Patrick O'Connell, Kevin O'Connor, Celeste Ogburn, Spencer Paige, Jonathan Pakan, Kimberly Parker, Stephen Patterson, Hadley Quish, Jonathan Rea, Karlin Revoir, Nathan Riley, Trisha Ritchie, Darcie Robinson, Sheila Rodriguez, Ann Sargent, Chelsea Sauve, Christopher Skeels, Linnea Smolentzov, April Spearance, Stephanie St. Joseph, Michael Stafford, Valerie Stucker, Adam Tapply, Lindsey Taylor, Sammie-Jo Therrien,

Alexa Unser, Christopher Wall, Alexis Webb, Shawna Weeks, Erin Welch, Alison Welsh, and Melinda Zocco.

Finally, I would like to thank the several editors and publishers who have allowed me to include previously published material in this volume. I would like to thank the editor of *Evolutionary Psychology* for permission to include material from my article (with contributions from St. Lawrence University students) "The Heroine with a Thousand Faces: Universal Trends in the Characterization of Female Folk Tale Protagonists" (2005) volume 3, pages 85–103. I would like to thank Northwestern University Press for permission to include material from my article, "Quantitative Literary Study: A Modest Manifesto and Testing the Hypotheses of Feminist Fairy Tale Studies," which appeared in the edited collection *The Literary Animal: Evolution and the Nature of Narrative* (2005), edited by Jonathan Gottschall and David Sloan Wilson. I would like to thank Springer Science and Business Media for permission to include material from my article (with contributions from St. Lawrence University students), "The Beauty Myth is no Myth: Emphasis on Male–Female Attractiveness in World Folktales," which was published in the journal *Human Nature* (2008) volume 19, pages 174–188. I would like to thank the editor of *Philosophy and Literature* for permission to include material from my article (coauthored with Marcus Nordlund, and with contributions from St. Lawrence University students), "Romantic Love: A Literary Universal?" (2006) volume 20, pages 432–452.

*   *   *

It is a convention of the acknowledgments genre that a writer should, having copiously thanked his benefactors for their contributions, close by absolving them for the book's shortcomings. In the present case, however, stressing my personal responsibility is not a *pro forma* exercise. This book operates in politically sensitive territory and its total message is certain to be controversial. There are many in my intended audience who will feel queasy, or personally outraged, by my diagnosis of maladies in literary academia, by my prescriptions for change, or by my mustering of illustrative case studies. The students who contributed to the case studies of Part II helped shape the conclusions of those chapters; they mulled with me, long and hard, over the meaning of our results, and those deliberations are reflected in the case studies. However, the original inspiration for the studies, the choice of questions to be addressed, the specific study protocols, the ultimate decisions about interpretations of results, and the final compositional efforts were mine alone. Further, while I received copious support from colleagues and friends, this reflects their common commitment to free inquiry and their inability to resist importunate pleas for help, not their endorsement of any claim of this book. I acknowledge *Literature, Science, and a New Humanities* as my baby, and I am responsible for her, flaws and all.

Introduction: Shrinking Possibility Space

People agree that the academic field of literary studies is in trouble. Writers in the venerable "crisis in the humanities" genre—of which I am now one—fret over some of the following indicators. Decades of downward trends in undergraduate humanities enrollees and majors mean that the humanities generally, and literary study specifically, "have become a less and less significant part of higher education" (Kernan 1997, 5). Funding trends among private and public subsidizers show that "people, including Congress, think of the humanities as increasingly marginal contributors to the sum of knowledge and the well-being of society" (Kernan 1997, 5). In fact, systematic "disinvestment in the humanities" means that higher education is going through a decades-long phase of "dehumanization" (Engell and Dangerfield 1998, 111). As humanities enrollments have fallen and professorial jobs have evaporated, the production of new PhDs has not fallen apace, producing yearning masses of adjunct working poor (see Stanton et al., 2007). At the same time, the cultural prestige of the humanities is undergoing "momentous decline" (Hunt 1997, 17). In literary study, things may be worst of all. It seems that literary scholars are to be the laughingstocks of the academic world (see Delbanco 1999, 32; Patai and Corrall 2005b, 18; Oakley 1997, 67). We are savagely parodied in academic novels, humiliated by hoaxers, and held up to ridicule by satirical journalists, who richly feast themselves at the discipline's main conferences. This is all revenge for our perceived pretentiousness, for the impenetrability of our verbiage, for our unearned moral vanity, and for our apparent contempt for reality.

While fewer students hear us in the classroom, far fewer still can be bothered to read what we write. If you visit your local mega bookstore you will probably find, as I have, shelves groaning under the weight of serious yet lively books about biology, political theory, physics, history, economics (economics!), religion, mathematics, and so on that are pitched to the interests of intelligent lay readers. Yet, Harold Bloom's prodigious output aside, successful trade books in literary study are few and far between. The whole Literary Studies section at my local megastore consists of a single eight-foot length of shelving, and most of that consists of reference work and the sprawling corpus of Harold Bloom.

This is obviously not because people have lost interest in literature. My local megastore stocks an impressive array of contemporary literary fiction, the whole range of canonical classics, and tons of genre stuff. People still take great satisfaction in reading; they just don't need academics mediating between them and their texts of choice. While this failure to connect to the public at large is worrying, an even more alarming and poignant indicator of the current troubles is our increasing inability to communicate with each other. Life in the profession of letters is complicated by soaring publishing demands (one harvest of the runaway buyer's market for professorial labor) and a concomitant publishing "crisis" in which academic presses are slashing production of books and journals. There are several important reasons for the cutbacks, but they all come down to the bottom line: books about literature are very likely to lose money because consumers, including academic consumers, are not interested in reading them (Stanton et al. 2007; Harpham 2005a, 388; Greenblatt 2003). This situation—"a piling up of books [and articles] that hardly anybody reads" (Kermode 2005, 613)—is palpably absurd. The field has reached the point where even literary scholars are increasingly indifferent to one another's production.

Given these and other indicators (for data-based summaries of all the gloomy trends, see Stanton et al., 2007; Engell and Dangerfield 1998; Kernan 1997; for further references see footnote on page 6), there is remarkably strong agreement among all the squabbling tribes of literary critics and theorists that the field is floundering, aimless, and increasingly irrelevant to the live concerns not only of the "outside world" but also to the world *inside* the ivory tower. Many have gone so far as to say, in hope or in dread, that the discipline is in the midst of an extinction event—that it is nearing its twilight, its death, or its abolition. Jeremiads, obituaries, threnodies, and eschatological meditations abound. Not everyone thinks we are living at the end of days (and these writers are more likely to describe the "crisis" as a "malaise"), but almost everyone seems to agree that the field has "lost a sense of purpose" (Appiah 2005, 447), "has run out of steam" (Latour 2004), "has lost its authority" (Menand 1997, 201), is "uncertain of its role" (Macey 2000, v), is "desperate for a rationale" (Cunningham 2005, 24; see also Menand 2001 on the "crisis of rationale"), and is suffering "an epochal loss of confidence" (Deresiewicz 2008); almost everyone seems to agree that all of the trends are bad and that deep change is urgently required. But there is far less agreement on root causes and the most hopeful prescriptions for change.

* * *

This book locates the source of the current troubles not in the surface phenomena that have milked pure vitriol from polemicists, like jargon-clotted language or extremes of political correctness. Rather it identifies deep, elementary weaknesses in the theories that guide literary investigation, in the methods used to explore and validate hypotheses, and in certain prominent attitudinal constellations. In other words, the prognosis is bad: the primary theoretical, methodological, and attitudinal struts that support the field are suffering pervasive rot. If the discipline of literary study ultimately collapses, it will be because of the rot in these primary struts.

This book does not and cannot prescribe a panacea for these ills, but its ambitions are high. It seeks to sketch rough outlines of a new paradigm in the study of literature. It seeks to show how literary analysis can be founded on theoretical, methodological, and attitudinal struts that are strong, and driven in bedrock. The message, which will soon be given at length, can first be given in short: Literary studies should move closer to the sciences in theory, method, and governing ethos. In the long view, this scientific turn represents the only responsible and attractive correction of course—the only correction with the potential to lift the field from its morass. What I am finally proposing is a bold experiment that, like any experiment, is worth doing only because it might fail.

The Liberationist Paradigm

English established itself as a formal academic discipline little more than a century ago, and throughout this time it has suffered painful anxieties about its *raison d'etre*. In a world of viciousness and lack, of epochal scientific discovery, how can the literary scholar *possibly* justify (excuse?)

4   LITERATURE, SCIENCE, AND A NEW HUMANITIES

a (usually) impressionistic study of the landscape of make believe? Is it by initiating students into the priceless expansions of attentive and sensitive reading? Is it by providing a criticism of the culture as a whole, partly as a means of producing raw material for creative artists? Is it by making valuable and durable contributions to human knowledge for its own sake? Is it by transforming drawing room natter about stories and poems into an autonomous and rigorous science of the forms, themes, and deep structures of literature? Is it by using literature as a vehicle for advancing political and social goals that the critic holds dear? Is it through good stewardship of culture's sublimest monuments?

While the list of possibilities could be extended, the point is clear: the conscience of the field has been hounded by hard questions about utility; scholars have expended a lot of time, anxiety and ink trying to produce a satisfying and self-justifying response.

What use are literary scholars? Beginning in the late 1960s, and especially since around 1980, many literary scholars have envisioned themselves striding in the vanguard of noble movements of social liberation and transformation. Drawing energy and impetus from the great emancipation movements of the1960s and 1970s, from the radical epistemology of post-structuralism, and from immediate catalysts like the Vietnam War and the student uprisings of 1968, literary scholars embarked upon a great project of *denaturalization*. They set out to show that almost everything that people considered to be "natural"—gender roles, sexual orientations, suites of attitudes, ideologies, and norms—were actually the local, contingent, and endlessly malleable outgrowths of specific historical and social forces. In Roland Barthes sense, they were all "myths," designed to "transform history into nature," to give "a historical intention a natural justification," and therefore to make "contingency appear eternal" (Barthes 1972, 29).

The denaturalization process reached its apogee in concerted efforts to identify—like explorers searching out undiscovered countries, chemists seeking new elements, or biologists hunting up the last undescribed mega fauna—the specific historical provenances of core aspects of human psychological and social life: romantic and parental love, concepts of homosexuality and heterosexuality, the idea of "man" and of childhood, the modern sense of selfhood, not to mention our very ability to *think* about a multitude of specific concepts and ideas (for a large sample of putatively unthinkable thoughts see Levin 2003; see also Headlam Wells 2005). In this respect, I think Frederic Jameson's terse definition of the Postmodernism is very apt: "Postmodernism is what you have when the modernization process is complete and nature is gone for good" (1991, ix).

The liberationists sought to show—sometimes convincingly—that "natural" was simply what privileged men of Western European descent named their artificial and inherently oppressive sociopolitical inventions. The victims of the doctrine of naturalism (and of scion doctrines of essentialism and humanism) were all the "others": the non-male, the nonwhite, the nonhetero, the disabled, the colonized, and all the other huddling subalterns. There was no reference point from which you could judge the "truth" of anything: Objectivity was just a synonym for white male subjectivity (see Gitlin 2005, 404).

Liberationist praxis represented an audacious response to the problem of utility. It was a rebuke to the ivory tower fuddy-duddyism of the historical, philological, and formalist scholars who had dominated academic criticism for most of its history, and it was a repudiation of the psychoanalytic and structuralist dreams of establishing sciences of the literary. In the wake of the great social upheavals of the 1960s and 1970s, sheltering in the cool, echoing halls of academe to ponder, to scrawl, and to shrewdly declaim on the themes, structures, meanings, or historical backgrounds of stories seemed positively indecent—it was to compound key problems instead of working toward their solution. Literary scholars would therefore march with the revolutionaries; they would shout truth to power in the classrooms and in the journals until the hegemons toppled and the masses were free.

The liberationist paradigm has changed over time, mellowing with age. But buzzing rumors of the demise of Theory (which roughly corresponds to what I am calling the liberationist paradigm) are clearly premature. Simply skimming the contents of prominent humanities journals, or the abstracts for the annual convention of the Modern Language Association, is enough to show that this is not the case. On the contrary, variants and offshoots of the liberationist paradigm remain the strongest forces on the contemporary theoretical and critical scene (for similar arguments see Slingerland 2008).

Surely, this paradigm is the furthest thing from an undifferentiated monolith. Not only are there real and deep differences *between* different liberationist schools, but there are also intense debates *within* predominantly Marxist, postcolonial, post-structuralist, new historical, queer, feminist, and psychoanalytic approaches. Indeed, viewed from up close, each school is a zone of pure and often bitter fracas—a zone of faction and fission where aggressive thinkers vie tirelessly for dominance of message. But, for the purposes of this discussion, what is important is not all of the things that divide these tribes (which have been subjects of countless commentaries, in any case), but the things that bind them in confederation. Almost every significant contemporary approach shares some key components (though in different degrees) that typify the liberationist paradigm:

1. Active commitment to achieving radical or progressive political ends *through* scholarly means.
2. A "nurturist" commitment to theories of strong sociocultural constructivism and a rejection of biological "essentialisms."
3. An epistemology strongly influenced by—if not directly based upon—post-structuralist antifoundationalism.

Yet for all of its staying power there remains a broad feeling that this movement in libratory scholarship has finally exhausted its force. There is a nervous sense that prime tenets of post-structuralism—which once seemed startlingly radical—amount to the endlessly rococo embellishments of a great banality: we can't be completely sure of anything. There is a feeling that scholars have gone much too far in reducing literary works to the power plays of the weak and strong, to "reading until you find the victim" or "reading for evil." As Robert Scholes, a recent president of the Modern Language Association, ruefully quips (2005), the urgent question now seems to be "wither, or whither"? That is, Scholes suggests, the academic study of literature will continue to wither away—perhaps deservedly so—unless practitioners eschew the smooth comforts of old grooves and move out in substantially new directions.

We have, in short, an emerging consensus that the dominant paradigm is spent, and that we are urgently in need of massive intellectual overseeding, if not a total break with the old modes.* But while those who are dissatisfied with contemporary critical theory tend to agree on its inadequacies, they have not espoused a new vision that matches the force of their critiques or the attractions of the status quo. For the liberationist paradigm cast literary scholars as academia's questing intellectual and moral heroes (see Conclusion). For all of its distortions

---

* The emerging consensus is visible in the thirty-odd papers read at the 2003 *Critical Inquiry* Symposium, described in the preface (Mitchell 2004). See also papers given in collections edited by Kernan (1997), by Patai and Corral (2005a), and in a special issue of *New Literary History* devoted to the crisis in the humanities (Cohen 2005, v36, 1). Also relevant are a number of recent books with titles like *After Theory* (Eagleton 2003), *Post Theory* (McQuillan et al. 2000), *After Poststructuralism* (Davis 2004), *Beyond Postmodernism* (Lopez and Potter 2005), and so on. Other representative examples include Boyd 2006; Butler 2002; Carroll 2004a; Ellis 1997; Delbanco 1999; Goodheart 1999; Kernan 1992, 1990; Lentricchia 1996; Scholes 1999; Woodring 1999; Weisbuch 1999.

and exaggerations, it provides many scholars with a self-image that would be absolutely painful to relinquish.

Shrinking Possibility Space

Our troubles are not new. We are simply in a particularly acute stage of a crisis that is as old as the professional study of literature itself. In his 1983 introduction to literary theory, Terry Eagleton notes that the familiar anxieties were already strongly present in the 1920s when "it was desperately unclear why English was worth studying at all" (27). Traveling back even further—to the last quarter of the nineteenth century, when English as an academic discipline was effectively invented (Graff 1989)—many of the modern concerns are already strongly represented. As Graff and Warner write in their collection of founding documents in the field of literary studies, "attempts to diagnose and cure humanities maladies are about as old as the discipline itself" (1989, 2).

In my view, the origins of the crisis, and its dogged permanence, are principally traceable to one basic cause: literary scholars only rarely succeed in accumulating more reliable and durable knowledge. As Goodheart writes, "Quarrels among critics have rarely, if ever, been adjudicated. Interpretations and evaluations abound and are often different from or in conflict with one another. The reputations of writers, determined by criticism, fluctuate, sometimes as wildly as the stock market in crisis" (2005, 509). In other words, literary studies is not a discipline where we reliably succeed in producing firmer and surer understandings of the things we study. In stark contrast to the sciences, in literary studies we have only argument and counterargument. Often these arguments center on "permanent questions" that have been in place, more or less, from the earliest Greek beginnings. And the debates seem to revolve in continuous circles, bending with fashions and the pronouncements of our charismatic leaders.

These are not really controversial observations, and they are not offered in a spirit of meanness. Few literary scholars would leap to refute this assessment of knowledge production in their field. They would be more likely to challenge the assumption latent in the assessment: That literary scholars actually *try*, as one of their primary goals, to generate more reliable and durable understanding (this book will make my own views clear: most do try, and others should). Or they might dispute my implicit sketch of knowledge progress in other fields, pointing out what they consider to be the main difference between humanities fields and "progressive" fields: we recognize that progress of knowledge is an illusion while researchers in most other fields do not.

Our failures to accumulate knowledge have not been total. There are things we know about different literary questions and phenomena that are as well established as good history. Yet, there is much more that we do not know, and both foundationalists (those who are persuaded that there is a real world that we can know in a reasonably objective way) and antifoundationalists (those who are not) typically agree that there is no decisive way to address our unanswered questions or to firmly resolve conflicts between two plausible arguments. In short, for many of the most vital questions in literary inquiry the space of possible explanation is vast, and we have devised no reliable way of shrinking it down.

*   *   *

Science can be understood as the most successful method humans have devised for shrinking the space of possible explanation. The work is carried forward by research communities whose members typically focus on little parts of big problems. Through their competitive, cooperative, and cumulative efforts, scientific research communities seek to narrow the range of plausible response to given questions. Sometimes this process is spectacularly successful and possibility space is reduced to a speck. This doesn't mean that we are certain about such issues. But science can achieve understandings that are so theoretically and empirically robust that all reasonable people must provisionally operate on the assumption that the explanation is correct. This spectacular narrowing of the space of possible explanation is what science has achieved in the theories of evolution, of a heliocentric solar system, of the circulation of the blood, of the germ theory of disease, of thermodynamics, of plate tectonics, of the cell theory in biology, of aspects of quantum mechanics, and of countless other phenomena. In other areas, for instance the attempt to derive a unifying theory in physics (the so-called Theory of Everything), the narrowing of possibility space has been more modest and the final result—given that adequately testing an idea like String Theory may be forever beyond human capacities (Woit 2006; Smolin 2006; but see Greene 2003, 2005)—is in doubt.

All scientists close off the space of possible explanation in much the same way. While the instruments, methods, and subject matter differ profoundly, they all proceed by systematically testing and ruling out competing hypotheses until (ideally) only the most robust possibility remains. The result is the triumph of the scientific method: a steady, usually slow process that often backslides or blunders into cul-de-sacs but, in the long view, results in an undeniable narrowing of the space of possible explanation.

These contractions of the space of possible *explanation* are not, of course, tantamount to contractions of *general possibility*. If anything, I would argue that genuine contractions of the space of possible *explanation* are more typically associated with rapid expansions of human possibilities, as the great imperium of ignorance, superstition, prejudice, and simple falsehood is robbed of reach and power (these points are further developed in chapter 3, "The Challenge of Inconvenient Results"; see also Sagan 1997). In any case, "shrinking possibility space" is the governing metaphor of this book, and it is intended to apply narrowly and strictly to the space of possible *explanation* for given problems and questions, and never to possibility more generally.

This ability to systematically and decisively narrow our allotted portion of possibility space—to zoom in toward truth in the immense, multidimensional hyperspace of error and vacuity—is precisely what literary studies, and other humanities disciplines, have always lacked. We have not developed ways of putting our ideas to rigorous tests. These tests—the core of scientific methodology—seek to limit the scope for various forms of bias (subjectivity, selection, confirmation, and so on) to distort human perception (see Kahneman and Tversky 1996).

Again, this is basically an uncontroversial position; actually, it is a self-evident one. I am saying that literary study is not a scientific field. Literary scholars may bemoan or celebrate this fact, but almost none dispute it. Most literary scholars proceed as though a universal and inexorable law of epistemology forever sunders the sort of questions they ask from those that scientists ask. Literary questions simply *do not* submit to falsifying tests: they are "unquantifiable" (Fludernik 2005, 64), "they cannot be captured by scientific reason" (Harpham 2005b, 105); and they cultivate mental activity that shares more in common with artistic or "religious consciousness" than with scientific consciousness (Fludernik 2005, 59; see also Delbanco 1999). For whatever intercourse is possible and valuable between the two cultures—for all the enriching cross-fertilization that can and should occur—the scientific method cannot be dragged across the divide. This is because, as Woodrow Wilson announced when he was still a young professor at Princeton University, the literary "expression of the spirit…escapes all scientific categories. It is not pervious to research" (Wilson 1893, 82).

As I will argue in chapter 2, this reasoning about methodological incommensurability is demonstrably wrong, demonstrably impoverishing (see also Mantzavinos 2005). It has helped mire the discipline in a deep rut where progress comes slowly if at all. I use the word "demonstrably" advisedly: the final four chapters of this book are case studies designed to show that the realms of the humanities and sciences are not riven by an unbridgeable methodological chasm.

This is far from arguing that all of our questions are within, or will come within, the practical reach of scientific methodology. I suspect that there will always be vital humanities questions that deflect every tool and device in science's organon. Moreover, I do not mean to hint that sound qualitative studies cannot help us generate more reliable knowledge. I have personally devoted a great deal of energy to this kind of work (e.g., Gottschall 2008), and I am not repudiating that work here. I therefore reject the adamantine positivism attributed to the bacteriologist Max Gottlieb, and other "scientific sharks," by the English professor Dr. Brumfit in Sinclair Lewis's *Arrowsmith* (see epigraph to this volume): "He says that knowledge is worthless unless it is proven by rows of figures." But I equally condemn the smug and slothful apriorism of Brumfit's mere fiat that phenomena such as literary genius and beauty are the products of a mysterious "vital force" that will forever frustrate scientific exploration. If I am more critical of Brumfits than Gottliebs in this book, it is because Brumfitian apriorism is a chief obstacle to knowledge generation in the humanities and Gottliebian positivism is not.

*   *   *

The position of this book, and the soul of the paradigm it seeks to inaugurate, is that we have been much too pessimistic about the capacities of humans—including even literary scholars—to produce durable and reliable knowledge. For decades, many literary scholars have expressed endless pessimism toward the possibility of knowledge generation, toward the "decidability" of anything save "undecidablity." Literary scholarship in the post-structuralist era has been aptly characterized as entailing "a kind of despair about the Enlightenment-derived public functions of reason" (Butler 2002, 11). At some point, literary academics began seeing themselves not as knowledge generators but as uncompromising knowledge dissolvers whose acid was perfect skepticism. The liberationists distinguished themselves from their predecessors through their special knowledge that none of the questions they were asking had real answers (it has often been asked: How, then, did *they know* the questions had no answers? How did they achieve certainty about uncertainty?). Starting in the late 1960s, claims of interest, insight, and political usefulness have been applied to distinguished literary investigations, more than claims of reliability, validity, or accuracy. Among the many flailing and contradictory attempts to define "Theory," one of the most incisive is Leitch's: "It's all too easy to think of Theory as a body of knowledge rather than as *an approach to insoluble problems*" (2001, 2318; italics added). Another major theorist, Jonathan Culler, concurs. In the concluding paragraph of his *Literary Theory: A Very Short Introduction,* he writes, "Theory, then, *offers not a set of solutions but the prospect of further thought.* It calls for commitment to the work of reading, of challenging presuppositions, of questioning the assumptions on which you proceed" (1997, 120; italics added).

Thus, praxis in the liberationist era has amounted to endlessly asking questions while despairing of more valid answers; to deconstruction without a clear sense of how to reconstruct once things are made to fall apart; to smothering the flame of Enlightenment without a clear vision of how to light a world that—deprived of reason—is "demon haunted" (Sagan 1997). The quintessence of the dominant paradigm is, then, constitutional and reflexive pessimism about the ability of humans to really know *anything.* Post-structuralism, which has so profoundly influenced every significant contemporary approach, has introduced a literally abysmal vision of the human capacity to understand—a vision of the "ultimate signified" skidding just beyond the fingertips and into the abyss. In general, literary scholars are not so naïve as to hope for progress of knowledge because, as Lyotard said, the idea of progress has disappeared (1986, 1612–1613).

But long before Derrida's neon declarations, the scientists had been pretty comfortable with the idea that it is not possible for humans to know the truth of something in the sense of its ultimate reality (See Boyd 2006). Popper's concept of falsifiability, which has been a guiding philosophical principle of scientific investigation for more than a half century, is an attempt to grapple with the fact that it is not logically possible to *prove* any scientific claim by experiment. But science's response to this realization was more reasonable and productive than that of the "great generation" of liberationist theorists (see Menand 2005). We can't know for certain what is true. Science makes no ultimate claims. But through a gradual process of rational thinking and falsifying tests, communities of scientists can show where the preponderance of evidence lies. This is the best that humans can do, and this is no small thing.

The argument of this book is that saving the field of literary study requires moving closer to the sciences. Of course, I am far from the first to feel dissatisfied with the soft modes of literary analysis. Nor am I first to propose that the study of literature should move in a scientific direction. Thus, in one sense, the message of this book sits snugly within a "tradition" of rebellion. Since the very beginning of institutionalized literary study, prominent thinkers have advanced specific plans for how the study of literature should become more serious, more systematic, more rigorous, and more scientific. Louis Menand goes so far as to describe the whole history of university literary study as a long sequence of "mood swings of the field—from attraction to controlled scientific methods to distaste for them and back again" (2005, 100). The philologists, the structuralists, the semiologists, the psychoanalysts, the narratologists, the Marxists, and others have bemoaned the failures of their discipline, derided the efforts of dilettante amateurs engaged in "chatter about Shelley," and sought to move toward a science of literary analysis. All along the way these systemizers have been opposed by belletrists who—like the New Critic Cleanth Brooks—have branded attempts "to be objective and scientific" as "quixotic" (1942, 235).

But Menand's thumbnail history of a field whiplashing back and forth between attraction to scientific methods and distaste for them gets it wrong in one important way. While literary scholars may have been, at various times, *attracted* to science's methods they have almost never *employed* them. The main attraction, in fact, has been to science's theories, vocabularies, taxonomies, and aura of logical rigor, not its methods. While different literary schools have attempted to apply strict systems to literature, and while they have imported concepts and impressive vocabularies from "more scientific" fields, each one has lacked utterly the *sine qua non* of a true science: the method. Science *is* the method. No matter how systematic the underlying conceptual structure, questions were ultimately explored with the old methods of careful reading and close argument (some exceptions to this rule will be discussed in chapter 2). What is more, some of the most prominent "scientific" approaches (branches of psychoanalysis and Marxism stand out) have, through their determined efforts to inoculate themselves against negative evidence, devolved into authentic antisciences ("more numerology than numbers," as Kernan [1992, 41] puts it).

The methodologically unscientific nature of previous "scientific" schools has convinced the great majority of contemporary scholars that the entire concept of "literary science" is risibly oxymoronic.

The frustrated scientific ambitions of previous schools are said to illustrate the fatuity of attempting to cram a nonscientific subject into science's alluring, but ill-fitting mold. As Roland Barthes wrote of his own transition away from structuralism, it may be said that most literary intellectuals are now wide awake from the "euphoric dream of scientificity" (1971, 97)—and they are grumpily disillusioned.

But I would argue that three important elements distinguish my proposal from previous attempts to establish a scientific study of literature. The first departure: I will describe an approach that is based in scientific theory and grounded, ultimately, in the bedrock of evolution by natural selection. Therefore, as I will explain in chapter 1, this approach will be based on theoretical foundations that blend seamlessly into scientific foundations, and that are, as a result, more robust, more accurate and—most vitally (if also most surprisingly)— more *supple and holistic* than those it displaces. The second departure: I will call for a much more vigorous branch of literary research based in the scientific method. As detailed in chapter 2, I will *not* merely suggest that literary studies should be "more scientific" (whatever that means), or that scholars should know more about science (as C. P. Snow averred in "The Two Cultures"), but that literary scholars should actually *do* science; where possible, we can and should make use of science's powerful methodology. In addition to these major theoretical and methodological shifts, in chapter 3 I will propose important adjustments in governing attitudes that will be necessary for the theoretical and methodological innovations to take hold.

In summary, the first three chapters (Part I) argue that by emulating aspects of scientific theory, method, and ethos, literary scholars can gather much more reliable knowledge about many of the questions we ask, and the discipline can be one where—along with all of the words— real understanding accumulates. In the four chapters of Part II, I move beyond argument and present case studies designed to concretely illustrate the values promoted in Part I. What is noteworthy about the chapters of Part II is not the questions they pose (which will be familiar in the main), but how my collaborators and I have sought to answer them. These chapters are based upon three multiple-coder content analyses (two of which were computer-facilitated) of large and cross-culturally diverse samples of world folktales. The studies were designed to gather data capable of empirically testing prominent hypotheses at the nexus of literary study and evolutionary science.

Part I

On Theory, Method, and Attitude

Chapter 1

On Theory

"Do you believe," said Candide, "that men have always slaughtered each other as they do today, that they've always been liars, cheats, traitors, ingrates and thieves, weak, fickle, cowardly, envious, greedy, drunken, miserly, ambitious, bloodthirsty, slanderous, lecherous, fanatical, hypocritical and foolish?"

"Do you believe," said Martin, "that Hawks have always eaten pigeons when they find them?"

"Yes, of course," said Candide.

"Well, then," said Martin, "if hawks have always had the same nature, what makes you think men have changed theirs?"

(Voltaire, Candide, 1759, trans. Lowell Bair)

The literary scholar's subject is ultimately the human mind—the mind that is the creator, subject, and auditor of literary works. The prime activity of literary critics of all theoretical and political slants has been to pry open the craniums of characters, authors, and narrators, climb inside their heads, and spelunk through all the bewildering complexity to figure out what makes them tick. Why does Hamlet hesitate? What is Marlowe telling us about the heart of darkness? And why do we respond as we do? In short, the traditional job of literary scholars has been to explore why characters act and think as they do, and to explain significances in the messages that texts convey to readers.

When engaged in these activities, literary scholars lean hard on theories of human nature. Sometimes these theories are explicitly codified, as they are, for instance, in some Marxist and psychoanalytic schools. Sometimes they are not, as when traditional literary critics base judgments on intuitions about the regularities and rhythms of human psychology. But at the core of all classes and orders of literary scholarship are assumptions about the nature of humans: our capacities, limits, and ultimate motives. Even those many scholars who boldly disavow the entire concept of human nature are—in this very disavowal—subscribing to a precisely codified theory of what human nature is: generally, that our nature is to spoon up whatever culture happens to feed us (and that we are what we eat).

For roughly four decades academic literary study has been dominated by exactly this nurturist understanding. For all of their important differences, post-structuralists, feminists, Marxists, psychoanalysts, postcolonialists, new historicists, queer theorists, and all of their teeming crossbreeds base their praxes on similar assumptions about the nature of human nature. With well-isolated exceptions literary scholars in the liberationist era have agreed that the human animal is almost entirely dominated and defined by nurture. Sometime in the depths of prehistory, culture asserted itself as an awesome coercive and constructive force, and the salience of evolved drives, biases, and inclinations steadily shriveled. The end result of this process was pithily described in a 2005 issue of *The Proceedings of the Modern Language Association*, by Robert Scholes, the outgoing president of the Modern Language Association: "We were natural for eons before we were cultural—before we were human, even—but so what? We are cultural now, and culture is the domain of the humanities" (Scholes 2006, 299). While most literary scholars might not phrase things so bluntly, critical theory in the liberationist era has been predicated on the nearly limitless capacity of what Durkheim (1895) called "the social factor" to dominate—to mold and manipulate—"the biological factor." In these various strains of denaturalizing social constructivism, human behavior, psychology, and culture are seen as products of arbitrary social conditioning with only diaphanous ties to evolved biology.

These "hard" versions of social constructivism cannot withstand the scrutiny of modern science. Theory and data from biology, behavioral genetics, developmental and cross-cultural psychology, cognitive science, endocrinology, neuroscience, anthropology, and a nexus of other fields and subfields have definitively shattered the tabula rasa (for overview see Pinker 2002). The psychoanalytic theories that have been so influential in the humanities have also been found badly wanting in parsimony and in theory–data fit; they appear in psychology textbooks only in sections providing historical overviews. In short, the theories of human nature that have dominated the recent history of literary theory and criticism now exist almost exclusively in the humanities. While literary scholars are often dismissive of concepts like "right" and "wrong," "true" and "false," most of our theories have been thoroughly discredited. This is a matter of scientific "fact," as the term is defined by Stephen Jay Gould: "Confirmed to such a degree that it would be perverse to withhold provisional consent" (1994, 254).*

Most will feel that Joseph Carroll goes too far in concluding that literary scholars' dependency on deficient theories of human nature means that,

> A very large proportion of the work in critical theory that has been done in the past twenty years will prove to be not merely obsolete but essentially void. It cannot be regarded as an earlier phase of a developing discipline, with all of the honor due to antecedents and ancestors. It is essentially a wrong turn, a misconceived enterprise, a repository of delusions and wasted efforts. (1995, 468)

Many scholars would burn with resentment over Carroll's sweeping dismissal, but they would also be hard pressed to dispute his central point: scholarship built on unsound theoretical foundations—on essentially faulty premises about human tendencies and potential—must itself be unsound, no matter how internally self-consistent. Or, to use my own idiom, these theories have not been able to produce work that reliably closes off the space of possible explanation. Is there a superior theoretical orientation available? I believe there is. It is represented in the concept of consilience.

Consilience

The natural sciences are mutually consistent: there are no major conflicts between the governing laws and theories of physics, chemistry, and biology (see Weinberg 1992). E. O. Wilson has argued for more than thirty years that extending mutual consistency beyond the natural sciences to other branches of knowledge, including the humanities, is the most fundamental intellectual challenge of our

---

*I like this definition of a scientific fact very much, so I decided to quote it even though I believe that Gould's positions on many scientific issues were, in fact, perverse. While Gould (who died in 2002) was the most prominent public biologist of recent decades, his reputation among his peers was shaky. Gould's prolific writings on evolution, and its intersections with political matters, have been so controversial, so visible, and so maddening to so many that they have spawned a vigorous genre entirely devoted to his systematic refutation (for representative examples, see Carroll 2004b; Alcock 2001; Dennet 1995; Smith 1995).

time. Wilson's term for the unification of knowledge is "consilience," literally "a 'jumping together' of knowledge by the linking of facts and fact-based theory across disciplines to create a common groundwork of explanation" (1998, 8; see also Tooby and Cosmides 1992; for advocacy of consilience from within the humanities see Slingerland 2008; Carroll 2004a; Mantzavinos 2005). The concept of consilience can be illustrated through the metaphor of a tree of knowledge (see Gottschall 2003). The trunk of the tree is physics; chemistry and biology branch off from it. But the tree of knowledge does not end with the trunk and the main scientific branches; it ramifies into a canopy of smaller branches, sprigs, and leaves that impart much of the fullness and beauty to the tree. The branches at the apex of the tree of knowledge are the social sciences and the humanities. Both branches emerge from the more fundamental principles of biology (and, more immediately, from the biologically grounded principles of psychology). Humans are biological organisms. Everything we do socially and artistically is both allowed and constrained by our biology (and, as we will see below, what we do socially and artistically has also influenced our biology).

The higher one climbs in the tree of knowledge, the more complicated things become. The trunk of the tree is smooth, straight, and broad, as are the laws of physics. But as one climbs higher, past the trunk and main boughs, branches twist, intersect, and slap the face, leaves and creepers block the view. In the rioting life of the canopy, explanatory principles are more difficult to discern. Because of this wild complexity, disciplines at the apex of the tree of knowledge may never equal the muscular mutual consistency that is the power and pride of the natural sciences. However, social scientists who have recognized continuities with lower branches of the tree of knowledge have discovered salient and heretofore unrecognized patterns in the tangled canopy of the tree of knowledge. They have found a way to extend many of the benefits of mutual consistency to the social sciences.*

---

*The most impressive results have emerged in the field of evolution and human behavior. Some of the main theoretical works in this area include Darwin 1859, 1871, 1872; Williams 1966; Wilson 1975; Hamilton 1964; Dawkins 1976; Barkow et al. 1992; Trivers 1971, 1972, 1974. Good popularizations of some of this work include Pinker 2002; Pinker 1995; Ridley 1995, 2003; Wright 1995. For an especially welcoming introduction to the field, see Wilson 2007. The most compendious and up-to-date surveys of research in the field of evolutionary psychology are Buss 2005 and Dunbar and Barrett 2007.

But humanists have typically failed to see the tree of knowledge. Concentrating on their own specialized branches, mastering every notch and knot, they have not noticed that their branch is part of a larger system. This is part of the "sheer loss" that C. P. Snow bemoaned in his identification of the two cultures. Because of the segregation of knowledge communities, because scholars have often failed to see the tree for the branches, disciplines have been denied the benefits of mutual consistency. As Wilson writes in *Consilience,* these benefits are not negligible: "Units and processes of a discipline that conform with solidly verified knowledge in other disciplines have proven consistently superior in theory and practice to units and processes that do not conform" (1998, 198). In other words, a concept that can survive a brutal sprint down the gauntlet of disciplines, all of them probing for vulnerabilities from different angles, must be hardier than one that wilts under the blows from all sides.

More than thirty years after Wilson's earliest calls for consilience in *Sociobiology*—what he then described as a "new synthesis"—the humanities remain overwhelmingly isolated from developments in the biologically grounded human sciences. The main orientation of literary scholars has retained more in common with the influential anti-consilience of the late-nineteenth-century philosopher Wilhelm Dilthey, who wrote that human studies "cannot be a continuation of the hierarchy of the natural sciences, because they rest upon a different foundation" (qt. in Freeman 1983, 22; for modern examples of anti-consilience see Dupré 1993; Cartwright 1999; for criticism of Dilthey's views see Mantzavinos 2005).

*   *   *

Committing to consilience means making our theories of literature and culture consistent with the best scientific understandings. Of course, we can still focus on textual depictions of gender, economic conflict, and psychological development; but, for the scholar who cares about shrinking the space of possible explanation, these investigations must be founded on a firm grasp of current knowledge in relevant scientific fields. This might be considered an unobjectionable prescription, even a self-evident one, except for the point noted above: for workers in the humanities the most constraining branch of the tree of knowledge is not, practically speaking, particle physics but evolutionary biology. In some quarters, this inspires deep dread (Louis Menand calls consilience "a bargain with the devil," 2005, 14; see also Goodheart 2007), and an embrace of theories of mind and behavior that verge on to "secular creationism" (see Ehrenreich and McIntosh 1997).

I believe that this response is based not on a sober assessment of the theories and the data supporting them, but on historical baggage, misunderstandings, and rancorous volleys of polemics by soldiers on both sides of the "sociobiology wars." Before suggesting what a consilient approach to literary study might look like, it is necessary to first clear the air. The next two sections of this chapter discuss the leading reasons why, more than three decades after evolutionary models of behavior and psychology burgeoned in other human-related fields, they have failed to locate a welcoming humanities niche. What are the main barriers to a consilient literary study? They are (1) doubts about the scientific status of evolutionary psychology and (2) concerns about the political and ideological ramifications of Darwinism applied to human psychology, behavior, and culture.

Barrier One: The Scientific Status of Evolutionary Psychology

The failure of evolutionary thinking to thrive in literature departments cannot, of course, be attributed to hostility toward evolutionary theory itself. Literary scholars are not creationists, nor are they agnostic about how human beings came to be constituted as they are; the overwhelming majority are committed evolutionists who grasp the theory's resistless logic if not its fine details. Most literary scholars have been suspicious of, if not openly hostile to, Darwinism applied to human behavior and psychology. But, in this new century of biology—in this "age of Darwin" (Shermer 2006, xxii)—few contemporary scholars would seriously contend (Robert Scholes' comment notwithstanding) that the behavior of the human primate alone, among many millions of distinct animal species, can be fully explained by the culture concept. Most would reject this statement of *omnis cultura ex cultura*, if not for the vacuity of its tautology, then for its proximity to the narcissistic creationist placement of *Homo sapiens* above and outside the natural order (or at least lording atop the chain of being). Further, since they are neither creationists nor proponents of the Cartesian "dogma of the ghost in the machine" (Ryle 1949), they would almost all embrace some form of this syllogism: the human brain is an evolved biological organ shaped by natural selection to address the problems of survival and reproduction that plagued the lives of our ancestors; the human brain produces the human mind; therefore the mind, and the behavior and psychology it promotes, also bear the impress of natural selection. Most literary scholars would accept this syllogism because there is simply no viable scientific alternative to the hypothesis that psychology evolved.

Then why are literary scholars so suspicious of evolutionary psychology? While many evolutionists attribute this suspicion solely to ideological bias (Carroll 1995; Storey 1996; Pinker 2002), much resistance stems from honest qualms about the scientific credentials of evolutionary psychology and related fields. Evolutionary psychology is based on the simple premise that human psychology evolved—the structures of the brain and mind, like those of the rest of the body, gradually taking shape under relentless selective pressures over millions and millions of years of mammalian, primate, and hominid existence. From this perspective, human behavior and psychology are adapted to the life conditions of our hunting and gathering Pleistocene ancestors (see Barkow et al. 1992). Humans act and think as they do, not because these patterns of thought and action enhance survival and reproduction in novel modern environments (though they often may) but because they enhanced survival and reproduction in the band and tribal communities of our ancestors. Just as our greed for sweet, salty, and fatty foods is no longer adaptive in food-rich modern environments, so too may psychological and behavioral tendencies that promoted the fitness of our ancestors actually reduce the fitness of us, their modern descendants. Evolution is usually a grindingly slow process, and even champions of punctuated equilibrium (Eldredge and Gould 1972) would not argue that natural selection could affect a massive overhaul of the human brain and mind in the mere 10,000 years since the advent of agriculture. The world has changed immensely since the agricultural revolution. Technologies have bloomed and populations have boomed—expanding from bands of dozens to nation states of millions and billions. But plodding evolution trails behind the rapid pace of cultural change, and the universal psychological and behavioral tendencies exhibited in modern humans are basically the same ones our ancestors carried out of Africa tens of thousands of years ago. Or so argue evolutionary psychologists.

From these basic premises, evolutionary psychologists proceed exactly like evolutionists interested in the development of bodily characteristics: they ask, how did the psychological or behavioral trait in question facilitate survival and reproduction in the environment in which the trait took shape? On the basis of theory, they generate hypotheses to account for the selective value of the trait in question. All evolutionists, including evolutionary psychologists, produce hypotheses that take the form of "historical narratives." This is a historical scenario that provides a plausible explanation for the origin and maintenance of given traits. The next step is to "test the various possible adaptive advantages of the feature, and its adaptedness is confirmed when all attempts to disprove these advantages are unsuccessful" (Mayr 2001, 155). The methods used by evolutionists to attempt to falsify their hypotheses are as diverse as evolutionary biology itself and include experimental and observational approaches. When adaptive hypotheses fail, evolutionists must conclude that (1) the trait is a result of chance, (2) the trait is a nonadaptive by-product of other adaptations, or (3) the trait was adaptive but because of changes in the environment it is now nonadaptive (Williams 1966).

So there is nothing wrong with the construction of "just-so stories." Steven Jay Gould, who (along with Richard Lewontin) applied this brand to sociobiology, was an evolutionist himself, so part of his career was given over to the telling of such stories. Generating just-so stories (otherwise known as historical narratives) is the first step in evolutionary hypothesis testing, whether the hypothesis concerns the function of a fossilized bone fragment, the origin of bipedal locomotion, or the evolutionary significance of a psychological or behavioral trait. Just-so stories are reckless only when investigators fail to follow through with rigorous attempts to falsify the narrative, accepting them on the basis of simple plausibility and consistency with theory. Evolutionists of all bents and specialties have sometimes confidently proclaimed that a given historical narrative is the correct explanation without going through the trouble of rigorous falsification efforts. (For instance, consider Gould's own controversial and quite tendentious insistence that the mammalian clitoris—not to mention the sexual pleasure it promotes—is a nonadaptive by-product, in effect a vestigial penis [1991]). This is a basic breach of scientific protocol and it is deserving of censure.

However, critics have often maintained that evolutionary psychological hypotheses cannot be falsified and are therefore fundamentally unscientific. The answers to evolutionary psychological questions usually depend upon whether a given trait was adaptive in the environments of our remote ancestors and, skeptics argue, the environments of our remote ancestors are gone and behavior (unlike bone) does not fossilize. Exactly these same arguments have been leveled in the past by creationists and other doubters against all of evolutionary biology (see Mayr 2001). Unlike chemistry, physics, or astronomy, where pertinent phenomena can be directly observed and where carefully controlled laboratory experiments can decisively falsify hypotheses, evolution is a historical science. The evolutionary process cannot usually be observed directly; it must be inferred on the basis of various evidence streams. The reason natural selection is scientific, contrary to the arguments of creationists, is that it generates a priori predictions that can be confirmed or disconfirmed by many different sources of evidence. Therefore critics should be cautious: the same arguments used to deny scientific status to evolutionary psychology would also deny it to the historical sciences of evolutionary biology, cosmology, geology, as well as other fields, such as theoretical physics, where answers cannot usually be verified directly but must be sought via inference.

Moreover, evolutionary psychologists would object to criticisms based on the poverty of evidence, the fact that we cannot directly observe ancestral environments, and the claim that behavior does not fossilize. It can, in fact, be argued that evolutionary psychologists draw on an enviably rich base of evidence relative to other fields of evolutionary inquiry. For instance, paleontologists depend on the fossil record to reconstruct the evolution of the earth's life forms. But they acknowledge that the fossil record is full of gaps, jumps, omissions, and discontinuities; for most lineages the fossil record, despite providing virtually unassailable evidence for evolution, is clearly incomplete. For example, there is a gaping hole of about ten million years—from roughly 14.5 million years ago to about 5 million—in the lineage that resulted in human beings; and the fossil remains of early hominids are fragmentary and incomplete, requiring uncomfortably large measures of subjectivity in reconstruction (and constant, jarring adjustments to our historical narratives). These facts do not represent problems for the theory of human evolution— the record is complete enough to tell the basic story—rather they reflect the facts that fossils are only formed under special and rare conditions and, because they are buried in the earth, they make elusive quarry for fossil hunters who must be as lucky as they are good.

While evolutionary psychologists may lack "fossils" of ancestral human behavior, they would claim to have access to something even better: numerous, well-studied groups of Stone Age hunter-gatherers and tribal peoples who were living in conditions approximating the human "state of nature" well into the twentieth century. World ethnography, especially of relatively "uncontaminated" hunter-gatherers, is a precious repository of information about the lives of our ancestors. It is as though paleontologists had a record—painstakingly compiled by teams of specialist observers—describing dinosaurs as they lived and walked. In addition to cross-cultural anthropology and ethnography, evolutionary psychologists rely on comparative zoology (especially on comparison with our closest primate cousins), archaeological artifacts, the whole panoply of psychological methodology (including the tools of neuroscience), and more.

None of this is meant to imply that evolutionary psychology is beyond censure, that its challenges are few and slight, or that its premises and findings should be swallowed unskeptically. It is to argue that many of the philippics against evolutionary psychology end up in the same place. They are not arguments for constructive reform in theory, data, or method. Rather, many suggest that the whole enterprise faces insoluble difficulties, that it is hopelessly ideologically compromised, and that it should therefore be repudiated and abandoned. But humans are inquisitive apes and we are not going to stop trying to map the details of human psychology or wondering how it came to be constituted as it is. Psychology evolved. Evolutionary psychology is therefore an indispensable scientific discipline, the only one that is equipped to grapple with elemental questions about why we are the way we are.

However, it is essential to acknowledge that evolutionary psychology has not yet reached a stable, mature form. Evolutionary psychology is not a monolithic enterprise or an assemblage of accepted facts; rather it is a young science where most of the exciting questions are hotly contested *within* the field. Many who believe that psychology evolved (me included) are nonetheless uncomfortable with the very term "evolutionary psychology" because it implies a misleading degree of uniformity and a prematurely rigid way of thinking about the evolution of the mind associated primarily with the psychologists John Tooby and Leda Cosmides (for examples of a different and exciting approach to evolutionary psychology that is now on the rise, see Wilson 2007; Wilson and Wilson 2007).

All who study human behavior from an evolutionary point of view share at least one conviction: human minds, just like human bodies, were shaped by the processes of natural selection; psychology evolved. But beyond this shared conviction there are many disagreements about the way that evolution works, how we would expect it to shape our minds, and the best way to test competing possibilities. Those who know evolutionary psychology only through racy journalistic accounts, glib popular books, or the polemics of its most rhetorically gifted and indefatigable antagonists are not likely to appreciate the broad diversity of views within evolutionary psychology itself and the fact that many of the most common external criticisms are debated with finer subtlety within the field.

But the question I have set out to address is not so much, *Why is evolutionary psychology controversial?* but *Why is it controversial in literature departments?* As mentioned above, modern literary scholarship stands out for its eager interdisciplinary impulse. At the risk of offending through overgeneralization, the first reflex of literary scholars is not extreme, hard-nosed skepticism but an eager openness to fresh and interesting perspectives. In fact, literary scholars have frequently been satirized (sometimes justly, sometimes not) for their eagerness to embrace and defend perspectives that outrage common sense. There are many ideas that are all the rage in literary studies that, at least superficially, seem less robust in theory, data, and harmony with common sense than evolutionary psychology. So, while scientific doubts are important, they do not tell the main story. The main story is less about science than politics and ideology.

Barrier Two: Political and Ideological Ramification of Darwinism

There can be no doubt that Charles Robert Darwin was a committed evolutionary psychologist almost from the instant he conceived his theory, and that he remained one for the rest of his life. For him, evolutionary theory was always as much about brain as body, mind as morphology. His earliest notebooks for what he called his "big species book," commenced more than twenty years prior to its 1859 publication, unmistakably convey his intention to apply his theory to all aspects of human behavior, psychology, cognition, and culture. Darwin saw that natural selection had profound implications for the origins of the most trivial aspects of human nature–why do people laugh when tickled?–as well as for the most exalted of our higher faculties— whence and wherefore human logic, reason, intelligence, imagination, spirituality, morality, and emotion? Young Darwin's journal entries on the evolution of what he sometimes called the "mental organs" are breathless, unguarded, and instructive; it is worthwhile to reproduce a few of them here:

- My theory would give zest to recent & Fossil Comparative Anatomy, & it would lead to study of instincts, heredity & mind-heredity, whole metaphysics (Notebook B, # 227–229, in Barrett et al. 1989).
- To study Metaphysic, as they have always been studied appears to me to be like puzzling at Astronomy without Mechanics. – Experience shows the problem of the mind cannot be solved by attacking the citadel itself. – the mind is function of the body. – we must bring

some *stable* foundation to argue from (Notebook N, #5, in Barrett et al. 1989).
• Origin of man now proved. – Metaphysic must flourish. – He who understands baboon would do more toward metaphysics than Locke (Notebook M, # 84e, in Barrett et al. 1989).

Yet Darwin pointedly avoided discussing the evolution of human physical and mental faculties in the main body of *On the Origin of Species*. However, "in order that no honorable man should accuse me [him] of concealing my [his] views" (1877a, 130), the famous conclusion presaged the rise of an evolutionary science that would illuminate the workings of the human mind:

> In the distant future I see open fields for *far more important researches*. Psychology will be based on a new foundation . . . that of the necessary acquirement of each mental power and capacity by gradation. Light will be thrown on the origin of man and his history. (449; italics added)

Darwin helped to bring this prophecy to fruition in the *The Expression of the Emotions in Man and Animals* (1872), in his essay "A Biographical Sketch of an Infant" (1877b) and, especially, in *The Descent of Man and Selection in Relation to Sex* (1871), which was the first work of evolutionary psychology. In *The Descent of Man*, Darwin discusses all issues of human physical and mental evolution that he suppressed in *The Origin of Species* for fear that they would "add to the prejudice against my views" (1871, 1). *The Descent of Man* is in many ways a bolder and more radical book than *The Origin of Species*. Darwin daringly contended that *all* of our higher powers–our intelligence, our imagination, our yearning for spiritual fulfillment, our language, our reason, our capacity for sympathy and morality—in short, everything that supposedly distinguishes us from brute creation and testifies to the favor of divinity—are end products of a strictly blind and purposeless churning of natural laws. For Darwin, establishing the evolutionary origins of "the highest psychical faculties of man" (1871, 100), like the human moral sense, was just as important as showing how "organs of extreme perfection" (1859, Chapter 6), like the human eye, were formed through slow gradation. In contrast to Alfred Russel Wallace, the codiscoverer of natural selection, who eventually invoked a higher power to explain human intelligence, Darwin felt it would be necessary to reject the whole theory if it failed to account for any aspect of human mental life. When Wallace announced his views on human intelligence (1867), Darwin wrote to his friend in disappointment, "I hope you have not murdered too utterly your child and mine" (F. Darwin and Seward 1903, 2.39–40).

However, while Darwin was founding the science of evolutionary psychology, he was inadvertently helping to plant the seeds of its twentieth century difficulties. Darwin was liberal by the standards of his age and, in some ways, by the standards of ours. His abhorrence of slavery was so virulent that as a young naturalist aboard the HMS Beagle he was almost put off ship after violently arguing the issue with Captain Fitzroy, a defender of the institution's benevolence (see Darwin 1877a). And while he acknowledged in *The Descent* that some of his theories could lead to the consideration of eugenic policies, he rejected eugenics in bold terms. Darwin wrote that we cannot check the proliferation of "less fit" people because of our natural sympathy for our fellow man. He continued, "Nor could we check our sympathy, if so urged by hard reason, without deterioration in the noblest parts of our nature. . . . If we were intentionally to neglect the weak and helpless, it could only be for a contingent benefit, with a certain and great present evil" (138–139). In *The Descent* (and also in *The Expression of The Emotions in Man and Animals*), Darwin arrayed forceful arguments against the then popular idea that the "so-called races of men" (2) could be classified as different species; he produced physiological and behavioral evidence for an early version of the currently ascendant "out of Africa" theory and against the notion that the different races were scions of different hominid progenitors. *The Descent of Man* and *The Expression of the Emotions* are festooned with subtle, almost tender observations of physical, mental, and emotional characteristics shared by all human beings everywhere.

Yet, for all of its prescience and brilliance, *The Descent* is a document of its age. One of the main questions Darwin addresses regards "the value of the differences between the so-called races of man" (2). Darwin asks, "whether man, like so many other animals, has given rise to varieties and sub-races, differing but slightly from each other, or to races differing so much that they must be classed as doubtful species" (2). Darwin's opinions were shaped by the sensational ethnographies of his day and by the violence of his own culture shock upon encountering, on the Beagle voyage, unassimilated tribal peoples in Tierra del Fuego—"man in his lowest and most savage state" (1871, 122). Darwin would conclude that the "varieties" and "sub-races" of men were arrayed on an evolutionary scale from the savage or lower races to the civilized or higher races. The savages, while far superior to the apes, were still intermediate between apes and civilized men.

The conditions and modes of life among the Fuegians, which so shocked the young Darwin, did not result primarily from chance or culture but from differing hereditary endowments—savages had "insufficient powers of reason" and "weak power of self command" (1871, 123) that reflected their "retention of a primordial condition" (1871, 230). Darwin's thinking about sex differences likewise reflected the thinking of his epoch; he accepted cousin Galton's sweeping conclusion, in *Hereditary Genius,* that "the average standard of mental power in man must be above that of woman" (1871, 584).

Little research was conducted into the evolution of the mind during Darwin's lifetime. In fact, Darwin was a thinker fully one hundred years ahead of his time: evolutionary psychology, sexual selection theory, and research on human expressions progressed very little until the 1960s and 1970s and, while the historical fact of evolution was widely accepted by scientists soon after the publication of *The Origin of Species,* it took another eighty years before Darwin's proposed evolutionary mechanism, natural selection, was fully accepted.* But, toward the end of his life and soon after his death, much effort was expended considering the biology of racial and sexual differences. By the first decades of the twentieth century a large number of intellectuals in Europe and America, influenced partly by Darwin but more by Herbert Spencer's vision of evolution progressing inexorably toward perfection, forsook Darwin's emphasis on the importance of environmental influences and concluded that the importance of nature dwarfed nurture (see Freeman 1983; Degler 1991). Biology determined the destinies of individuals and groups, and the observable differences between sexes, races, and ethnicities could be explained almost solely in terms of differing hereditary endowments.

The resistance against biological determinism was led by Franz Boas, the man responsible for developing the culture concept and for defining the research programs of twentieth-century anthropology. Early in his career, in *The Mind of Primitive Man* (1911), Boas rejected biological determinism as a viable explanation for ethnic and racial differences, arguing for the prime importance of culture in producing differences across populations.

Boas did not deny the role of biology; rather he adopted the moderate position that the similarities among human groups resulted

---

* For slow acceptance of evolutionary psychology, see Pinker 2002; of sexual selection theory, see Cronin 1993; of research on human expressions, see Ekman 1998; of natural selection, see Mayr 1982.

from a common genetic heritage whereas the differences were cultural in origin. What bothered Boas was *not* the concept of human nature, but the concept of *many human natures*—a separate and distinct nature for Africans, Aryans, Asians, and Anglo-Saxons. In this, Boas's position is virtually indistinguishable from the position of mainstream evolutionary psychology. Evolutionary researchers credit genetic research (see Cavalli-Sforza 2001; Olson 2002; Wells 2004) suggesting that, while there are real genetic differences across human populations, the differing fates of the races owe less to genes than to accidents of history, culture, and geography (Diamond 1997; Pinker 2002; Dawkins 2004).

Boas's students, however, took the fight against biological determinism much further, arguing that culture, not biology, determined *all* the qualities of individuals and populations. Boas' students—especially Alfred Kroeber, Robert Lowie, Margaret Mead, and Ruth Benedict—became the simple inverse of the biological determinists, coming to support a doctrine of total cultural determinism. They wrote that "culture is a thing *sui generis,* which can be explained only in terms of itself... *omnis cultura ex cultura*" (Lowie 1917, 4); that culture was "superorganic," in the sense of being above and disconnected from nature (Kroeber 1917); that human behavior was "apparently exempt from the operation of the laws of biological evolution" (Kroeber 1910, 437); and that human nature "was the rawest, most undifferentiated of raw material" (Mead qt. in Freeman 1983, 101). Boas's students, with the support of the older Boas, and protected at the flanks by Émile Durkheim in sociology and John Broadus Watson in psychology, policed a decades long segregation of biology from the study of human behavior, psychology, and society.

The fate of evolutionary analysis of human behavior and psychology was sealed when the Nazis supported their enormities, in part, with a grossly twisted version of Darwinism. From that point on, Darwinian explanations of human behavior and psychology were considered too dangerous to entertain, and the UNESCO statement of 1952 officially tabooed such approaches as morally, scientifically, and politically incorrect (see Segestrale 2000, 39–40).

However, it should now be obvious that evolutionary theory cannot be blamed for these outcomes. There is nothing intrinsically dangerous about evolution: the theory provides a set of conceptual tools that, like all tools, can be manipulated by human agents for good or ill. In fact, it is becoming clear that twentieth-century iniquities underwritten by radically constructivist theories of human nature rival those based on nativist theories (see Singer 1999; Ridley 2003).

Early critics of sociobiology routinely cited the Darwinian rhetoric of the Nazis in order to warn that sociobiology was a slippery slope to similar evils (e.g., Lewontin et al. 1984). Yet, as the cognitive scientist Steven Pinker reminds us:

> The Nazi Holocaust was not the only . . . ideologically inspired holocaust of the twentieth century, and intellectuals are only beginning to assimilate the lessons of the others: the mass killings in the Soviet Union, China, Cambodia, and other totalitarian states carried out in the name of Marxism . . . Historians are currently debating whether the Communists' mass executions, forced marches, slave labor, and man-made famines led to one hundred million deaths or "only" twenty-five million . . . And here is the remarkable fact: though both Nazi and Marxist ideologies led to industrial-scale killing, *their biological and psychological theories were opposites.* Marxists were averse to the notion of genetic inheritance, and were hostile to the very idea of a human nature rooted in biology. (2002, 155; italics in original)

*   *   *

This brings us to the most important reason for the failure of evolution to gain a place in literature departments, even after it had securely established itself in other human-related fields. Literary scholars have clung to obsolete *tabula rasa* theories of human nature because they consider these theories to be consistent with a socially and politically progressive orientation while theories that invoke biology are viewed as socially and politically retrograde. Starting in the late 1960s the dominant schools of literary study have been as much about agitating for progressive social change as about anything else. To scholars committed to the realization of better worlds, more equitable divisions of resources, and more harmonious human relationships, the theory that the human psychological endowment is infinitely pliant seems more attractive than the theory that significant aspects of this endowment will stiffly resist manipulation. The environmentalist theory suggests hope, while the nativist theory seems to suggest—as Martin bleakly suggested to young Candide—that we are the heirs to, and prisoners of, an ancient legacy of human viciousness. When forced to choose between what Mary Midgley calls "the rival fatalisms" of cultural and biological determinism, it is not surprising that literary scholars have virtually unanimously chosen the former alternative.

However, the choice between biological and cultural determinism has been definitively exposed as a false one. The biological determinism of Galton and Spencer, as well as the cultural determinism of the

"Boasian" paradigm, are failed theories. As Derek Freeman concludes in his history of twentieth century nature–nurture debates:

> We may thus identify biological determinism as the thesis to which cultural determinism was the antithesis. The time is now conspicuously due for a synthesis in which there will be, in the study of human behavior, recognition of the radical importance of both the genetic and the exogenetic and their interaction, both in the past history of the human species and in our problematic future. (1983, 302)

Modern evolutionary approaches to human mind and behavior stress the fully coequal roles of genetic and environmental (read sociocultural) influences and are thus seeking to embody this synthesis.

Critics often accuse evolutionists of hungrily conquesting through the disciplines, seeking to place all aspects of human behavior and culture within a biological framework. Indeed, they are not wrong. Making sense of all human behavior and culture from a biological perspective *is* the ambitious goal of the "adaptationist program." But this does not mean that all other approaches are thus subsumed and rendered irrelevant. Nor does it mean renouncing or demoting "nurture." An evolutionary biology that ignores or de-emphasizes the importance of physical and sociocultural environments is, in fact, *profoundly un-biological*. Environments—social and physical—shape, constrain, and elicit the behaviors of organisms.

Adopting this "biosocial" stance does not represent a retreat into wishy-washy platitudes for the sake of keeping everyone happy. Rather, it is based on scientific information about how genes interact with environments: genes have a strong influence on behavior, yes, but behavior and environment also exert strong influence over genes (a classic example of the latter fact is adult lactose tolerance in populations with a history of herding dairy animals, and lactose intolerance in populations lacking this cultural practice; see Richardson and Boyd 2005 for more examples). As Matt Ridley writes in *Nature Via Nurture*, "The more we lift the lid on the genome, the more vulnerable to experience genes appear to be . . . Genes are not puppet masters or blueprints. Nor are they just carriers of heredity. They are active during life; they switch each other on and off; they respond to the environment . . . They are both cause and consequence of our actions" (2003, 4).

The philosopher Peter Singer argues, in *A Darwinian Left*, that progressives are not asked to make a Faustian choice between the theory of human nature that is most consistent with their political goals and the theory that seems most likely to be scientifically correct. If we wish to affect social and political change, Singer writes, we must embrace the theory that accounts for the most information most parsimoniously, not the theory we would most like to be true: the left must "accept that there is such a thing as human nature, and seek to find out more about it, so that policies can be grounded on the best evidence of what human beings are like" (1999, 61). Thus evolutionary study of human behavior and psychology is not—contrary to a common allegation*—an ideology of pessimism, defeatism, or conservative defense of the status quo. The Delphic imperative, *know thyself!*, rings as a great moral of the evolutionary exploration of human nature. As the biologist-philosopher Richard Alexander writes: "The value of an evolutionary approach to human sociality is not to determine the limits of our actions so that we can abide by them. Rather it is to examine our life strategies so that we can change them when we wish, as a result of understanding them" (1987, 9).

Acknowledging that Darwinism has a significant role to play in explaining human behavior and psychology does not mean accepting that all people are bad and selfish, that women are weak and passive objects awaiting exploitation, that human life must be *bellum omnes contra omnes*, or that we should sit idly by while the strong feed on the weak. Accepting Social Darwinism means subscribing to this vision; accepting modern Darwinism means rejecting these views, not only on moral grounds, but also on the grounds of staggering scientific error.

*   *   *

I think we can be confident that, were he alive today, Darwin would readily concur. Darwin knew that his initial speculations into the natural history of the human mind were highly preliminary and "want[ed] scientific precision" (1871, 628). With characteristic humility he concluded *The Descent of Man* with the following acknowledgement:

> Many of the views which have been advanced [in this book] are highly speculative, and some no doubt will prove erroneous . . . False facts are highly injurious to the progress of science, for they often endure long;

---

*This charge is at the heart of much criticism of sociobiology and evolutionary psychology. For representative examples of this criticism, see Lewontin et al. 1984; contributors to Rose and Rose 2000. These criticisms have been answered in Alcock 2001; Alexander 1987; Dennett 1995; Ridley 2003; Pinker 2002.

but false views, if supported by some evidence, do little harm, for every one takes a salutary pleasure in proving their falseness: and when this is done, one path toward error is closed and the road to truth is often at the same time reopened. (549)

The history of the twentieth century shows that Darwin was wrong about false scientific views causing "little harm." Harm was done to those branded "unfit" and, as Darwin warned in 1871, putting Social Darwinist theory into practice represented a "deterioration of the noblest parts" of our natures. However, we should now be at the point of being able to take "salutary pleasure" in pointing out the falseness of the crude doctrines of biological and cultural determinism. With these paths to error finally closing, there is reason to hope the "road to truth" may finally be opening, though we must remain vigilant for further errors that doubtlessly lurk along our way.

The Lunacy of One Idea

As Brian Vickers (among others) has pointed out, literary analysis has been dominated by intellectual "Masters": Marx, Freud, Jung, Saussure, Barthes, Derrida, Frye, Lyotard, Althusser, Kristeva, Butler, Lacan, Jung, Foucault, and so on. The "master narratives" composed by these thinkers and elaborated by their devotees are typically determinist, reductionist, and highly aggressive. They suggest that all aspects of human conscious and unconscious life are determined by language, early childhood trauma, class striving, the conspiracies of patriarchs or plutocrats, or competing discourses of power. Even post-structuralist theory—which was famously defined by Lyotard as skepticism toward grand narratives and as a "war against totality"— provides an especially aggressive, deterministic (with human beings defined not as relatively free agents but as "subjects" of cultural and linguistic forces), and reductive narrative that embraces all totality. As Cunningham writes, while post-structuralists set their faces "against Grand Narratives and Keys to All Mythologies, as delusive and imperialist, and all that, Theorists have managed to erect the Grandest Narrative of all—Theory—the greatest intellectual colonizer of all time" (2005, 28).

A more sympathetic commentator, Madan Sarup, reaches the same conclusion, and asks: "Why is Lyotard telling us yet another grand narrative at the end of grand narrative" (1993, 146)? I think that the answer to Sarup's question is that grand narrative is inescapable. Human cognition operates by devising large narratives and reducing phenomena to the terms of those narratives (see Gazzaniga 2000). And would we really wish it otherwise? Are the subjects we study—to borrow the idiom of creationist pseudoscience—really irreducibly complex? Is "reductionism" really a nasty word? Does it deserve its status as a term of opprobrium? The alternative to some form of reductionism is, I think, well described in Darwin's letter to Henry Fawcett: "About thirty years ago there was much talk that geologists ought only to observe and not theorize; and I well remember someone saying that at this rate a man might as well go into a gravel pit and count the pebbles and describe the colors. How odd it is that anyone should not see that all observation must be for or against some view if it is to be of any service!" (F. Darwin and Seward 1903, 194–196) This is not to argue that reductionism is appropriate in every situation or always properly carried out; it is to argue that truly eschewing big theory for "little stories"—Lyotard proclaimed this to be the essence of the postmodern—is a lot like squatting in a ditch to count up pebbles.

In any event, we literary scholars have almost always claimed to abhor determinism and reductionism—attributing these sins to intellectual opponents—while savagely practicing them ourselves. As Denis Donoghue has eloquently phrased it, adapting his statement from the Wallace Stevens poem "Esthétique du Mal," literary scholars have always veered toward a "lunacy of one idea" (2005, 257). Lunatics of one idea know the answer to all of their questions at the outset. And they never fail to find evidence that supports narrow conceptions about what literature or culture or history is *really* all about.

So, is my call for a consilient literary theory grounded in evolutionary biology just the next candidate in a long string of grand, conquesting, determining, and reducing master narratives—the next candidate to enjoy a short vogue before turning sterile and repetitive, and joining its predecessors in the dustbin of disciplinary history? Is this merely to replace the sociological and linguistic imperatives of Lacan, Derrida, and Foucault with Darwin's biological imperatives? What will be the upshot of this? Will literary scholars now be asked to tally the babies of authors and characters, to robotically translate old interpretations into the new vocabulary of inclusive fitness? Will the acid test of good literature and bad be how well it meshes with the predictions of evolutionary psychology (or cognitive science or some other emerging scientific paradigm)? To paraphrase Frank Lentricchia (1996, 64), once consilient literary theory is established, will it be easy to predict in advance what its advocates will say about works of literature, especially those they have not read?

I hope not. Evolutionary theory is a source of rich and nontrivial perspectives not only on human nature generally but on literature specifically. These perspectives genuinely challenge some of the field's deepest understandings; they raise new and provocative questions that deserve concerted exploration. There is now a significant body of work that follows the drama of survival and reproduction as it unfolds in literature generally, and as it is inflected by different cultural milieus and authorial sensibilities.* But, even though evolutionary theory has inspired most of my personal investigations, I would not insist (or even hope) that all literary scholars follow this course.

Consilient literary theory—as I hope to see it develop—is a new form of old-fashioned pluralism. Pluralism, as defined by Richard Levin, is a "Recognition that there are a number of fundamentally different philosophical or intellectual perspectives that generate quite different approaches to a literary work, and that these approaches should be respected as equally valid, since each of them can give us insights into valuable aspects of the work that are obscured or ignored by other approaches" (2003, 10; see also Booth 1979). While Levin is expressing an inclusive understanding, he elsewhere makes it abundantly clear that anything does *not* go. All approaches are *not* equal in validity; we need not tolerate—much less esteem—perspectives for which there is no real evidence and for which, in fact, proponents have made strenuous attempts to writhe away from compelling disconfirming evidence.

Consilient literary theory might evolve in weak and strong forms. The minimum qualification for the weak form is that a statement by a humanist not conflict with well-established knowledge in lower branches of the tree of knowledge. Thus a requirement for any consilient approach is a firm grasp of contemporary understanding in relevant scientific fields. In this minimal sense, consilience consists of gaining freedom from obvious and readily avoidable error. A more robust consilience encourages explicit integration of literary knowledge with theory and data from more fundamental fields of inquiry. In either case, I would strongly argue the following: a consilient viewpoint that acknowledges the influence of biology *and* culture in human affairs (including how biology and culture *each* influence the other's evolution, see Richardson and Boyd 2005) *is manifestly more*

---

* For example, Carroll 1995, 2004a; Barash and Barash 2005; Flesch 2008; Gottschall 2008; Gottschall and Wilson 2005; Nordlund 2002, 2007; Cooke 2002; Boyd 2005b; for field overviews, see Max 2005; Whitfield 2006; for a review articles, see Carroll 2003, 2008.

moderate, holistic, and inclusive than the master narratives that have dominated literary analysis for most of its institutional history. It acknowledges the power of acculturation while resurrecting *Homo sapiens:* the mammal, the Old World Catarhine primate, the great ape; the hominid who has known agriculture and civilization for only about 10,000 years; the big-brained, featherless, bipedal critter that has been placed under erasure by a quasi-creationist project in denaturalization.

Consilience is a catholic philosophy. A consilient perspective encourages and endorses historical, biographical, linguistic, economic, philosophical, psychological, anthropological, biological, and socio-logical approaches to literary study. For instance, exploring gender relations and sexual identity in literary works is a worthwhile endeavor, but to assert—as canonized saints of literary theory regularly have—that human beings are neutral as to sexual and gender orientation at birth is outrageously unconsilient. This flouts great swaths of theory and data from biology, psychology, cognitive science, anthropology, endocrinology, comparative zoology, neuroscience, and so on. Far from narrowing possibility space, unconsilient perspectives like these can only fuel the metastasis of ignorance.

Above all, the advantage of a consilient literary theory that blends seamlessly into the sciences is its supple, evolving nature. By basing our theories of literature in science (or at least ensuring their consistency with the best scientific understandings), we can hope to avoid the rigid dogmatism that has ended up characterizing most previous approaches. As suggested above, most schools of literature have been ruled by the grand assertions of intellectual Masters. The followers internalize the dictates of The Master, faithfully stake their intellectual and professional reputations on His (or, more rarely, Her) teachings, and vigorously defend against dissenters and apostates (see Vickers 2005; Evans 2005). In so doing they have often gone to great lengths to insulate themselves from the very possibility of wrongness. It is fair to ask, What data would committed followers of Althusser, Foucault, Lacan, Butler, or almost any other Big Name accept as disconfirming the Master's premises?* Indeed, when challenged with negative evidence, proponents will often proclaim by fiat that such theories are beyond

---

* Of course, doubters, usually of creationist stamp, suggest that Darwin's theory has hardened into an unchallengeable article of secularist faith. But when challenged for evidence that would falsify the theory of evolution, the biologist J. B. S. Haldane had a ready answer, "fossil rabbits in the pre-Cambrian era" (qt. in Dawkins 2006, 128).

disproof: they "cannot be adequately tested, falsified, or objectified" (Leitch 2001, 913). The outrage of commentators like Brian Vickers has so far made little difference:

> Freud's work is notoriously speculative, a vast theoretical edifice elaborated with a mere pretense of corroboration, citing "clinical observations" which turn out to be false, with contrary evidence suppressed, data manipulated, building up over a forty-year period a self-obscuring, self-protective mythology. The system of Derrida, although disavowing systematicity, is based on several unproven theses about the nature of language which are supported by a vast expanding web of idiosyncratic terminology...Lacan's system, even more vastly elaborated is...a series of devices for evading accountability...Foucault places himself beyond criticism. (2005, 249)

The common denominator of almost all major contemporary approaches to literary theory is, according to Frederick Crews, "A refusal to credit one's audience with the right to challenge one's idea on dispassionate grounds" (2005, 228). Psychoanalysts have argued that citing evidence against their belief system is quite transparently—in itself—evidence *for* that system; criticism of Marxist or neo-Marxist notions can be dismissed as craven attempts to bolster the critic's economic interests; and any criticism of the so-called race-class-gender-sexuality movements can be brushed off as spasms of rightist political reflexes (which accounts for the scarily servile protestations of good liberal credentials that accompany so many critical treatments of these movements; I won't be doing that here, make of it what you will). While these prophylactics against negative evidence have been potent, and while they help explain the impressive resilience of the dominant paradigm, they have also been primary obstacles to the generation of reliable knowledge.

It is not that the theories, when devised, were transparently defective. They were the thrilling dreams of genius and they deserved exploration. But time and great accumulations of evidence have exposed fundamental and irresolvable shortcomings. Literary scholars cannot be justly assailed for their initial attraction to these ideas. After all, most of the big theories in the liberationist paradigm were initially consistent with a scientific consensus that biology minimally influenced human behavior and psychology (see Tooby and Cosmides 1992). But, the way that many scholars continue to cling to defunct theories long after the strong nurturist consensus has disintegrated is indeed blameworthy.

A Dogma of Partial Skepticism

This evasion of strong disconfirming evidence is accompanied by an acute irony. For, above all, the liberationist movements presented themselves as principled skeptical movements—movements that sought to embody Marx's vision of "*a ruthless criticism of everything existing*" (1977, 13; italics in original). The project of denaturalization, the quintessence of the liberationist paradigm, constituted a breathtaking challenge to all received wisdom. As Culler writes, "It [Theory] encourages you to be suspicious of what is identified as natural, as a given. Might it not, on the contrary, have been produced by the discourses of experts, by the practices linked with discourses of knowledge that claim to describe it?" (1997, 4).

Of course, the answer to Culler's question is a thundering "Yes!" Skepticism is a wholesome habit of mind that all true questors for knowledge must possess in abundance. (This value is pithily transmitted in the motto of the The Royal Society of London, the world's first modern scientific society—*nullius in verba:* on the words of no one). But it is now apparent that skepticism toward the whole category the Natural was based not so much on hard critical thinking and sober assessments of evidence as on *a dogma of partial skepticism* born, ultimately, from perceived political needs. While deploying a method of near-total skepticism toward competing schools of thought—and above all toward the category Natural—the liberationists evinced uniform credulity toward claims for the tyranny of nurture. They simply assumed and asserted that nothing human (gross physiology aside) was natural. Skepticism has been nowhere in evidence when it has been averred that folk wisdom and common sense are almost always misplaced, or that in humans alone genetic components of behavior, psychology, and culture are exiguous or nonexistent. The skepticism of literary scholars toward the category Natural turned into a dogma when it became apparent that the liberationists would never turn Culler's question around and interrogate their own nurturist convictions.

There is good reason to hope that literary theories grounded in consilient science will be appreciably less vulnerable to this creep of dogmatism. Scientists are human and thus fully capable of falling disastrously in love with this idea or that. But scientists also recognize that the nature of their institution, and the soul of its power, is change. Once scientists begin proceeding as though their arguments are beyond practical disconfirmation (as literary psychoanalysts often do) or that there are no ideologically neutral grounds for challenging them (as many activist scholars do), they are no longer dealing in the realm of science. The history of science gives stern lessons in humility: many aspects of our contemporary understanding *will* be proven inadequate by future investigators. For instance, we *will* discover frailties in understandings of evolved psychology that currently seem firm. But as the science of human nature evolves, so too must a responsibly consilient literary theory.

In short, the paramount advantage of anchoring literary theory in consilient understanding is the advantage that accrues to theory that must update itself based on clear shifts in the preponderance of evidence. It must do this or be instantly forced to relinquish claims to genuine consilience.

Chapter 2

On Method

The way that literary scholars continue to take guidance from discredited theory is only one part of the problem. An equally important factor is method. Literary methods are weak when compared to the power of the theories—the former seem almost incapable of demonstrating that the latter are wrong. The role of method is not simply to enable investigators to demonstrate the correctness of their ideas; the role of method is also to act as a *check* on the explanatory greed of all theory. Literary methodologies largely fail in this latter duty: theory is the bully of method.

Richard Levin writes that a dominant method of arguing literary hypotheses has been "enumerating the positive evidence" (Levin 2003, 138). Going back more than a century to the "old" historicists and the early formalist critics, and then traveling gradually forward to focus on the contemporary era, Levin reveals, in more than a dozen specific examples, a disturbing trend whereby literary scholars tout evidence in accord with their theses while flagrantly minimizing or ignoring "negative evidence." A methodology that focuses on enumerating positive evidence is one where tests of hypotheses cannot fail—one where, as Frederick Crews has written in a similar vein, the "bogus experiments succeed every time" (Crews 2005, 229). Thomas H. Huxley defined scientific tragedy as what happens when a beautiful hypothesis is slain by an ugly fact (1870, 244). Levin, Crews, and others (see contributors to Patai and Corral 2005a) have shown that this is precisely what too many literary scholars will not allow: they exert themselves to keep ugly evidence from marring the beauty of their ideas.

Levin hastens to add that he is not indicting the whole field (and neither am I!). Very many scholars *do* take pains to carefully weigh the negative evidence along with the positive. Levin writes of his education at the University of Chicago:

> [We were taught] a respect for the kind of rational argument that was necessary to demonstrate interpretations of literary works. For we learned that every interpretation (including our own) must be treated as a tentative hypothesis that must be supported by arguments, and that each of these arguments must be tested rigorously to see if it holds up—if it is logically coherent and consistent, and proceeds *a posteriori* from the facts, and takes into account all the relevant ones, especially those that might seem to conflict with it or support a different interpretation. (2003, 10)

Few could fault this philosophy, and perhaps fewer still would acknowledge that their own critical practice substantially differs from it. Levin's teachers sought to sow a mental habit that would prompt pupils to ask of their beautiful idea, "Okay. Now. Step back. Is it true? What consequences are predicted by this idea? What is the most efficient and rigorous way of determining if those consequences are in effect?" Levin's teachers were not the authors of this wisdom. Almost 120 years ago the Shakespearean Richard Moulton offered the same advice as a "foundation axiom" for literary study: *"Interpretation in literature is of the nature of a scientific hypothesis, the truth of which is tested by the degree of completeness with which it explains the details of the literary work as they actually stand"* (Moulton 1888, 69; italics in original).

Reestablishing Moulton's axiom as a guiding imperative for modern literary investigation would make for an excellent beginning in establishing more responsible literary methods. However, while literary hypotheses have often been *formed* in a scientific spirit, they have almost never been *tested* in the same way. And there remain very large classes of problems that cannot be adequately addressed even with the most scrupulous application of conventional humanistic methods. Are there methods that can enable us to do a better job of addressing such questions? The point of this chapter is that there are. I'll begin illustrating this point through a deliberately simple example.

Are the Beautiful Good?

Consider the physical attractiveness stereotype (PAS)—the "lookist" tendency for people to attribute positive personality characteristics to the physically attractive and negative personality characteristics to the physically unattractive. Social psychologists refer to this tendency as the "beautiful is good" stereotype (see Dion et al. 1972; Eagly et al. 1991; Feingold 1992; Langlois et al. 2000).

On the surface, there appears to be good evidence that traces of this psychological tendency have found their way into literature. Literary characters who are both beautiful and good are legion. A few memorably unattractive "bad" characters include Shakespeare's Richard III, Homer's Thersites, Dickens' Uriah Heep, and Cinderella's stepsisters. Moreover, the hideous appearances of monsters, ghouls, goblins, gargoyles, and witches symbolize their unwholesome natures. On the other hand, examples may almost as readily come to mind of characters who violate this pattern. The physical appearances of Quasimodo, Cyrano de Bergerac, and numerous other unattractive characters belie their essential goodness, while the beautiful Queen in "Snow White" and lovely Duessa in the *Faerie Queene* are but two in a long line of femme fatales who approach evil incarnate. In short, in literature the beautiful are obviously not always good, and the ugly are not always bad.

So the task of determining whether there *is* a PAS in literature—not in the sense of being represented in individual works but as a salient phenomenon running through whole literatures and genres—may not be as straightforward as it first appears. When asked if the stereotype is broadly reflected in literature, the scholar must respond by cudgeling his brains for examples and counterexamples and, in this fashion, try to provide an accurate response. But, when awash in the whole universe of literary characters, amidst all the characters who fit the stereotype and violate it, how is it possible to arrive at a firm answer? Any scholar citing a proliferation of characters who fit the pattern can be countered by another scholar citing droves who do not. The winner of this hypothetical debate will not necessarily be the scholar who more closely approximates "the truth," but will just as likely be the scholar who is more rhetorically fluid or who happens to be able to conjure from memory a larger or more resonant set of examples.

In a debate of this kind, the traditional qualitative methods of the humanities quickly collapse beneath the burden of selection and confirmation biases. Believers and nonbelievers in the reality of a literary PAS can volley examples and counterexamples, but it is difficult for them to actually determine if the phenomenon exists in literature or if it is only a phantom produced by an unrepresentative set of examples (My colleagues and I [Gottschall et al. 2007] addressed this very question in a quantitative analysis of a large and random sample of Western literary works. We found solid evidence for the PAS, but, perhaps contrary to intuition, the stereotype applied with much more force to *males* than to females).

It may be objected that I am pushing too hard. Perhaps many scholars would guess that something like a PAS operates in literary works, and that the many counterexamples represent cases of authors toying with the prejudices of audiences. But the implications of this argument radiate beyond the confines of attractiveness prejudice. The problems of confirmation and selection bias discussed above are not unique to the question at hand; they are primary obstacles to the progress of literary knowledge.

The work of literary scholars has been hounded, above all, by one enormous methodological obstacle. The problem derives from an ancient defect of human psychology, and it was perfectly understood and described by Francis Bacon in the 46th aphorism of the *Novum Organum* (1620):

> The human understanding when it has once adopted an opinion (either as being the received opinion or as being agreeable to itself) draws all things else to support and agree with it. And though there be a greater number and weight of instances to be found on the other side, yet these it either neglects and despises, or else by some distinction sets aside and rejects; in order that by this great and pernicious predetermination the authority of its former conclusions may remain inviolate.

Bacon was describing a phenomenon that psychology would eventually define as confirmation bias: the tendency to find (or unconsciously manufacture) evidence that confirms what one already believes. This has been a leading problem in all fields of inquiry. But some fields, especially scientific fields, have recognized the dangers of confirmation bias and have made aggressive attempts to diminish its power. In literary study, confirmation bias is *the* leading methodological problem responsible for our failure to generate more reliable knowledge. Moreover, as noted above, this weakness is also a principal reason for the survival, in our field, of theories that have already died in the sciences; instead of challenging our favorite notions, our methods allow us to sift out whatever evidence seems to confirm them. This is blatantly true of work that settles for "enumerating the positive evidence"—of work, as Elrud Ibsch puts it, that is not animated by "the ethical impulse inherent in the search for a counter-example" (1989, 399). But, it can also infect, more subtly, the scrupulously scholarly approach Levin advocates. Two honest and doggedly responsible researchers could easily reach opposite and equally defensible conclusions on questions like the reality of a literary PAS, and probably every academic can readily list many examples where exactly this has occurred.

In short, an honest, rigorous, and conscientious approach to our questions is not enough to tame the problems of bias—confirmation, selection, and other kinds. Of course, most literary scholars understand this. They are aware of the weaknesses of their methods, but live with them because the methods also have salient strengths and because they believe the issue is moot in any case: qualitative methods are the only ones that *can* be applied to the sorts of questions we ask. This chapter argues strongly to the contrary. There are large areas of literary investigation that will probably never yield to the scientific method. For these questions, the conscientious approach advocated by Levin and Moulton is the best thing going. But I will argue here— and then attempt to show in the case studies—that there are other territories in literary study, large and important ones at that, where scientific methods can play an important role. The great methodological wall sundering the sciences and the humanities has no substance; the wall is a figment—a failure—of our imaginations.

Literary Science: A Modest Manifesto*

Around 1660, a London haberdasher of small wares named John Graunt—a self-made and self-educated man—had an inspiration. Since the sixteenth century, London's Bills of Mortality had listed all "The Diseases and Casualties" of the week, partly to serve as an early warning system during the time of plague. For instance, during the week of April 11–18, 1665, one died from cancer, twenty-one from "dropsie," six from the hangman, fourteen from "griping in the guts," eight from "rifing of the lights," eight from "stopping of the stomach," one from "wormes," and none from plague. Five months later, during the week of September 12–19, more died in almost every category and 7,165 died of plague (See Graunt 1665). The bills also provided sex ratio information on the total numbers of burials and christenings, the net increase or decrease in burials, and, strangely, the amount of white and wheaten bread to be purchased for a penny or a halfpenny.

In his *Natural and Political Observations Mentioned in a Following Index and Made upon the Bills of Mortality* (1662) Graunt noted that while rich people used the bills at plague time to better "judge the necessity of their removal," most read them only to see "how the burials increased or decreased; and among the Casualties, what had happened rare, and extraordinary in the week currant; so as they might take the same as a Text to talk upon, in the next Company."

---

* Some of the material in this section was originally published in Chapter Ten of *The Literary Animal*, edited by Jonathan Gottschall and David Sloan Wilson. Evanston, IL: Northwestern University Press (2005).

Graunt suspected that the bills had potentially "greater uses" and proceeded to do something unprecedented: he went to the Hall of the Parish-Clerks and gathered copies of all bills on record. He meticulously compiled the information and organized it in tabular form so that it would be possible to compare births, diseases, and causes of death "by year, by season, by Parish, or other Division of the City." Based on his tables Graunt made 106 natural and/or political observations, "some concerning Trade and Government, others concerning the Air, Countries, Seasons, Fruitfulness, Health, Diseases, Longevity, and the proportions between the Sex, and Ages of Mankinde" (Graunt 1662, 1, 2, iv). Here are some of Graunt's discoveries, in his own words:

• That about one third of all that were quick die under five years old, and about thirty six per Centum under six.
• Annis 1603, and 1625, about a fifth part of the whole died, and eight times more than were born.
• That Purples, small-Pox, and other malignant Diseases fore-run the Plague.
• That not one in two thousand are Murthered in London.
• That Plagues always come in with King's Reigns is most false.
• That there are about six millions, and a half of people in England and Wales.
• That there are fourteen Males for thirteen Females in London, and in the Country but fifteen Males for fourteen Females.
• There being fourteen Males to thirteen Females, and Males being prolifique fourty years, and Females but twenty five, it follows that in effect there be 560 males to 325 Females.
• The said inequality is reduced by the latter marriage of the males, and their employment in wars, Sea-voiage, and Colonies.
• Physicians have two Women Patients to one Man, and yet more Men die than Women.

As might be inferred on the basis of this list, Graunt is now esteemed as a pioneer in fields as diverse as medicine, political science, sociology, demography, statistics, criminology, biology, and others where the systematic study of populations (human or other) is vital. The methodology Graunt established allowed him "not only to examine the Conceits, Opinions, and Conjectures, which upon view of a few scattered Bills I had taken up; but did also admit new ones, as I found reason, and occasion from my Tables" (Graunt 1662, 2). This was a watershed moment in the development of the modern medical, life, and social sciences. Graunt was among the first to see that compiling and analyzing population-level data allows a researcher to systematically test the validity of his or her preconceptions and to discover relationships in data that might otherwise have been invisible.

Observations helped inaugurate a true and revolutionary Age of Discovery in the sciences of man and society. Graunt and his more mathematically sophisticated successors would discover, over the next 150 years or so, vast and unanticipated regularities in rates of birth, death, trade, mortality, murder, theft, disease, suicide, insanity, and more. These findings were often wholly unanticipated or perfectly opposed to expectation. For instance, Graunt himself discovered that, contrary to common prejudice, members of "the weaker sex" perished at lower rates in virtually every age cohort. Edmund Halley (1656–1742), of Halley's Comet fame, reported in astonishment that half of the souls in a sample of English towns perished before the age of seventeen (see McDonald 1993). The self-styled "social physicist" Adolphe Quetelet (1796–1874) found many striking regularities in important areas of social and life history data, and he also discovered things that were more trivial but amazing nonetheless (see Porter 1986). For instance, he found that different breeds of intellectuals tended to have different average life expectancies. My readers may be interested to learn that the natural philosophers in his sample tended to live the longest, outliving the shortest lived intellectuals, the poets, by fully eighteen years.

Impressed with these regularities, many nineteenth-century thinkers welcomed "the exciting prospect that the application of probability to empirical social data could produce a social physics to stand beside Newtonian natural philosophy" (Stigler 1986, 67; see also Stigler 1999; Porter 1986; McDonald 1993). Social scientists are more sober minded now; they have largely abandoned the extravagant Newtonian hopes of the statistical "age of exuberance" (Porter 1986, 163). But, in a real sense, the glacially paced development of what is known as "modern statistical methodology" over the course of 270 years—the conventional dates stretch from around 1650 to 1933—rivals those revolutions associated with the names of Darwin, Newton, and Einstein (see Stigler 1986, 381). The slow creep of quantitative and statistical methods across disciplines of the natural and social sciences radically and irrevocably altered the way that human beings seek, process, and evaluate information.

My argument is that literary studies is now in something quite like the position of those areas of knowledge that would become the social sciences before the advent of quantitative analysis of mass social phenomena. To read the history of the gradual coalescence of modern statistical methodology is to be constantly confronted with these salient facts: quantitative and statistical analyses have consistently revealed knowledge that could not otherwise have been known or, oftentimes, even suspected; these methods have continuously forced deep revision or outright abandonment of the most deeply seated and intuitively held convictions. To phrase my argument in the form of a prediction: if the community of literary scholars will make limited and judicious use of quantitative methodology, it will experience precisely the same benefits that have accrued to other human-related fields. Literary scholars will discover important things about literature that were previously unknown or unsuspected, and some of our most comfortable assumptions will be proven illusory or in need of significant revision. We can be confident in this prediction because this is precisely what has occurred in all other human-related disciplines that have wed quantification to their traditionally qualitative approaches, no matter how vigorously some thinkers initially protested that the subjects under study were fundamentally unquantifiable.

Quantifying the Not Easily Quantifiable

Those who seek to study literature quantitatively are frequently presented with two objections. The first is based on the conviction that all of the really intriguing questions in our field just *cannot* be quantified. Andrew Delbanco's easy confidence about this is typical: literary studies "will never be able to submit its hypotheses to the scientific test of replicable results" (1999, 37). The second concern is that even if challenges associated with quantifying literary information *could* be overcome, quantitative analysis scrapes away the fine texture of individual characters and texts—and that fine texture is the main object of literary examination. Statistical generalization entails stark reductions of complexity and nuance and, in literary studies, complexity and nuance are bread and butter. In these objections, one hears ringing echoes of William Blake: "To Generalize is to be an Idiot. To Particularize is the Alone Distinction of Merit—General Knowledges are those Knowledges that Idiots possess" (1988, 641).

Statistical thinking has transformed the way economies and governments are managed, the way illness is tracked, the way the efficacy of drugs and medical procedures are established, and the way crime is studied and punishment assessed—in short, it has changed the way investigators of strikingly diverse phenomena seek order in chaos. It is therefore interesting to see that precisely the same concerns literary scholars voice about quantification have been raised in *nearly every* human-related field to which it has been introduced (the single clear exception is psychology) (Stigler 1986, 189–199). As the premier historian of statistics Stephen Stigler writes:

> In the 300 yrs since Newton's *Principia,* mathematical probability and statistics have found application in all the sciences—social, physical, biological. In each area where these ideas have been introduced there has been resistance as the protectors of the different realms have sought to prevent the "Queen of Sciences" [mathematics] from conquering new territory. The arguments against quantification have at times been sound and irrefutable, at other times ignorant and self-serving. At times, the battles have been vicious, scorched earth affairs; at others, they have been carried out on the highest intellectual planes. This tension, between those who appreciate and wish to extend quantitative analysis and those who argue that only qualitative description can deal with the essence of all but the most limited questions that touch our lives, persists today. (Stigler 1986, 203)

Quantitative methodologies were eschewed even in fields where all would now agree that they are absolutely vital. For example, few people today would be keen to ingest a drug or submit to a medical procedure that had not been tested in a large-scale, double-blind study, and few would choose to consult a physician who relied purely on intuition, ignoring statistical studies on the characteristics of illnesses, the efficacy of treatments, and so forth. We would all prefer to consult the physician who combined excellent medical intuition, a firm and broad foundation in the scientific literature, and a deep sensitivity to our individual medical histories. Yet quantification initially met with almost overwhelming resistance in the field of medicine. Opponents objected that "the numerical method" denied "the variability of medical facts, which could only be fully appreciated through induction and medical intuition" (Porter 1986, 159). In short, opponents argued that medicine was an art form and that studies of populations were not useful because the physician's ultimate responsibility was to the individual patient. Statistics were good at describing the composite features of a population—an abstraction that Quetelet dubbed *l'homme moyen* (the average man)—but real patients weren't average men, they were all unique individuals (and not a few were women and children). Old-guard artists of the physic worried that the incursion of mathematics and empiricism would rob medicine "of all rational induction" and reduce it to "a position among the lower grades of experimental observations and fragmentary facts" (Warner 1998, 183–184). Yet it was only in the nineteenth century, when substantial numbers of physicians stopped relying purely on observation and "rational induction," and began implementing scientific methods, that medicine began making dramatic progress beyond Hippocrates and Galen (Barry 2004, 14–35).

A very similar description of the initial reaction to quantitative methods could be constructed for almost all other human-related fields where the value of those methods now goes all but unquestioned.

Critically, the point is *not* that investigators in these fields eventually discovered that everything could be reduced to numbers after all. Rather, they came to realize that a diverse methodological toolkit was utterly indispensable for a reasonably complete exploration of the diversity of their fields; quantitative and qualitative tools were right for different types of questions. For example, a large body of quantitative data about human societies provides anthropology's skeleton while qualitative ethnography gives it flesh. Without qualitative work anthropology would be merely skeletal; without quantitative work anthropology would be shapeless and spineless. It is in this latter condition—sagging from the absence of empirical spine—that literary studies finds itself now.

Thus, while concerns about statistical generalization in literary study are perhaps natural, more quantitative research will be valuable for two principal reasons. First, and most obviously, quantitative analysis may help us do a better job of seeing patterns in complex literary works, or large populations of literary works, that might otherwise have been overlooked or underappreciated. As Anthony Kenny writes, the value of this sort of quantification can be likened to the value of aerial photography:

> Photography from the sky can enable patterns to be detected which are obscured when one is too close to the ground: it enables us to see the wood despite the trees. So the statistical study of a text [or texts] can reveal broad patterns, macroscopic uniformities in a writer's work [or a population of works] which can escape notice as one reads word by word and sentence by sentence. (1986, 116; a recent example of work in the "aerial" vein is Moretti 2005)

Overgeneralizing *can* lead to a sort of idiocy in which the importance of minute particulars is ignored. But William Blake was spectacularly wrong: all virtue obviously does not reside in minute particulars. Generalities are important too and concentrating only on the minute particulars—while denying that the trees form a forest—represents an equally abject kind of idiocy.

Second, the addition of a quantitative dimension to literary scholarship will substantially improve the power and precision of strictly qualitative work. By way of illustration, consider practice in fields of the social sciences where, despite sometimes-uneasy relationships between mainly qualitative and mainly quantitative researchers, there is a general appreciation of the complementarity of the two methodologies: some important questions yield to quantitative methods and some do not. But those social scientists who work with qualitative tools still reap great benefits from the rich body of data developed on the quantitative side (and of course it works the other way too, with the quantitative work bolstered and inspired by the qualitative). At present, literary scholarship cannot draw on these synergies because, for all intents and purposes, there is no quantitative branch of literary analysis. Therefore, in addition to the direct knowledge produced by a quantitative branch of literary inquiry, indirect benefits would also accrue to qualitative researchers whose work would be disciplined and inspired by empirical information. We can anticipate a ratcheting effect, whereby a scientific branch of literary analysis would improve the power of qualitative studies, which, in turn, would improve the depth and precision of the scientific branch, and so on.

This is very far from arguing that scientific quantification is, as a rule, superior to traditional humanistic methods of careful reading and reasoning. Both sets of methods are tools: like hammers and screwdrivers they are exquisitely fashioned to address narrow ranges of tasks. For the scholar and the scientist, the challenge is to select the right class of tools for the problem. Sometimes the hammer is called for, sometimes only the screwdriver will do, and for complex problems a diverse methodological toolkit is frequently needed to do the job right.

In sum, it is a mistake to see quantitative and qualitative methods as competing alternatives; they are, on the contrary, entirely complementary. Each set of tools helps to make up for the inadequacies of the other. The Shakespeare scholar mentioned above, Richard Moulton, emphasized a similar point in his own call for a scientific branch of literary study that would thrive alongside the belletristic, "Scientific criticism and the criticism of taste have distinct spheres: and the whole of literary history shows that the failure to keep the two separate results in mutual confusion" (1888, 68). Nearly 120 years later, "the whole of literary history" still shows precisely the same thing: much "mutual confusion" arises from the failure to comprehend that different types of problems require different types of tools.

(However, I differ from Moulton in one important respect: Empirical and nonempirical questions do not form separate, nonoverlapping magisteria, the former being pervious to scientific analysis and the latter not. Moulton's formulation suggests that the spheres are neat, clean, geometric, and distinct. But the reality is a lot messier. There are questions of empirical fact that resist methodologically scientific analysis and, as I will argue below, there are "softer" questions of judgment and meaning where quantitative methods may be fruitfully applied.)

*   *   *

The objection may arise that these arguments, like those of nineteenth-century "social physicists," are based on a false or strained analogy between literary study, where data are messy and complex, and fields where data are simpler and more straightforward. The abortive field of "social physics" failed to reduce human social life to a few fundamental laws because, in contrast to the phenomena studied by physicists, the forces governing human social life are vastly complex. But there is not a similar gulf in the complexity of phenomena studied by social scientists and literary scholars. Both fields explore exactly the same complicated things, although in different types of data sources: human social behavior, psychology, culture, creativity, and cognition. Literary study *does* often deal in the unquantifiable and the not easily quantifiable, but in this it is not different from most other human-related fields, where many important questions are always best approached qualitatively. Sociologists, anthropologists, cognitive scientists, economists, and psychologists all face daunting challenges in attempting to assign numbers to different aspects of human behavior, society, culture, and psychology. These problems are never fully resolved. Rather, ideally, the problems are confronted, difficulties are minimized as much as is practical, and potential inadequacies are frankly acknowledged. These shortcomings can be addressed in follow-up studies, and researchers can be most confident in their knowledge when unaffiliated investigators applying different methods converge on the same results.

Before moving on, I must also address the distressingly common objection that scientifically studying beautiful things is simply vulgar; instead of exalting beauty, such study diminishes and deadens it. I side with Richard Dawkins, who has argued—eloquently and at book length—that this objection gets it almost exactly backwards: scientific understanding is not at odds with aesthetic or artistic appreciation. In fact, the most intriguing contention in Dawkins' *Unweaving the Rainbow* (1998) is that artists and scientists are not the opposites portrayed in the stereotypes: they are attracted to the same types of questions, big ones and small, and are impelled by the same emotions of wonderment and awe. Dawkins draws the title of his study from Keats' poem "Lamia." At a dinner party, Keats complained that Newton had "destroyed the beauty of the rainbow by reducing it to a prism" (recorded in Haydon 1876, v.2, 54–55) and then wrote in "Lamia" that "cold" natural philosophy had clipped the wings of angels, conquered all mysteries, and "unweaved" rainbows. Blake felt similarly: he distrusted natural philosophy and ranted against the ethic of reductionism. He described Bacon and Newton (and Locke) as teachers of "Satan's doctrine" (recorded in Robinson 1869, 306) and, according to Northrop Frye, this "unholy trinity," "this three-headed Gerberus of hell," is "constantly in Blake's poetry a symbol of every kind of evil, superstition and tyranny" (see Frye 1949, 377, 189, 17). Similarly felt Wordsworth: "Sweet is the lore which Nature brings; / Our meddling intellect / Mis-shapes the beauteous forms of things:- / We murder to dissect" (*The Tables Turned*, 25–28).

These romantic prejudices are well represented in contemporary culture by images of warm and sensitive poets juxtaposed against coldly rational scientists; the former celebrate the beauty and mystery of nature and the latter seek to dissect it (and in the process of carving Beauty at the joints, of course, the scientist murders it). John Ross inhabits this position in a recent commentary on the study of literature from a biological perspective:

> The danger of this rather grandiose scheme is that, by reducing culture and art to biological phenomena, we may lose our sense of wonder at the strangeness, extravagance, and glory of language, art, and creativity. Evolutionary literary criticism tends to diminish rather than exalt the highest productions of the human spirit. Demystified, these things lose their fascination. (Ross 2006, 1457)

But Dawkins and other thinkers have exposed this thinking as facile. Newton may have used his prism to unweave the rainbow, but this did not reduce by a single jot his prostrating sense of humble, religious awe at all that nature had revealed and all that she kept resolutely hidden. Learned astronomers such as Carl Sagan have felt little ring of truth in Whitman's poem: knowledge of the movement of the stars does not dull the shine of the nighttime sky; the heavens are as bright and many new mysteries are born for each that is solved. When told that scientists miss out on the beauty of flowers by studying them, the physicist Richard Feynman retorted:

> The beauty that is there for you is also available for me, too. But I see a deeper beauty that isn't so readily available to others. I can see the complicated interactions of the flower. The color of the flower is red. Does the fact that the plant has color mean that it evolved to attract insects? This adds a further question. Can insects see color? Do they have an aesthetic sense? And so on. I don't see how studying a flower ever detracts from its beauty. It only adds. (2001, 2)

As a final example in this vein, *The Origin of Species* ends with a famous poem in prose—a meditation on the beauty and the "grandeur in this view of life":

> It is interesting to contemplate an entangled bank, clothed with many plants of many kinds, with birds singing on the bushes, with various insects flitting about, and with worms crawling through the damp earth, and to reflect that these elaborately constructed forms, so different from each other, and dependent on each other in so complex a manner, have all been produced by laws acting around us… Thus, from the war of nature, from famine and death, the most exalted object which we are capable of conceiving, namely, the production of the higher animals, directly follows. There is grandeur in this view of life, with its several powers, having been originally breathed into a few forms or into one; and that, whilst this planet has gone cycling on according to the fixed law of gravity, from so simple a beginning endless forms most beautiful and most wonderful have been, and are being, evolved. (Darwin 1859, 397–398)

*   *   *

As should be clear by now, I claim no priority in my call for a methodologically scientific dimension to literary study. In contrast to most previous scientific approaches to literary study (where the word "scientific" really meant something like "systematic"), the last three decades have seen attempts to establish a methodologically scientific arm of literary study (e.g., De Beaugrande 1989; Schmidt 1982, 1992; Martindale 1990, 1996; Miall 2006; Van Peer et al. 2007). But despite their best efforts, advocates have never come close to mustering the critical mass required to move quantitative methods from the far fringes to the mainstream. The reasons for this are small and large. There are fears about the ease of "lying with statistics" (as though there were no sophists or charlatans prior to the mid–seventeenth century rise of statistical methodology); there is significant concern in some quarters about the political and ideological ramifications of scientific method-ologies (as though the "values" of science were mainly inherent in the tools rather than their wielders); and there is the practical fact that a stunningly high proportion of literary scholars honestly believe them-selves to be mathematically disabled (as though concepts taught in undergraduate statistics courses are beyond the faculties of people with the brains and discipline to earn doctorates).*

While these issues, and those discussed above, are contributing factors, the most important impediment is the old and largely unexamined assumption that the objects literary scholars study, and the questions we ask, are of a fundamentally different kind than those addressed in all nonhumanities disciplines (for sustained criticism of these views see Mantzavinos 2005; see also Slingerland 2008). The traditional role of the critic has been to provide trained but ulti-mately subjective evaluations of literary beauty and value. As Arnold wrote, "judging is often spoken of as the critic's one business" (1864, 823) and Emerson defined critics as "esteemed umpires of taste" (1844, 215).

But the kinds of questions literary intellectuals address have changed radically since the days of Arnold and Emerson. Literary scholars still participate in the old forms of belletristic criticism, as well they should, but "pure" literary criticism—questions of trained taste, valuation, and intensely subjective response—recruit smaller and smaller proportions of the discipline's total energies. I would

---

*The common feeling that the minds that gravitate toward language and literature are unsuited for math receives an interesting challenge from the history of statistics. A surprising number of the most influential figures in the development of "modern statistical methodology" were also competent scholars or producers of literature. For example, Quetelet wrote the libretto to an opera, a historical survey of romance, and much poetry. Karl Pearson (1857–1936), who is ranked among the greatest statisti-cians of all time, wrote plays and published articles on medieval German literature. Francis Ysidro Edgeworth (1845–1926), an important statistical innovator, had an outstanding literary mind. He studied classics at Trinity College, Dublin, where he took first prizes in Greek prose and verse composition and was considered by his tutors to be the best student in his class. Graunt's contemporary and close friend William Petty (1623–1687), a founder of "political arithmetic," was a professor of music at Gresham College who dabbled in the composition of Latin poetry (biographical details from Johnson and Kotz 1997; Stigler 1986).

suggest, in fact, that *most* of the questions contemporary literary scholars address are vitally contingent on specific fact claims about empirical reality. While many scholars have dismissed the entire idea of "facts" in the course of a larger ideological critique, this has not stopped them from making copious fact claims about the nature of gender, race, ethnicity, human psychology, economics, politics, or, for that matter, the factuality of facts themselves. In its hard swerve toward cultural critique, the field has moved rapidly and decisively away from arguments over aesthetic taste and valuation—so rapidly that many believe (and others fear) that the field has become, "inadvertently but surely ... social science without statistics" (Perloff 2005, 677). Leaving aside qualms about the sort of questions literary scholars *should* be asking—Harold Bloom grumbles that we are becoming just one more "dismal social science" (1995, 17)—if we are going to address questions that overlap those of the social sciences, surely we should do an excellent job of it. That is, our investigations should be guided by the best theory and we should use the most rigorous methods we can practically apply.

In short, the problem could not be more elementary: the questions literary scholars address have changed dramatically, but we have not altered our methods. We attack our new questions with almost the same methodological panoply connoisseurs deployed in their battles over the musical dissonances and harmonies of this or that poem.

Those willing to accept this characterization will now reasonably inquire, How, *exactly*, are we to proceed differently? How can there be a science of the literary? How do we begin to assign numbers to the riot of information conveyed in a text? In confronting this challenge—and it *is* a high challenge to which we must rise—we can begin by consulting examples from the social sciences. For example, a common problem across these fields is that many types of valuable information come only in text form: government documents, political speeches, personal romantic advertisements, subject interviews, ethnographies, and so on. Traditionally, investigators have attempted to extract information from these sources qualitatively, in much the same way that literary scholars extract information from their texts. However, over the past half century, "content analysts" from diverse disciplines have been developing an increasingly sophisticated suite of methods—and software—for reducing some aspects of the information in text messages to a form suitable for scientific analysis (for a historical survey, see Neuendorf 2002, 27–46). Thus the encouraging answer to the questions posed at the head of this paragraph is that many different methods for quantifying text are already widely in use in other fields—to make a start, all we need to do is adapt them for our purposes.*

I am lingering over the example of content analysis because it happens to be the method employed in the case studies of this book. But I fear that this narrow focus may give readers the mistaken sense that when I speak about scientific approaches to literary study what I am really talking about is content analysis. I'm not. Content analysis is just one tool among very many. For example my collaborators and I—Joseph Carroll,** John Johnson, Daniel Kruger—have recently completed a large-scale study of readers' emotional and analytic responses to the depiction of many scores of characters in 144 British novels of the "long" nineteenth century (Jane Austen to E. M. Forster). The full results of this study will soon be published in a book titled *Graphing Jane Austen: Human Nature in British Novels of the Nineteenth Century* [under consideration]. Here are just a few of the findings:

- True to conventional wisdom, authors systematically distort the depiction of opposite sex characters. Male authors masculinize female characters, and female authors feminize their males. Interestingly, however, the distortions appear to be most extreme in the works of female authors.
- The norms of the novels are gynocentric. That is, the "good" characters—the characters respondents "root for" and code as protagonists—possess overall personality profiles that are closest to the averages for female characters.
- Contrary to our theory-based expectations, the differences between antagonists and protagonists are far larger and more distinct than differences between males and females. The personality profiles show that male and female protagonists share *much* more in common with each other than they do with antagonists of their own sex. As we conclude in *Graphing Jane Austen*: "Being male or female matters, but being good or bad matters more."

---

* The best single guide to quantitative research in the humanities is Van Peer et al.'s *Muses and Measures* (2007). This book combines an apologia for quantitative methods with a "how to" manual that instructs humanists in the basics of scientific study design, statistical testing, and use of common statistical software. Especially welcome is Van Peer et al.'s list of responses to dozens of common misconceptions about scientific research in the humanities (see pages 24–32, 350–357).

** Primary investigator.

Further, since all of the case studies in this volume reflect my personal fascination with world folktales and with the intersections of literature and evolutionary science, I fear that readers may get the sense that quantitative methods are only applicable to these narrow classes of investigation. They aren't. For example, *Graphing Jane Austen* is designed to address a variety of questions in the fields of psychology and behavioral biology. But this survey of 500 avid readers and scholars was also designed to address traditional questions of literary meaning and interpretation. For example, our data allow us to weigh in on *the* big question in reader response: Generally speaking, how successfully do authors constrain the meanings and significances that readers take away from texts? At one end of the continuum, scholars have proposed that literary texts function like Rorschach tests: the words on the page serve as ink blots that encourage readers to project and create meanings and significances that are profoundly idiosyncratic. Others have claimed that authors are highly successful in orchestrating response to their works, and that the only locus of true meaning is authorial intention (e.g., Hirsch 1967). Debates over this question have been very loud and very long (sound and fury, by the way, is a predictable outcome of debates almost totally lacking a foundation in data). But, like many other issues literary scholars ponder, questions of reader response cannot be much advanced (much less settled) by more assertion, argument, or arrangement of anecdotes. Our survey data revealed some variation among our readers (of course, it is to be expected that a veteran of the Marine Corps might well experience a war novel differently than a veteran of the Peace Corps; that a person who has experienced sexual abuse may relate differently from the average to *Tess of the D'Urbervilles*), but that variation was well contained within tight normative ranges. These data suggest that authors expertly constrain not only the analytical, but also the *emotional* range of response to their creations. The results presented in *Graphing Jane Austen* suggest that—at least as far as nineteenth-century British novels go—the author is alive and well.

Similarly, interpretation. The study of British novels was partly designed to explore whether, and how far, quantitative methods might be fruitfully extended into the realm of traditional literary interpretation. We generated predictions from prominent interpretive hypotheses of specific novels, and we have sought to use our survey data to address them. Consider the history of critical response to Hardy's *Mayor of Casterbridge*. Over decades, the main interpretive models for *Mayor* presuppose the reader's *passional* involvement with a protagonist. Passional involvement is indeed a common way in which novels work, but it is not the only way, and, according to our response data, it is not the way *Mayor* works. Our eighty-five respondents (who were mostly Hardy specialists) did not care deeply about the plights of the characters. On the contrary, *Mayor's* characters received especially low scores on the response factor Interest (which basically means that readers expressed indifference toward the characters). About 80 percent of all characters in the sample of nineteenth-century novels had higher Interest scores than the six main characters in *Mayor*. Though Henchard is the story's main character, his score on Interest is just average among all characters in the study, including those identified as "minor" characters. In short, these results cast doubt upon a dominant notion in the history of the criticism of the novel—the notion that the novel does its work by involving the reader, at a deep emotional level, in the struggles of the protagonists. On the contrary, our data suggest that readers experience *Mayor* with an attitude of reflective detachment. Overall, our work on *Mayor* suggests something quite radical: not only is it possible to be wrong about a literary critical judgment, but it is possible to gather data and use it to *demonstrate* that a judgment is likely to be wrong.

Finally, while this aspect of the study does not lend itself to bullet points, *Graphing Jane Austen* illustrates the potentially synergistic relationship of quantitative and qualitative tools. The survey data allowed us to create detailed personality profiles for dozens of characters and of reader's emotional and analytic responses to those characters. A portion of *Graphing Jane Austen* is given over to using this data to produce "re-readings" of major characters and works. Franco Moretti has called quantitative literary study a kind of "distance reading" (2005) that has usually focused (so far) on the literary macrocosm. But what fascinates us about distance reading is the way that it can sharpen the acuity of close reading—helping to accentuate microcosmic, fine-grained aspects of literary character, theme, and tone.

*   *   *

Of course, these are not the first experiments in applying quantitative methods to literary questions. For example, a number of interesting stylometric studies have been used to show—decisively according to some observers (Boyd 2003)—that many of Shakespeare's plays were written with coauthors. These designs were not only able to identify who his collaborators were, but to strongly suggest which passages were written by the Bard and which by his helpers (for a book-length study, including a good critical history of stylometry, see Vickers 2002; for the uses of computers in stylometric analysis see Hockey 2000). Richard Janko addressed age-old debates about the origins of the Homeric compositions through a statistical study of Homeric linguistic forms compared to linguistic forms in more precisely datable texts; Janko's studies are a bright star in a constellation of evidence that leads most contemporary Homerists to date the *Iliad* and *Odyssey* to somewhere around eighth century BC (1982). More recently, a research team led by Cambridge University *biochemists* have made important contributions to our understanding of the Chaucerian manuscript tradition (Barbrook et al. 1998; Windram et al. 2005). The researchers traced the evolutionary history of the manuscripts in almost precisely the same way they trace common ancestry in different biological lineages—they studied rates of error in the manuscripts in the same way they study rates of mutation in the genetic "text" of A's, C's, T's, and G's. As Howe and colleagues explained in a recent review article in the journal *Trends in Genetics*,

> Clearly, the model of changes being introduced during copying [of manuscripts by hand] and then propagated in subsequent rounds closely resembles the introduction of mutations into DNA and their subsequent propagation. Similarly, the process of using comparisons between texts to infer a tree of relationships has a close parallel in the use of nucleotide or amino acid sequence data from a range of different organisms to construct a phylogenetic tree showing how they are related. There is a wide range of powerful methods and computer programs available to handle the sequence data used for phylogenetic inference, and these can be used more or less unchanged to handle manuscript data to generate credible stemmata. (2001, 147)

In a different vein, researches have done work that gives some preliminary support to the hypothesis of an *écriture féminine*. Moshe Koppel and colleagues (2002) devised an algorithm that can process writing samples and accurately infer the author's gender 80 percent of the time. Colin Martindale was among the first to use survey methodology to begin addressing questions of reader response (1996), and his bold, feisty book, *The Clockwork Muse* (1990), employs computer algorithms to translate literature into statistical data. Martindale's results challenge the conventional view that art traditions change rapidly, and mainly in response to large-scale sociopolitical shifts. Martindale found that literary traditions actually change gradually and predictably—like clockwork, in fact. From this he concludes that the principal driver of artistic change is not social, political, or religious upheaval, but the simple pressure on individual artists to "make it new." Eric Rabkin, Carl Simon, and their many coder-collaborators have quantitatively analyzed thousands of twentieth-century science fiction stories, and have used that data to test prominent academic claims (there was no 1960s "boom" in SF by women) as well as to evaluate a major hypothesis of their own about the Darwinian nature of genre evolution (Rabkin 2004). While reader response theorists like Wolfgang Iser and Stanley Fish were growing famous for their speculations about the responses of a platonic form known as the "ideal reader," others, such as David Miall and his colleagues, were conducting laboratory studies of how actual, ordinary people think, feel, and respond as they read (Miall 2006).* Scholars such as Franco Moretti (2005) and William St. Clair (2007) have embarked upon ambitious, quantitative studies of literary history and book history that, although at early stages, indicate that critical issues can be addressed in a responsibly numeric fashion and that the findings will often challenge our expectations. Finally, scientific approaches are making some headway in other fields of the humanities like history (e.g., Sulloway 1996; Diamond 1997; Turchin 2003, 2005) and, perhaps most interestingly, in an emerging approach to analytical philosophy called experimental philosophy (or X-Phil, as it has been shrewdly marketed). Experimental philosophers have applied the methods of experimental psychology to generate quantitative data with a direct bearing on ancient debates about the foundations of intuition, free will, morality, and intention (for overviews see Knobe, forthcoming; Nichols 2004; Lackman 2006).

*   *   *

This short survey is obviously not intended to be exhaustive; it is intended to provide a brief glimpse of large, fertile fields for research programs in quantitative literary analysis that are currently lying fallow. But as interesting as these studies are, they all represent early,

---

* In addition to survey methods, reader response hypotheses can also be tested with the use of technologies like the fMRI (and its developing successor technologies), which can spy into reading brains and compare their activities. Moreover, potentially useful data on emotional states can be gathered from instruments that measure the autonomic responses of readers (heart and respiration rate, perspiration, even sexual arousal), and from simple salivary swabs that can provide hormonal indicators of emotions experienced during reading.

sometimes awkward applications of scientific methods to humanities questions—often by scholars who are learning those methods on the fly. Moreover, it would be at least as easy to assemble a parallel list of inept scientific investigations of literature. It cannot be denied that humanistic attempts to apply scientific methods have often been guilty of amateur errors in data selection, basic study design, and statistical procedures (for discussion see Vickers 2002; for similar criticism of experimental philosophy see Bernstein 2007). But these deeply flawed studies cannot be responsibly deployed as warnings against the folly of a science of literature, or as illustrations of an inherent and unbridgeable methodological divide. They are nothing of the sort. They are merely warnings against shoddy work. One should remember that it would be easiest of all to compile endlessly depressing bibliographies of startlingly inept work based on purely qualitative approaches. In either case, shoddy qualitative or quantitative approaches should not lead us to dismiss the whole approach; they should challenge us to do better.

*   *   *

All of the above examples have something in common: They all feature literary hypotheses that make testable predictions about empirical reality. Recognizing that a large percentage of literary hypotheses are based, at least in part, in claims about empirical reality does not mean that testing those claims scientifically will be an easy or straightforward process. The methodological model for the humanities will not be the clean one of physics or chemistry; it will entail the messier, probabilistic triangulations of the life and social sciences. In these fields, progress rarely emerges from sweepingly definitive experiments; it emerges when slow accretions of independent findings converge in support of a hypothesis.

Granted, testing literary hypotheses presents challenges that are unique to the field. Perhaps foremost among these are the length and sheer variety of literary works, as well as the undeniable challenges of translating words and concepts into the language of statistics. But all fields of inquiry face unique, field-specific challenges that researchers must struggle at high costs to overcome. For instance, there are also huge barriers to reconstructing human prehistory on the basis of scattered fossils, artifacts, and molecular analysis; or deriving the organizing principles of human sociality; or solving the mystery of why most of the world's inhabitants believe in some form of god; or deriving a unifying theory in physics; or really understanding the language of the human genome (sequencing it was the *easy* part); or solving the great unanswered question of the brain sciences: What is consciousness? But these difficulties have not deterred researchers from devoting the energies of their careers to resolving them. To the contrary, the difficulty of these questions has added to their glamour and attracted the best minds in the respective fields. Are the obstacles to testing literary hypotheses so much more formidable than these?

If you respond, with me, *Surely not!*, then another question arises. Why, at bottom, have we totally eschewed such a successful method for gaining reliable answers to certain types of empirical questions? Given the scientific method's spectacular successes in shrinking the space of possible explanation, why is it that only a tiny fraction of literary scholars have experimented with its application? This is part of what I'll be exploring in the next chapter.

Chapter 3

On Attitude

In what is perhaps history's most influential meditation on the role of literary criticism, "The Function of Criticism at the Present Time," Mathew Arnold advised critics to strive "to see the object as in itself it really is" (1864, 806) and he defined criticism as "the disinterested endeavor to learn and propagate the best that is known and thought in the world" (823). For Arnold, things were quite simple:

> [The governing rule of criticism] may be summed up in one word *disinterestedness*. And how is criticism to show disinterestedness? By keeping aloof from what is called "the practical view of things.".... By steadily refusing to lend itself to any of those ulterior, political, practical considerations about ideas which plenty of people will be sure to attach to them, which perhaps ought often to be attached to them, which in this country at any rate are certain to be attached to them quite sufficiently, but which criticism has really nothing to do with.... Its business is to do this with inflexible honesty, with due ability; but its business is to do no more, and to leave alone all questions of practical consequences and applications. (1864, 814–815)

Trilling called Arnold the founding father of modern literary criticism (1939) and, until the advent of the liberationist paradigm in the late 1960s, most literary scholars would have been more or less comfortable with Arnold's "elementary laws" (1864, 822). Scholars generally conceived of themselves as striving to make real and lasting contributions to the fund of human knowledge; they saw the pursuit of disinterestedness as a worthy, if elusive, goal. The liberationists, however, questioned—and continue to question—both the desirability and the possibility of disinterested inquiry. According to the liberationist creed, not to be actively fighting Injustice is to be Injustice's sneaking accomplice. A scholar who claimed not to take sides in the great political struggles *through* his academic work had, in fact, already cast his lot with the wrong one. Soon the guiding Arnoldian precepts—that progressive understanding was possible, but only if thinkers worked to keep inquiry pure of practical (i.e., sociopolitical) considerations—were aggressively derided for their preciousness and their de facto conservativism; no one would be so naïve (or reactionary) as to seek to "establish a current of true and fresh ideas" (1864, 823).

In fact, the liberationists inaugurated an approach to literary investigation that would be an incarnation of Arnold's most terrifying nightmares. Consistent with his boldly expansive concept of the objects within criticism's scope, they enacted a criticism that would become the boundary-wrecking juggernaut of Theory. But it would also be a criticism where practitioners, instead of struggling to suppress their biases, would proclaim, accentuate, and celebrate them. Many critics of the contemporary paradigm, myself included, would feel justified in transferring Arnold's assessment of criticism in his day to ours:

> For what is at present the bane of criticism in this country? It is that practical considerations cling to it and stifle it. It subserves interests not its own. Our organs of criticism are organs of men and parties having practical ends to serve, and with them those practical ends are the first thing and the play of the mind the second. (1864, 815)

But in some respects, the revolt from Arnold was healthy and necessary. The liberationists pointed out, rightly, that it is very hard for humans to be truly disinterested and it is hard to say which, if any, of all those fresh ideas generated by Arnoldian critics were actually true. Arnold's own analysis, in "The Function of Criticism at the Present Time," illustrates some of the limitations in the program he proposes. In the course of the essay, Arnold applies his disinterested critical faculties to make overconfident, highly contestable assertions about the ultimate sources of creativity in given historical milieus, and strident value judgments about the poets Shelley ("so incoherent") and Wordsworth ("profound but lacking in completeness and variety") (809). Is *this*—this "chatter about Shelley"—the current of "true and fresh" ideas that will be the harvest of disinterested attempts to see the object as it really is? Given the shortcomings in Arnold's own arguments, and of others working in the Arnoldian mode, it is hard to blame the liberationists for their dissatisfaction, for their skepticism, and for seeking a different way.

Perissons en resistant!

To this point, I have suggested that sundry maladies afflicting literary academia emerge from a persistent failure to generate a "current of fresh and true ideas" capable of progressively shrinking the space of possible explanation. I've so far identified two large factors—theory and method—that contribute to this failing. The third factor is attitude. Contemporary literary study has been preoccupied with sociopolitical advocacy and—in its extreme forms—by "a studied refusal to acknowledge any criteria of judgment except sheer subversiveness toward an imagined establishment" (Crews 2006, 211). As Bromwich writes, "Since the 1960s the place of advocacy in teaching and research has become so prominent as almost to constitute in itself a separate description of what scholarship in the humanities is" (1997, 220). In this milieu, to hew to the Arnoldian line of neutral inquiry was almost the same as blazoning reactionary political sympathies. As they used to tell me in graduate school, not having an agenda *is* an agenda (and, it was implied, probably a baleful one at that).

Thus, activist scholars did not neutralize charges of bias by denying it. On the contrary, they proudly proclaimed their biases and openly lauded them in the works of others (so long as those biases ran in the proper direction). At the same time, however, they absolutely denied the *possibility* of work that did not take a side in the liberationist struggle. All intellectual investigations—especially in the human related fields—were inflected by the acknowledged or unacknowledged ideologies of the investigators. The main difference between the liberationists and more traditional investigators was that the former were honest about their biases while the latter developed elaborate conventions to conceal theirs—usually even from themselves.

In short, in recent decades the strongest and most populous tribes of literary intellectuals have seen their work as part of something very big and important. They have seen their teaching and their writing as a place for raising consciousness about injustice and agitating for progressive or radical social transformations. For whatever social progress has resulted from this work (and the amount of progress, or lack thereof, has been much debated), the hyper-politicization of the field has been a decisive factor in its failure—relative to other disciplines and to what might have been—to generate more reliable and durable knowledge (for related arguments see Fish 2008).

The problem is not only that literary scholars have been biased, but also that they have all been biased in the same direction. Of course there have been many real and intense skirmishes among the various tribes of liberationist scholars, but these are all debates from within the Left. The most influential dissent has not emerged from the marginalized traditionalists at the National Association of Scholars—with their flaccid "geriatric rage"—it has emerged from the far Left. Leftish thinkers attack other leftish thinkers for failing to do work that is *really and truly* socially and politically engaged. The recently published *Norton Anthology of Literary Theory and Criticism* is a hefty monument to the most influential thinkers in the field over the last 2500 years. The last fifty years occupy about half of the volume's 2600 pages, and the overwhelming majority of the collected writers are explicitly defined in the editorial introductions, and/or by themselves, as enlisting their academic studies in service of the sociopolitical programs of the progressive or radical left. Most are defined, at least in part, through politics, but no one is described as an advocate of conservative or rightist causes.

So over the last decades the field—with its ideological homogeneity, its intolerance for dissent, and built in vulnerabilities to groupthink—has possessed none of the checks on shoddy thinking that come with rich intellectual and political diversity. Because literary scholars so rarely address general readerships, they are almost always and only speaking (1) to students who can usually be trusted to suffer meekly whatever they say, or (2) the choir of right-thinking literary academics. They can be confident that their formulations will be handled pretty gently so long as they are on the right side (that is, the left side) politically.

To use a Darwinian metaphor, we have created an environment where there are few selective forces countering the emergence of sheer intellectual peacockery. In the absence of counter-selective forces, positions and rhetoric grow ever gaudier—good for making personal display of wit, erudition, and proper political emotion, but not for shrinking the space of possible explanation.*

---

* After writing this, I came across John Ellis's *Literature Lost*, which develops a similar analogy between the displays of literary scholars and the extravagant excesses of sexual selection: "This is rather like the Irish elk syndrome…competition for dominance within the species led to the evolution of ever larger antlers, but the larger antlers caused the species as a whole to become dysfunctional and dragged it down" (1997, 211).

To understand the malignancy of this situation, all that is required is an intensely simple, if terrifying, thought experiment: imagine that the political situation was reversed. Imagine that university English faculties were dominated by conservative activists. The rightist activists jam all literary and cultural production through narrow ideological filters, and they evangelize from the lectern and the page about their dearest political causes (although stressing how scrupulously they avoid indoctrinating their students): the end of the welfare system, the scientific status of Intelligent Design, a moratorium on embryonic stem cell research, the sanctity of marriage, an end to the genocide of the unborn, demystifying the leftist ideology of global climate change, and so on. A dictatorship of traditional virtue asserts itself; "lib" dissenters are beyond the pale and are effectively forced into hiding. The radical conservatives conduct erudite, rhetorically scintillating, theory-rich readings of literary texts that always locate troves of evidence brilliantly supporting their political positions.

For most academics (including most conservative academics), this is a fanciful sketch of what life would be like in hell's inner ring. Clearly these political dynamics would distort and disfigure the discipline so absolutely that its production would be indistinguishable from travesty; in such an environment there could be no current of fresh and true ideas and no progressive shrinking of possibility space.

This is my point: a travesty almost as extreme *has* been enacted over the past decades. The fact that those within earshot of this book are so much more apt to personally *like* the ideas espoused on the left more than those on the right is immaterial. Either way, standards of scholarship and intellectual integrity are mocked; the field's status as a rigorous and responsible discipline erodes as it is subsumed in a larger political machine; all that matters is that your side vanquishes the other; knowledge does not accumulate, though much agitprop does.

*   *   *

The point of this chapter is that *if* shrinking the space of possible explanation is considered a worthy goal, we simply must rehabilitate and revamp the concept of disinterestedness. Moreover, of the three major changes to the current paradigm that I have proposed, this attitudinal shift may be most important. For, as was suggested in the first chapter, the political interests of literary scholars have helped dictate the paradigm's deficient theories and methods; theories and methods that challenge the complacency of liberationist thinking, whatever their virtues, have lacked traction because they threaten ideas that are considered vital to "the struggle." Arnold was not as naïve as he has sometimes been portrayed. He believed in progress and expressed a faith—impossible to countenance today—in human perfectibility. However, he recognized that perfect disinterestedness, though a noble goal, was perhaps also an unreachable one. Moreover, as a committed liberal himself, he also acknowledged the strong temptation to subsume the critical mission within the practical one. But he insisted that the "critic's duty is to refuse, or, if resistance is vain, at least to cry with Obermann: *perissons en resistant!*" [let us die resisting].

I believe that this is exactly the attitude that contemporary literary scholars should seek to cultivate. I would not advocate a naïve regression to the fantasy that intellectual inquiry (scientific or humanistic) can be purely objective and value-neutral. But, for decades *literary scholars have mistaken the fact that it is not easy to be objective in one's intellectual work for a license to give up trying.* What is needed is a generation of scholars who would recognize, and seek to occupy, the middle area between the strong relativism of the liberationist paradigm and the naïve Enlightenment dream of "wholly disinterested knowledge" (Eagleton 1983, 62). Through the *pursuit* of more objective knowledge combined with better governing theories and better analytic methods, we can begin establishing (to quote Arnold once more), "an order of ideas, if not absolutely true, then true by comparison with that which it displaces" (1864, 809).

I would also argue—counter to the intuitions of most—that this is the *only* way our work can begin having real consequence in the social and political sphere.

Engagement through Disengagement

The best way to communicate this last point is through a comparison with the sciences. Scientists are not, as a rule, less political than humanists, and the issues they confront do not roil with lesser political fury. Scientists, in fact, help shape our responses to issues of momentous sociopolitical significance. Just to pluck a few dramatic examples from recent headlines, scientists have played leading roles in *political* debates over responses to global climate change, the teaching of creationism in public schools, and the efficacy of ballistic missile defense; they have also weighed in on the multitudinous ethical and practical dimensions of genetic engineering, embryonic stem cell research, and the "right to die." Of course, the list of examples where scientists play consequential roles in influencing how we respond to major sociopolitical issues could be extended *ad nauseam*.

Now let's consider a bitterly contentious question: What has been the actual, practical effect of literary academia's decades-long struggle to refashion the intellectual and social landscape of Western society? Has the impact been large, moderate, or small? Have we played a substantial role in the important social transformations that have occurred, or have we merely piggybacked onto changes that were already well underway (for variations on the latter view see Boyd 2006; Fish 2004, 1995; Poovey 2004; Levin 2003, 11)? This debate will continue. But one thing seems beyond debate: In comparison to the prominence of scientists on the political stage, humanists, despite their professed ardor for engagement, play a minuscule role. This is not to deny that literary scholars have had penetrating things to say about globalization, racial or gender or religious prejudice, income inequality, immigration reform, or many other topics of the day. But how many people have been listening? Relative to social and natural scientists (or historians), how often have literary scholars appeared on the evening news, on Terry Gross's *Fresh Air*, or in the pages of popular magazines to discuss issues of sociopolitical import? How can the political profile of literary studies be so low when its whole direction—almost its whole purpose—has been engagement with our thorniest cultural problems?

Part of the reason, indubitably, is that scientists happen to possess expertise about big, dramatic, even apocalyptic issues (global warming, natural disasters, nuclear proliferation, etc.). But literary scholars engage with big issues too—issues that arguably have more immediate implications to the daily struggles of ordinary people. It is just that fewer people care to hear what we have to say about the "war on terror," the scourge of global corporate empires, income inequality, or the nature of gender roles. (On these issues, people are more likely to seek out the opinions of historians, political scientists, economists, and psychologists.) So why do scientists—who devote far less *professional* energy to direct political struggles—possess most of the political heft (not to mention most of the intellectual acclaim) while literary scholars have comparatively little?

I believe that the answer to this question is simple. Both the wider intelligentsia and the general public feel that the institution of science—for whatever flaws must hound a human institution—has *earned* great respect. People generally trust scientific information, not because they are naïve, but because they understand that science is an Arnoldian institution: investigators are animated by "the scientific passion, the sheer desire to see things as they are," and they have developed a set of powerful tools for checking (though never eliminating) all of the biases that cloud sight; these tools include the conventions of peer-review and replication, and they are known collectively as the scientific method. This isn't to suggest that scientists are purer of motive than nonscientists. Scientists also have their grimy hopes for professional advancement and for the power and prestige that goes with it. But the incentive structure of scientific institutions is set up so that these rewards are more likely to fall upon individuals who make the most progress in seeing things as they actually are.

Thus in contrast to the scientists who are credited with producing relatively disinterested knowledge for policy makers to act upon, people understand that literary scholars have not made reasonable efforts to counteract their biases. Scientists have political relevance and we do not, because they have made reasonable—even heroic— *attempts* to keep their findings pure of politics and we have done precisely the opposite. In short, most people (excluding many liberationist scholars) trust that science gives us the most reliable information humans are capable of producing.

Am I suggesting that all political content should be stripped from critical endeavors? Emphatically I am not. There really are important political dynamics at work in literature that deserve analysis; and the new historicism, cultural studies, feminism and other approaches deserve thanks for bringing these dynamics to light. To rule out discussions of the way that different identity groups, classes, genders, and ideologies are portrayed in literature and other "readable" cultural products would be hugely impoverishing. But literary scholars must find a way to do a better job of exploring all of their questions—and *especially* those with direct political implications—in a reasonably disinterested fashion.

How are we to dispassionately study the things we are passionate about? We can begin, once more, by consulting existing practices in the modern human sciences. Researchers who study human behavior and culture scientifically never succeed in erasing themselves as political beings; instead they seek to devise methodologies that limit the distorting role that their biases can play. To give just one example, consider the illuminating work of the psychologists Jim Sidanius and Felicia Pratto. In *Social Dominance: An Intergroup*

Theory of Social Hierarchy and Oppression (2004), Sidanius and Pratto study precisely the same phenomena that obsess contemporary literary scholarship: oppression, sexism, hierarchy, group dominance, prejudice. But they conduct their studies in the most rigorously objective fashion that they are capable of. They study these phenomena disinterestedly *not* because they are in fact without biases. On the contrary, they do so because they are deeply committed to egalitarian principles and because they believe those principles can never be fully enacted while we remain in ignorance of the ultimate origins of oppression and hierarchy in our species (see Sidanius and Pratto 2004, 309–310).

If literary scholars wish to be considered seniors, trustworthy, and politically consequential, we must approach our questions in a similarly disinterested way. Until then, much of what we write will continue to be dismissed by the broader public (including the broader intelligentsia and the class of political actors) as hopelessly tainted by ideology.

Is Literary Study Important?

If it isn't worth doing, it isn't worth doing well.
(Donald Hebb)

In this book I am arguing for a massive restructuring of literary analysis and for fundamental changes in how scholars do their work. On the bright side, I suggest that we don't have to struggle very hard to see how our approach should be restructured. Insofar as possible, literary scholars should emulate the scientific virtues of caution, humility, and the pursuit of disinterested inquiry; we should develop a more diverse methodological toolkit; we should update our critical theories to make them consilient with the best scientific understandings. On the negative side, this transformation would be extremely costly. It would mean changing what literature departments teach and how students are trained; it would require *real* interdisciplinarity (not the cherry-picking of confirming evidence and the importation of jargon that have often passed for interdisciplinarity), and regular cross-listings with departments like statistics, psychology, and biology. It would require the investment of enough energy to overcome the methodological inertia of centuries and the entrenched professional interests of the tenured and the promoted. It would require much education in scientific thinking, in the processes of hypothesis testing, and in the intricacies of statistics and probability.

Literary academics should, *of course*, retain their long shelves of books, their methods of close reading, and their word processing software, but they should also avail themselves of other tools: sophisticated text analysis software to exploit the vast and almost completely untapped potential of having access to *all* the world's texts in digital form (see Hockey 2000; Popping 2000; Siemens and Schreibman 2008; Schreibman et al. 2004); knowledge of statistics and manipulation of data bases; access to appropriate lab apparatus and research subjects; and far more regular and intensive collaboration and consultation with researchers from scientific fields. The field needs its logicians and lofty theoreticians, but it also needs dogged lab rats and grubby empiricists—it needs some Gottliebs to go with all of the Brumfits. In short, restructuring will require very large outlays for new intellectual capital. This may simply be too much to ask of established scholars who would have to repudiate too much of their vitas and learn too many new tricks. Whether graduate students, younger scholars, and ambitious established scholars take up this challenge depends, I think, on how they would answer a single direct question: *Is the study of literature important?*

If the study of literature is important, then the expensive changes I have proposed are worth it. That literature itself is important, we will accept as given. Individual readers and societies as wholes reap from literature benefits of delight and edification. But, as noted earlier, the scholarship of literary intellectuals deserve few plaudits for this. By far the greatest bulk of our research and writing consists of arcane arguments within narrow specialist communities. This work—in contrast to specialist work in most other fields—is almost never repackaged for the benefit of general readers. If literature itself is important for its direct and/or ineffable gifts, but its organized study is not, then the radical reforms proposed here can be ignored because it doesn't really matter whether we do a good job or a bad one.

Phrasing the issue this way may seem like a crude rhetorical gambit: I force scholars to side with me or admit that their intellectual work is really not that important. But the question of whether or not literary scholars *really* do an important job that enriches individuals (*other* individuals) and society is an old and intense professional anxiety. Are we *really* making an indispensable contribution to human knowledge generally, to broadening student minds, or to the pursuit of social justice? Or are we today what we were yesterday: A class of well-fatted elites whose claims of social utility mainly further *our* interests in having high status jobs that, once tenure is achieved, usually become lifetime sinecures (to boot: with summers off, subsidized travel, top-tier health care insurance, precious tuition waivers for children, and so on)?

As I argued at the outset of this volume, the malaise among literary intellectuals emerges in large part from the feeling that our work does not have the kind of direct, practical utility that can be ascribed, at least in principle, to most nonhumanities fields. Probably most of us feel a keen stab of recognition in reading Wilde's aphorism, "All art is quite useless." Even correcting for his overstatement, how much more useless must it be to devote millions of scholar-hours to stockpiling commentaries on art (especially commentary that almost nobody, even other specialists, cares to read)? Still worse, if Theodor Adorno is right and it is barbaric to write poetry after Auschwitz, how much more barbaric must it be to defend the frivolity of its institutionalized critique?

The way literary study is currently being practiced represents an implicit answer, I feel, to the question of import. Many literary scholars are proceeding as though their subject is not important enough to study in a disciplined, principled way. The devotion to discredited theory, the eschewal of empiricism, the insulation from inconvenient findings from other fields, and the subordination of scholarship to politics are all indicators of the unseriousness of much current work. This is communicated, perhaps above all, in our basic unconcern about whether our responses to questions are right or whether they are not. As Wilde wrote a century ago, "Who cares whether Mr. Ruskin's views on Turner are sound or not? What does it matter?" (1888). Modern scholars have made parallel statements, including Stanley Fish who famously wrote of Theory, "It relieves me of the burden to be right . . . and demands that I only be interesting" (1976, 195; Fish would later revise his thinking somewhat, 1980, 174).

But in fields of human inquiry that matter, people are very much concerned about getting things right. In medicine, history, political science, computing, rocket science, psychology, and journalism—in all fields, in other words, where the workers really believe in the importance of their jobs—efforts are made to apply the best theory, methods, and governing attitudes available for getting things right, or at least moving in that direction. Not a few literary scholars will snicker into the backs of their hands at my seemingly ingenuous use of words like "best" and "right"; but even extreme antifoundationalists proclaim the fundamental unseriousness of their positions when it comes to things they consider *really* important (for instance their own medical care: Derrida perished of pancreatic cancer, not at home but in a modern Parisian hospital experiencing the kind of treatment and palliative care only found in affluent and scientifically advanced societies). Literary scholars may deny the special validity of science, sneer at the idea knowledge progress, and so on. But when it comes to getting important things right—Did the holocaust actually occur or was it just more dazzling propaganda from the world Jewish conspiracy? Was Paul de Man a Nazi-sympathizing anti-Semite or not? Does HIV cause AIDS or not? Is creationism (or intelligent design) science or not? Is global warming happening or not? Did the Bush administration think that the Iraqi regime possessed Weapons of Mass Destruction or not? Do IQ tests tell us something valid about native intelligence in different populations or not? Will this vaccination increase my child's likelihood of autism or not?—they are as outraged as everyone else to see loose play with the facts. When the field is important—when the field is not a humanities field—literary scholars are as keen as everyone else to see that the best processes are used to reach findings.

Literary scholars won't put up with shoddiness in other fields: tattered theory, incomplete methods, extreme and unapologetic ideological bias. So why, if the study of literature is important, do we countenance it in ours? Or, to paraphrase an incredulous journalist commenting on the state of affairs in literature departments, How can we allow ourselves to get away with this stuff? (Siegel 2005, 435).

* * *

For one thing, we have been slow to grasp the consequences of the fact that fewer and fewer of us are discussing value judgments about Wordsworth or Shelley where it can be frankly asked (and not in a mean spirit): Who really cares whether this or that judgment is right or not? The implications of Arnold's judgment that Wordsworth is "profound but lacking in completeness and variety" are very narrowly proscribed. But more and more contemporary literary scholars are asking empirical questions, and not just about art. The answers to these questions have potentially broad and serious repercussions. The movement of literary questions over the last forty years has been from the New Criticism's disciplined focus on the internal dynamics of "the text itself" to an intense absorption with the cacophonous social, political, and economic contexts in which texts are produced and consumed; the move has been from textual to contextual analysis, from discussion of "the words on the page" to moral and factual judgments about history, society, and politics. In other words, literary scholars aren't harmless (see Nanda 2005; Latour 2004). It matters whether we are right or wrong in the strong claims of fact we regularly make about the nature of gender, sexuality, human competitive tendencies, ethnocentrism, language, oppression, and so on.

Leaving aside the contentious issue of whether the field's migration from aesthetic judgments about texts to big empirical claims about contexts is a good thing or not, the migration *has* occurred. It is important, therefore, that our modes of inquiry adapt to our new questions. This part of the problem is simple: Over the last decades our questions have changed radically but our methods have not.

But there are bigger factors at work than a field's sluggish adaptation of ancient modes to rapid disciplinary changes. To see this, we must return to ground that we began covering in chapter 1.

The Challenge of Inconvenient Results

The spine of my position is that it is possible, with improved disciplinary foundations, for literary scholars to do a much better job of shrinking the space of possible explanation. But even if literary intellectuals can be convinced that this is possible, can they be convinced that it is desirable? After all, how better can we characterize the last four decades in literary academe than as a massive, determined effort to challenge all limits, deconstruct all barriers, and *explode* the space of possibility? Literary scholars have been committed, above all else, to expanding the possibilities for all people to express the diversity of their humanity with utmost completeness, liberty, and dignity. The whole project has centered not on contraction of possibility space, but on expansion of horizons so that we can first imagine, and then create, a better world—a world with less cruelty and more freedom.

For the many participants in this movement, the effort to shrink the scope of possible explanation can seem initially threatening, and for understandable reasons. The problem with a scientific approach to empirical questions of sociopolitical relevance (and which investigations of humans and their products are devoid of all such relevance?) is that of inconvenient results. While activist scholars will sometimes claim that there is no necessary conflict between their scholarly and political agendas, it is easy to see that the mandates of scholarship and activism will often clash. The former mandates aggressive and uncompromising commitment to the goal of more precisely understanding the universe and everything in it; the latter mandates aggressive and uncompromising commitment to advancing ideas that promote The Cause. Obviously, serving one of these masters can mean betraying the other.*

What are activist scholars to do when confronted with data that seems to shrink possibility space in the "wrong" direction? For example, what if—in contradiction to one of the most inflexibly propounded tenets of the liberationist paradigm—behavioral genetics, endocrinology, cognitive and developmental psychology, pediatrics, and neuroscience began carving a deep consensus that gender is not only, or even mainly, environmentally determined? What if data from these fields suggested, instead, that both genes and environments play important determining roles? Further, what if some scientists began to suggest, to the surprise of almost everyone and the dread of some, that the dominant environmental factor may not be the house-hold or society of rearing but the hormonal environment experienced by the developing fetus *in utero*? For literary scholars generally—and particularly for those who have grown comfortable with the simplicity of the dichotomous "sex-gender system," which formally segregates almost all aspects of gender from biological sex—these findings seem not only to close off the space of possible *explanation* (e.g., for the origin and maintenance of patterns of gendered behavior), they also seem to close off the space of possible human *expression*—for men, for women, and for those individuals who do not feel fully at home in their sex of birth.

In short, activist scholars have frequently been torn between sets of research findings that seem robust and important sociopolitical goals that seem to require different facts. Given that literary scholars associated with the race-class-gender-sexuality movements have often explicitly described their scholarly efforts as subserving larger political causes, it is no wonder that they have often placed those causes first. In this, I believe that activist scholars enact intellectual errors *and* ham-fisted political strategy. Both mistakes are based in the naturalis-tic fallacy—the notion that things that are natural are both necessary

---

* Paul Boghossian believes that this is precisely what occurred when the editors of *Social Text* published Alan Sokal's notorious parodic essay, despite admitting that they did not really understand it: "And this, it seems to me, is what's at the heart of the issue raised by Sokal's hoax: not the mere existence of incompetence within the academy, but rather that specific form of it that arises from allowing ideological criteria to displace standards of scholarship so completely that not even considerations of intelligibility are seen as relevant to an argument's acceptability" (1996, 14).

and good. But it should be easy to see that there are elements of physical biology (cancer, for instance) and evolved human nature (lower thresholds for physical violence in men, for instance; for overview of research see Gottschall 2008, Chapter Three) that are not good, and that all decent people have a stake in seeking to change.

How do we best pursue change? This is a difficult question, but I think we can be confident that the way to cure cancer or diminish male violence is *not* by standing in the way of a better scientific understanding of these phenomena. Before we can change who we are, we must first understand *what* we are and how we got this way; we cannot understand human minds, much less persuade them to change, if we remain ignorant of the biases and predispositions built into them not only by social pressures but also by the pressures of natural selection. Obvious analogies present themselves: It is like trying to fix an arrhythmic heart or a misfiring engine or a hemorrhaging brain without possessing the best understanding of how hearts, internal combustion engines, or brains work. In this I am just echoing the wisdom of Mathew Arnold, who admonished the activists of his own day that "acting and instituting are of little use, unless we know how and what we ought to act and institute" (1864, 827).

Those literary scholars who would contribute—directly or indirectly—to changing human behaviors and attitudes have badly handicapped themselves through dogged promotion and defense of distorted reality pictures. The question arises for me, as it has for many others before me, about how serious the average literary activist really is about affecting these changes. (It is dangerous to question another's underlying motives, but since it is pretty certain that mine will be impugned, I'll get the ball rolling.) If an activist wants to help affect major sociopolitical transformations, is a literature department (if one is lucky, at an elite university where one has every opportunity to publish and jet set, while helping the children of privilege capitalize upon their advantages) actually the best place to do this work? Terry Eagleton has framed the problem with typical concision, "How is a Marxist-structuralist analysis of a minor novel of Balzac to help shake the foundations of capitalism" (1981, 65)? Especially when that analysis is quite likely to be read only by a few dozen Balzac specialists, and to be written in a densely forbidding Theorese that is indecipherable not only by the proletariat it seeks to free, but also by the well-educated class of political decision makers.

As Eagleton's question suggests, the existential crisis presently gripping the field is partly instigated by concerns about the purity of our motives. If literary scholars are so ardent for sociopolitical change, then why is our form of activism so weak and why does it cost us so little? Activism that confers tangible benefits upon the activist, while extracting few costs, demeans the word. Isn't it possible that however passionately the average scholar proclaims his devotion to this or that noble cause, he is at least as interested in conspicuously displaying his righteousness *within* the academic community, accruing moral capital (which is the true coin of our realm), and growing his prestige along with his career? As Margery Sabin has written, the liberationist paradigm—that which helped to produce a profoundly inegalitarian academic "Star System" with its shrinking "middle class," its grandees, and its swollen ranks of helots—has been characterized by "rampant careerism from beginning to end" (1997, 86; see also Ellis 1997).

All of this represents another way of saying that doing work that is consequential (intellectually, socially, politically) means first becoming more responsible scholars. The way we have mixed defunct theory, inadequate methods, and unrestrained advocacy has condemned us to the sidelines of the important debates of our time. Almost no one outside of our field thinks that our perspectives have earned serious consideration when it comes to actually deciding "how and what we ought to act and institute." We have silenced ourselves. If we want back in the game, we simply have to start doing a better job. This is the paradox: real engagement comes only with disengagement.*

Coda: On Communication

One doesn't know whether to laugh harder at the charlatan who spreads all this fog…or at the audience which naively imagines the reason it cannot clearly recognize and grasp [his] masterpiece of insight is that new masses of truth are being hurled at it. (Kant, *Critique of Judgment*, 1790, section 47)

Before moving to the case studies, a short digression on communication is necessary. Starting with the French *maîtres à penser*, literary intellectuals, who once prided themselves on the precision of their prose, have adopted a style that flouts all the canons of good writing.

---

* Psychologist Phillip Tetlock has the same idea: "The lesson I've drawn from my encounters with the world of power is that credibility is our most important asset. When we lose our credibility we become just one more activist group clamoring for public attention….And if we lose our credibility [by allowing our research to be tainted by political partisanship] we won't be in a position to help any cause. It is as simple as that!" (1995, 153).

The conventional language of literary intellectuals has been described as gaseous, pompous, painful, turgid, incoherent, just plain bad, and fulsome with "polysyllabic...crapification" (Booth 2004, 351). It has been parodied in journalism and academic novels, and very effectively pilloried in *Philosophy and Literature*'s "Bad Writing Contest." A computer programmer even created a program or "bot" that works in a semi-Homeric fashion by stringing together combinations of intimidating big names and profound-sounding stock phrases to produce spookily convincing examples of High Theorese (try it at http://www.elsewhere.org/pomo.). Below are three sentences, two composed by humans and one by the bloviating postmodern bot. Can you determine which one was generated by the bot?

- "Sexuality is intrinsically meaningless," says Derrida. Thus, the main theme of Dietrich's model of postdialectic modern theory is the common ground between sexual identity and narrativity. An abundance of theories concerning not discourse per se, but neodiscourse may be discovered. However, the subject is contextualized into a Lyotardist narrative that includes truth as a totality. Baudrillard's analysis of semantic discourse suggests that the task of the poet is significant form, but only if culture is interchangeable with truth; otherwise, we can assume that discourse is created by communication. In a sense, Sartre uses the term 'Lyotardist narrative' to denote the meaninglessness, and some would say the defining characteristic, of postdeconstructive class. The primary theme of the works of Gibson is a mythopoetical paradox.
- The move from a structuralist account in which capital is understood to structure social relations in relatively homologous ways to a view of hegemony in which power relations are subject to repetition, convergence, and rearticulation brought the question of temporality into the thinking of structure, and marked a shift from a form of Althusserian theory that takes structural totalities as theoretical objects to one in which the insights into the contingent possibility of structure inaugurate a renewed conception of hegemony as bound up with the contingent sites and strategies of the rearticulation of power.
- If, for a while, the ruse of desire is calculable for the uses of discipline soon the repetition of guilt, justification, pseudoscientific theories, superstition, spurious authorities, and classifications can be seen as the desperate effort to "normalize" *formally* the disturbance of a discourse of splitting that violates the rational, enlightened claims of its enunciatory modality.

Perhaps it seems a little late in the day to have cheap fun at the expense of this sort of writing. But the fashion for impenetrable, essentially *anti-communicative* writing represents a huge and ongoing problem in the field, and I have a serious point about it. The snippets by humans were not results of authors having bad days at their word processors and happening to pump out meaningless (though smart sounding) sentences; then, through an unlikely but forgivable sequence of human errors, these sentences managed to survive peer-review and the editing process and to appear in print. These are examples of particularly bad writing: the second and third examples were celebrated as the very worst sentences of the year by *Philosophy and Literature* in 1998; the first sentence was produced by the postmodern bot. But people have taken the time to parody this sort of writing—to shame it with bots, bad writing contests, and other intelligent japery (for more of the latter see Crews 2001)—not because this writing is exceptional, but because it represents an exaggeration of conventional practice. This is a style of writing that literature graduate students are now—as I write and you read—striving to master as proof of professional competency. The sentences composed by humans made it into print because their authors are powerful and fashionable intellectuals, because they are on the "right side" of moral and political debates, and because many of their colleagues lack the nerve to say that *these* are the sorts of robes emperors don to hide the shame of their nakedness.

Here again, in the area of writing conventions, practice in the field of literary analysis makes for a sad contrast with the sciences. In the sciences, conventions of writing stress economy, clarity, and rhetorical restraint. Moreover, by convention, an example of scientific writing must take pains to show skeptics how they can find, and possibly rupture, its jugular. By writing clearly (if not always elegantly) about their questions, data, methods, and results, scientists agree to make their ideas vulnerable to critique. Scientific ethics demand that researchers reveal the weaknesses of studies along with their strengths, and the processes of peer-review and replication seek to hold individuals to this high standard.

This convention of scientific jugular-baring is embarrassingly at odds with what is tolerated in academic writing about literature. Literature scholars are much less likely to speak plainly and clearly. They are much less likely to raise the chins of their beloved ideas and expose the pale, tender flesh just below the jaw. Rather, rhetorical fireworks, gratuitous jargonizing, avoidance of negative evidence, interdisciplinary cherry-picking of only supportive evidence, and cunningly-placed thickets of impenetrable prose all serve to deter and intimidate dissenters and to conceal vulnerabilities in the thesis. Too many literary scholars scrunch chin to chest in order to protect the weakness and/or the triviality of their arguments. If literary scholars are to do a better job of narrowing the space of possible explanation, the epoch of anti-communicative writing must also come to an end.

Part II

Case Studies at the Nexus of Literature and Evolutionary Science

Introduction to Part II

I now shift to case studies that represent my first attempts, with the indispensable assistance of my collaborators, to embody the values promoted in this volume. In many ways, the contributions of these studies are quite humble in relation to the bold arguments of Part I. But I hope that, for all of their shortcomings (those I recognize will be discussed along the way), they will at least be acknowledged as *proof of concept*: Many of the questions literary scholars ask can be scientifically addressed; devising scientific designs is not easy to do, but it is certainly not beyond the capacities of smart and creative people; by moving closer to the sciences in theory, method, and ethos (not to mention transparency of communication) literary scholars can do a much better job of narrowing the space of possible explanation.

My examples are of content analyses of large and diverse samples of world folktales, which were designed to test specific hypotheses at the nexus of literature and evolutionary science. I hope that these studies amply suggest the potential of scientific methods in literary analysis, but I do not claim that they represent a full realization of this potential. The view of world folktales that materializes in these chapters is akin to a view of the nighttime sky through an early, low-powered telescope. The methodological lenses bring broad, and previously unglimpsed, celestial patterns into view. But they do not give us a focused sense for the contours of any specific constellation, and they leave much work for subsequent telescopists, as well as for workers who prefer the microscope.

For every aspect of theory, data, method, and interpretation featured in these studies, I am aware that legitimate concerns can be raised. For almost every paragraph, a critic could well counter, "Yes, but why didn't you try 'A,' and haven't you read 'B,' and how on earth could you conclude 'C' instead of 'D' or 'E'?!" But I am offering these studies as beginnings, not ends, in as yet hypothetical research programs; I do not claim to have addressed all or even most of the nuances of these issues. That is not, by and large, how science works; scientific progress depends on communities. Science's relentless narrowing of the space of possible explanation owes less to the celebrated icons of individual genius—Newton, Darwin, Einstein—and more to the synergy generated by members of large communities grinding obscurely away at the little parts of the big problems, as they hew to powerful shared principles and conventions. Even Newton, who saw further than any man who lived before him, acknowledged that he could do so only because he stood "on the shoulders of giants." The same would obviously be true of Darwin, Einstein, and all the other greats who planted their feet on the amassed findings of scientific communities, past and present. Those who would dispute my *interpretations* of results can do so through argument. But to effectively challenge the *results* themselves, disputation is just a beginning. To make an end of it, critics must themselves enter the trenches; they must design and conduct studies that are better and sounder—that are more creative and possess fewer blind spots and unexamined assumptions. Like scientists, they must seek—and possibly fail—to replicate my findings. If I am proven mistaken in this fashion (rather than being merely jeered from the safety of the sidelines), I will consider the highest purpose of this work achieved.

In segueing to these case studies, I cannot improve on John Graunt's humble introduction to his own *Observations*:

> How far I have succeeded in the Premisses, I now offer to the World's censure. Who, I hope will not expect from me, not professing Letters, things demonstrated with the same certainty, wherewith Learned men determine in their Scholes; but will take it well, that I should offer at a new thing...and that I have taken the pains, and been at the charge, of setting out those Tables, whereby all men may both correct my Positions, and raise others of their own: For herein I have, like a silly Scholeboy, coming to say my Lesson to the World (that Peevish, and Tetchie Master) brought a bundle of Rods wherewith to be whipt, for every mistake I have committed. (Graunt 1662, 2–3)

Chapter 4

The Heroine with a Thousand Faces: Universal Trends in the Characterization of Female Folktale Protagonists*

Introduction

Scholars have long remarked striking similarities in the depiction of male heroes in the world's folktale traditions. The most ambitious attempt to document and explain these similarities is Joseph Campbell's *The Hero with a Thousand Faces* (1936). Campbell's work differs in detail from other noteworthy attempts to define universal features of heroes (e.g., Dundes 1980; Fontenrose 1959; Rank 1909; Raglan 1936; Tylor 1871; Von Hahn 1876), but its grand thesis is much the same: wherever you travel in the world's folk literatures, and whenever you go there, heroes will share certain predictable patterns of characteristics; while the details of heroes "faces" may change as the investigator crosses geographical, cultural, and chronological borders, certain details of the hero's life and challenges are everywhere the same.

In contrast to the many determined efforts to generalize about heroes, scholars have expended little effort generalizing about cross-cultural features of heroines. This neglect is not mainly due to sexist disregard. In fact, a great deal has been written about female folktale characters (DeCaro's 1983 bibliography lists over 2000 studies). The

* An earlier version of this chapter was published in *Evolutionary Psychology* 3 (2005): 85–103 (http://www.epjournal.net/). Rachel Berkey, Mitch Cawson, Carly Drown, Matthew Fleischner, Melissa Glotzbecker, Kimberly Kernan, Tyler Magnan, Kate Muse, Celeste Ogburn, Stephen Patterson, Christopher Skeels, Stephanie St. Joseph, Shawna Weeks, Alison Welsh, and Erin Welch contributed to this research.

neglect of this subject reflects the difficulty of identifying and defining a "type" of heroine distinctly enough for cross-cultural analysis (see Ragan 1998b). Heroines are not merely heroes with some different body parts; as we shall see later in the paper, there are far fewer female characters who are heroic in the narrow sense we usually associate with male heroes. This chapter, based on a quantitative content analysis of folktales from 48 culture areas around the world, represents the first systematic attempt to identify, and account for, cross-cultural trends in the characterization of heroines. However, in order to avoid sticky problems of definition, and in order to attain a large and diverse sample, this study defines the term "heroine" in its most generic sense, as any main female protagonist. As we employ the term, there is absolutely no connotation of special grandeur, virtue, or courage.

While there is now a resurgence of interest in the subject of literary universals (Arleo 1997; Gottschall 2004; Gottschall et al. 2004, "Patterns of Characterizations in Folk Tales"; Gottschall et al. 2004, "Sex Differences in Mate Choice Criteria"; Gottschall et al. 2007; Hogan 1997, 2003a, 2003b; Jobling 2001; Mueller 1993; Richardson 2000; Sternberg 2003a, 2003b; Quasthoff 1996), the majority of literary scholars have, over the last several decades, viewed the entire subject with deep suspicion. This is in stark contrast to a long and prominent universalist tradition that argued for distinct regularities across the literatures of widely spaced peoples. There are both ideological and practical reasons for this state of affairs. For now I will only address the practical reasons, saving ideological concerns for the discussion.

Literary scholars have found it easy to dismiss the concept of literary universals largely because the most prominent research in the field has been rife with theoretical and methodological problems, and thus vulnerable to devastating skeptical critique (see Cook 1976; Jobling 2001). Prior to the twentieth century, universalist claims tended to be based on common sense claims about human psychology. For instance, the nineteenth century anthropologist Edward Tylor wrote:

> The treatment of similar myths from different regions, by arranging them in large compared groups, makes it possible to trace in mythology the operation of imaginative processes recurring with the evident regularity of mental law; and thus stories of which a single instance would have been a mere isolated curiosity, take their place among well-marked and consistent structures of the human mind. (1871, 281–282)

In the twentieth century, however, psychoanalysis emerged as an explicit and systematic theory of human psychology that attempted to codify and explain the universal "mental law(s)" taken for granted by men such as Tylor. Psychoanalysis became both the map and the legend for the twentieth century's most prominent universalists: the map that indicated where to look for universals; the legend that revealed how to interpret what was found. Thus the best-known attempts to define literary universals are heirs to the shortcomings of psychoanalysis and have often been guilty of implausible attempts to cram stories into Freudian or Jungian molds. In addition to theoretical weaknesses, previous attempts to define literary universals typically lacked methodological rigor. Conclusions were not based on statistical analyses of representative samples of texts but on highly impressionistic "readings" of handpicked texts, typically overrepresenting circum-Mediterranean content (Cook 1976; Jobling 2001).

The research presented in this chapter represents an attempt to improve upon previous work in literary universals by applying theory and methods that have invigorated the search for, and interpretation of, universals in other fields. By applying quantitative methods of data acquisition and analysis, an attempt is made to mitigate some of the problems of subjectivity, selection, and confirmation bias that plagued previous attempts. By taking evolutionary theories of human behavior and psychology as map and legend for this exploration, an attempt is made to identify universals that prove more valid than those based on psychoanalytic theory and looser methodology.

Predictions

This study sought universal patterns where evolutionary theory and research suggest one should find them. The first property of a literary universal is that the putative feature need not appear in *every* literary work or in *all* the world's literary traditions. An *absolute* universal is one that applies across all literary works and traditions. This is a special, and perhaps rare, phenomenon, which likely applies mainly at the highest levels of abstraction (e.g., "all peoples have literature," "all literature is focused on conflict," "all peoples have creation myths"). The study described in this paper sought to document features of female protagonist characterization that are *statistical*, not absolute, universals. These are features of characterization that recur at rates significantly greater than would be predicted by chance, and that cannot be convincingly attributed solely to diffusion (see Hogan 1997, 2003b).

The predictions were as follows. On the basis of kin selection theory (Hamilton 1964) it was expected that female protagonists would devote substantial effort to assisting their kin, especially their close kin, relative to non-kin and distant kin. On the basis of research into human mate preferences inspired by sexual selection theory, it was predicted that female characters, relative to their male counterparts, would place greater emphasis on a potential mate's wealth, status, and kindness (the last being a potential signaler of commitment) than on his physical attractiveness (Buss 1989; for elaboration of this logic see chapter 6). On the flip side, given the heavy emphasis males place on the attractiveness of potential mates in world cultures (see Symons 1979; Buss 1989, 2003; Geary et al. 2004), it was expected that there would be markedly greater emphasis on the physical attractiveness of female characters relative to male characters. On the basis of Darwin-Trivers sexual selection theory (Darwin 1871; Trivers 1972; see also Clutton-Brock and Parker 1992), it was predicted that female protagonists would be identified as less "active" and less likely to be defined as "physically heroic" than their male counterparts. This follows the logic of sexual selection: in *most* sexually reproducing animals, males will be more prone to risk-taking and status-striving behavior; males' higher likelihood of either reproducing prolifically or dying without issue gives them positive and negative incentives to strive intensely, even riskily, for mates, and for the social status and resources required to attract and retain them (for a review of sexual selection see Andersson 1994; for research suggesting that males have a stronger "social dominance orientation" across cultures, see Sidanius and Pratto 2004). Finally, it was expected that one side effect of the higher activity and heroism ratings of males would be an abundance of male relative to female main characters. We reasoned that audiences might find active characters (as well as the physically heroic) more compelling, and that one side effect of this might be male characters dominating the narratives.

While some of these expectations may seem obvious to some readers on the basis of common sense, they are at odds with the dominant humanities models, which predict strong intercultural variability given the largely arbitrary nature of human social and gender arrangements.

Data and Methods

Within the limits of availability, folktale collections were selected to maximize the geographical and cultural diversity of the sample. Specialized collections focusing on specific themes, plots, or character types (e.g., *Hopi Trickster Tales, Hero Tales of the South Slavs*) were rejected in favor of generic collections (*Hopi Folktales, Traditional*

Tales of the South Slavs). All collections were of traditional tales, originally transmitted through the oral tradition. In all, the study includes tales from 48 different culture areas from all inhabited continents. The cultures vary widely in ecology, racial and ethnic composition, political systems, religious beliefs, and levels of cultural complexity. All non-English tales had been translated into English, and the sample ran the gamut from polished fairy tales to literal transcriptions of tales told in traditional contexts (for collections used in this study, see Appendix A).

Once suitable collections were identified, each data collector (10 female and 5 male undergraduates at St. Lawrence University) scanned the 30 longest tales from each of 3 culture areas. (Several students coded tales from 4 culture areas. They volunteered to code collections of tales that only arrived through interlibrary loan after the main portion of the study had been completed.) The coders were participants in a seminar focusing on content analysis methodology and the depiction of female characters in world folktales (these seminars are described in the acknowledgments). All coding decisions were made independently; coders were told not to discuss judgments with colleagues.

Coders were, in content analysis parlance, kept "naïve": they were not appraised of controversies about human universals and they were not privy to the theory-generated expectations of the lead author. Coders were told that the study's aim was to determine whether or not there were cross-cultural patterns in the depiction of female characters. It was stressed that we had no favored outcome. Whatever we discovered—whether it was prevailing cross-cultural regularity or prevailing variability—would be an important contribution. While the use of student coders entails potential costs (can their diligence and judgment be counted upon?), for this project the benefits were judged to outweigh those costs. The coding questions were designed to be as simple and direct as possible. What these labor-intensive studies required was basic responsible effort, not highly trained judgment. Indeed, for this type of study, professional academic coders can be a liability because of their established intellectual and theoretical commitments (see Neuendorf 2002).

The 30 longest tales were chosen, rather than a random selection, to ensure a sample consisting of long, information-rich tales rather than short, information-poor tales. Since the emphasis of the inquiry was on the attributes of female characters, each of 1,440 tales was first scanned for the presence of a main female protagonist or a main female antagonist. A main female protagonist was defined as a character who plays a central role in the action and who the audience is led to root predominantly for rather than predominantly against. A main female antagonist was defined as a character who plays a central role in the action, who acts as an obstacle to the goals of the protagonist(s), and who the audience is led to root predominantly against rather than predominantly for. Any tale containing one or both of these character types was flagged for coding.

A coding form was developed to collect data on the main characters of all flagged tales (relevant coding questions are given in the results section). While male characters were not the principal targets of the study, coding forms were also filled out for main male protagonists and antagonists in order to establish a yardstick for measuring the characteristics of the females. A maximum of one coding form was filled out for each main male and female protagonist and antagonist per story. In the event that there were, for instance, two main female protagonists, coders focused only on the female protagonist who was judged most important and prominent. Thus between 1 and 4 coding forms were completed for each tale in the sample. In all, 1,307 coding forms were completed for 658 distinct tales. Of the completed forms, 568 were filled out for female protagonists, 392 for male protagonists, 197 for female antagonists, and 150 for male antagonists.

Unfortunately, while the sample is respectably large in aggregate, culture-by-culture samples were significantly smaller than we hoped for and anticipated. Not only did fewer characters meet our definitions of a main protagonist or antagonist than we expected, but many of the characters who did were minimally characterized, and we were often unable to gather information about them in many of our coding categories. As a consequence, statistically meaningful analysis at the single-culture level could not be accomplished. Instead, data analyses are reported for the sample as a whole and for 6 geographical regions: Europe, Western Europe, Asia, North America, South America, and Africa (for cultures represented in each region see Appendix A). Several collections of Middle Eastern and Oceanic folktales were coded but, because of especially small sample sizes, these results are included in the overall totals but not in their own geographic categories. Our division of cultures into geographical regions roughly follows Murdock's guidelines for large-scale cross-cultural studies (1957, 1981; for further discussion of potential problems in these groupings see the prefatory note to chapter 6).

The sample was also divided into two broad levels of cultural complexity. The first level consists of tales that circulated primarily in unassimilated band and tribal societies, though they may have only been written down after assimilation. The second level consists of tales that, while they may have originated in non-state societies, circulated for long periods in preindustrial state societies. Since the line between these categories can be fine, tales from culture areas that could not be confidently placed in one of these two categories were excluded from the calculation.

Finally, because a prominent claim of feminist scholars of folk and fairy tales is that patterns of characterization in European tale collections reflect the patriarchal biases of male editors, sub-analyses were performed for male-edited collections versus female-edited collections, and for data gathered by female coders versus data gathered by male coders (this issue is discussed in the next chapter).

A primary challenge in content analysis utilizing multiple coders is to maximize intercoder reliability—the frequency with which different researchers code the same variable, in the same text, in the same way. Content analysis of literary works presents special challenges to reliability assessment because of the length and complexity of the works and the time-consuming nature of the coding. Conventional measures (see Krippendorff 1980; Neuendorf 2002; Weber 1990) were undertaken to promote intercoder reliability, such as developing coding questions that were as simple as possible. And intercoder reliability was assessed in two formal tests. The first test assessed the coders' agreement in scanning the same assortment of 23 culturally diverse tales for the presence of a main female protagonist or a main female antagonist. The second test assessed agreement in coding an assortment of 11 culturally diverse tales previously identified as containing either a main female protagonist or antagonist. Most content analysis practitioners strive for reliability rates of 80 percent or better, and consider 70 percent to be the minimum level of adequacy (Krippendorff 1980; Neuendorf 2002; Weber 1990). Intercoder agreement in scanning tales was 89 percent while, for the variables discussed in this paper, agreement ranged from 75 to 94 percent, with an average agreement of 88 percent. This approach, in which reliability ratings are established prior to actual coding rather than having multiple coders read and code all or some fraction of the different works, is well established in content analysis and is discussed as an option in books on, and practical guides to, the subject. The advantage of this approach is that is allows the compilation of the largest data sets, though some content analysts argue that it does so at the cost of some degree of precision in reliability reporting (for discussion of different methods of reliability testing see Krippendorff 1980; Neuendorf 2002; Weber 1990).

We acknowledge, however, that the small number of tales examined in our reliability assessment must diminish confidence in the reliability of our overall results. At the same time, however, we believe that confidence in the results should also be influenced, in a positive way, by the fact that 15 naïve coders, working independently, found similar patterns of female versus male characterization in their individual collections. Such regularity would not be anticipated in the output of fundamentally unreliable coders (for further discussion of the coder reliability, see prefatory note to chapter 6).

Results*

Analysis of data reveals salient trends of female protagonist characterization in parameters associated with age, levels of physical attractiveness, frequency of representation as the main character, marital status, mating preferences, level of activity, propensity for physical heroism, and patterns of altruism.

Frequency of Representation as the Main Character

For each tale, coders were asked the following question: Is the main character in this story (1) male, (2) female, or (3) cannot answer. Across subsamples, female protagonists were significantly underrepresented as main characters. The representation of female protagonist main characters was estimated in two ways. The first estimation was reached by subtracting the number of tales with female main characters in the sample from the total number of tales scanned. In this estimation, male main characters outnumbered female main characters by a factor of three (see table 4.1). However, this method may underestimate the number of main female characters because it assumes that all of the sampled tales in fact had a main character whose sex was clearly determinable. To check the validity of this assumption, the senior author analyzed the tables of contents of all collections utilized in the study, determining the relative percentages of titles referring to male main characters versus female main characters. Any title that did not communicate definite information as to the sex of the tale's main character was excluded from the calculation. In this second estimation,

---

*Some of the results given here differ from previously published results. The differences are invariably minor and do not contradict the main patterns given in previous publications. Differences result from corrections of typos and computation errors and from refinements in methods of calculation and cultural grouping.

Table 4.1 Percentage of Male and Female Main Characters: Two Methods of Estimation

	Estimation 1			Estimation 2		
	Male	Female	Z-Score	Male	Female	Z-Score
Overall	75 (n=1084)	25 (n=356)	31.45**	68 (n=949)	32 (n=443)	20.59**
North America	82 (n=247)	18 (n=53)	20.77**	76 (n=151)	24 (n=52)	11.26**
South America	84 (n=176)	16 (n=34)	18.81**	76 (n=105)	24 (n=34)**	9.91**
Europe	76 (n=183)	24 (n=57)	13.5**	66 (n=267)	32 (n=134)	9.96**
Western Europe	77 (n=92)	23 (n=28)	9.77**	68 (n=130)	32 (n=65)	7.47**
Asia	76 (n=228)	24 (n=72)	14.91**	67 (n=216)	33 (n=107)	9.11**
Africa	62 (n=131)	38 (n=79)	5.24**	68 (n=172)	32 (n=82)	8.54**
Bands/Tribes	76 (n=466)	24 (n=149)	21.1**	68 (n=439)	32 (n=206)	13.91**
Preindustrial States	80 (n=477)	20 (n=123)	25.31**	68 (n=510)	32 (n=237)	15.18**
Male-edited Collections	***	***	***	***	***	***
Female-edited Collections	***	***	***	***	***	***
Male Coders	78 (n=288)	22 (n=80)	18.59**	***	***	***
Female Coders	76 (n=796)	24 (n=276)	25.68**	***	***	***

Note: Tests for statistically significant differences estimate the odds that an observed difference in scores could arise by chance alone. Two factors enter into testing significance levels: the size of the sample, and the magnitude of the difference in scores. The larger the sample and the larger the difference in scores, the easier it is to detect statistically significant differences. Significance levels are by convention usually registered at the .05 and .01 levels. A significance level of $p < .05$ (where "p" stands for "probability") means that the odds are less than 5 in 100 that the observed difference in scores between two sets arose by chance alone. A significance level of $p < .01$ means that the probability that the observed difference in scores arose by chance alone is less than 1 in 100. In statistics, z-scores represent a standardized way of representing the difference between two numbers when measurements are expected to follow a normal distribution.

The overall sample size is often larger than the sum of the subgroups. This is because a number of collections could not be efficiently placed in geographic subgroups and because not all collections could be assigned on the basis of editor sex or cultural level.

"n" is number of main male and/or female characters.

* indicates $p < .05$.

** indicates $p < .01$.

*** not calculated.

male main characters still outnumbered female main characters by more than 2 to 1. (The question of the relative representation of male and female characters is reconsidered at length in chapter 6.)

Age

Coders were asked the following question: What is your best estimate of the character's age: (1) prepubescent (0–13), (2) sexually mature teenager, (3) in her 20s, (4) in her 30s, (5) in her 40s, (6) in her 50s, (7) 60 or older, or (8) impossible to judge? Young women of reproductive age were vastly overrepresented in the ranks of female protagonists. Across subsamples, a striking majority of female protagonists were identified either as sexually mature teenagers or as 20–29-year-olds; just 8 percent were identified as 40 or older. This is in stark contrast to the depiction of female antagonists, 40 percent of whom were identified as 40 or older (see table 4.2). Interestingly, male protagonists, though rated slightly older than female protagonists overall (with more clustered in the 20–29 group than the teenage group), demonstrated exactly the same pattern: the antagonists are significantly older than the protagonists.

We did not predict the age discrepancies in the portrayal of antagonists and protagonists, but these groupings make some intuitive sense. As Carroll and colleagues write about a similar finding in nineteenth-century British literature: "The concentration of 'bad' characters in the older age groups forms part of a total dramatic structure in the world of the novels—a structure in which young people of good will are struggling against older people who are consumed by the desire for Social Dominance—for wealth, status, and prestige. It would stand to reason that older characters would be more established characters, would have more power, and would thus almost necessarily constitute the chief obstacles to the aims and ambitions of young protagonists" (manuscript under consideration). What also seems clear is that the youthfulness of protagonists is related to the prominent role of marriage in the tales.

Marriage and Mating Preferences

Coders were asked several questions about marriage and mating preferences. When the tale begins, is the character married? If not, does the character get married in the course of the tale? Is finding/keeping a mate a main goal for the character? Finally, they were asked: What *single* feature seems *most important* to the character in assessing

Table 4.2 Percentage of Female Protagonists and Antagonists Falling in Given Age Categories

	Sexually Mature Teens or in Twenties			Forty or Older		
	Female Protagonist	Female Antagonist	Z-Score	Female Protagonist	Female Antagonist	Z-Score
Overall	80 (n=531)	38 (n=174)	10.3**	8	42	8.68**
North America	71 (n=76)	38 (n=26)	3*	18	35	1.57
South America	71 (n=75)	52 (n=23)	1.58	8	30	2.22*
Europe	92 (n=114)	27 (n=44)	9.04**	8	73	8.35**
Western Europe	90 (n=59)	38 (n=21)	4.58**	8	62	4.77**
Asia	88 (n=117)	52 (n=31)	3.85**	8	42	3.72**
Africa	62 (n=78)	24 (n=25)	3.69**	12	48	3.43*
Bands/Tribes	70 (n=263)	41 (n=80)	4.64**	13	36	3.98**
Preindustrial States	88 (n=252)	38 (n=88)	9.12**	3	44	7.61**
Male-edited Collections	81 (n=319)	40 (n=106)	7.95**	13	56	8.2**
Female-edited Collections	81 (n=135)	27 (n=45)	7.42**	11	67	7.38**
Male Coders	82 (n=99)	35 (n=46)	5.86**	11	65	7.03**
Female Coders	79 (n=432)	39 (n=128)	8.47**	14	56	8.92**

Note: The overall sample size is often larger than the sum of the subgroups. This is because a number of collections could not be efficiently placed in geographic subgroups and because not all collections could be assigned on the basis of editor sex or cultural level.

"n" is number of male and/or female protagonists with age information.

* indicates $p < .05$.

** indicates $p < .01$.

the desirability of a mate: (1) kindness, (2) possession of wealth and/or other material resources, (3) high social status, (4) physical attractiveness, (5) other, (6) impossible to answer? While there was significant variability across subsamples, the majority of male and female protagonists were unmarried at the beginning of their tales (overall, 77 percent male, 78 percent female) and, of these characters, most were married by the end (overall, 64 percent female, 64 percent male) (see table 4.3). Fewer previously unmarried antagonists succeeded in marrying by the end of their tales, but the percentage was still substantial (33 percent female, 22 percent male).

In addition to questions about marital status and mating preferences, coders were asked a relevant question about the characters' main goals. First, they were asked if the character's primary motivation was to help others or to help himself/herself. For self-interested characters, a follow-up question was asked: What is the character's main goal: (1) survival, (2) finding/keeping a mate, (3) gaining wealth or material resources, (4) enhanced fame or social status, (5) other reasons. At about 50 percent for both sexes, finding/keeping a mate was the most common overarching goal for self-interested protagonists.

In short, a strikingly large proportion of folktales dwell upon the process of attracting and securing mates. Accordingly, the tales convey information on the attributes characters from the world's folktale traditions value in potential mates. Consistent with expectations, female protagonists were rated as placing the highest premium on a potential mate's kindness (a potential signaler of commitment). In contrast, while male characters also placed high value on kindness, they were far more likely to be rated as prioritizing the physical attractiveness of potential partners (see table 4.4).

Sex-differentiated trends in mate preferences were encountered across almost all of the subsamples, but they did not always reach the level of statistical significance. Moreover, we failed to find the predicted difference between male and female protagonists in preferences for wealthy and/or high-status mates. For protagonists of both sexes, the "extrinsic" mate qualities of wealth and social status paled in comparison to the "intrinsic" qualities of physical attractiveness and kindness. This finding would seem to be sharply at odds with well-publicized cross-cultural research indicating that women tend to place a higher premium on the wealth and social status of potential mates (e.g., Buss 1989). This anomaly may reflect a limitation of our coding instrument. Coders were instructed only to identify the single quality that seemed *most* important to each character in evaluating mates. If we had worded the question differently, asking coders to rate how

Table 4.3 Emphasis on Finding a Suitable Mate for Male and Female Protagonists

	Married at Start of Tale			Married at End of Tale			Mating Motive		
	Male	Female	Z-Score	Male	Female	Z-Score	Male	Female	Z-Score
Overall	23 (n=392)	22 (n=568)	0.38	64 (n=312)	64 (n=446)	0.07	53 (n=191)	48 (n=268)	1.11
North America	32 (n=72)	29 (n=83)	0.41	34 (n=53)	48 (n=60)	1.57	41 (n=22)	46 (n=26)	0.37
South America	35 (n=86)	38 (n=86)	0.48	57 (n=61)	66 (n=53)	0.95	55 (n=51)	54 (n=48)	0.07
Europe	11 (n=92)	8 (n=119)	0.4	90 (n=83)	89 (n=110)	0.68	60 (n=55)	51 (n=71)	1.05
Western Europe	7 (n=44)	7 (n=59)	0.01	90 (n=41)	89 (n=55)	0.18	54 (n=26)	50 (n=30)	0.29
Asia	15 (n=78)	14 (n=122)	0.28	83 (n=66)	72 (n=106)	1.84	54 (n=35)	47 (n=57)	0.65
Africa	27 (n=33)	34 (n=83)	0.69	71 (n=24)	64 (n=55)	0.64	44 (n=16)	42 (n=36)	0.14
Bands/Tribes	30 (n=192)	32 (n=285)	0.32	48 (n=141)	53 (n=195)	1.05	49 (92)	49 (n=124)	0.04
Preindustrial States	13 (n=184)	12 (n=259)	0.46	85 (n=160)	81 (n=230)	0.97	57 (n=96)	47 (n=135)	1.49
Male-edited Collections	17 (n=231)	20 (n=339)	1.05	70 (n=195)	69 (n=270)	0.84	54 (n=110)	47 (n=156)	1.2
Female-edited Collections	27 (n=75)	16 (n=141)	1.86	79 (n=56)	71 (n=120)	1.13	47 (n=31)	50 (n=58)	0.15
Male Coders	29 (n=78)	15 (n=111)	2.29*	64 (n=56)	65 (n=94)	0.08	47 (n=46)	53 (n=51)	0.72
Female Coders	21 (n=314)	23 (n=457)	0.72	70 (n=256)	70 (n=352)	0.09	40 (n=145)	60 (n=217)	5.46

Note: The overall sample size is often larger than the sum of the subgroups. This is because a number of collections could not be efficiently placed in geographic subgroups and because not all collections could be assigned on the basis of editor sex or cultural level.

"n" is number of male and/or female protagonists with information on marriage and motives.

* indicates $p < .05$.

** indicates $p < .01$.

Table 4.4 Percentage of Male and Female Protagonists Identified as Placing Primary Emphasis on Given Mate Preference Criteria

	Physical Attractiveness			Wealth/Status			Kindness		
	Male	Female	Z-Score	Male	Female	Z-Score	Male	Female	Z-Score
Overall Folk Tales	45 (n=206)	20 (n=243)	5.79**	8	12	1.44	37	51	2.93**
North America	16 (n=34)	3 (n=34)	1.1	3	15	1.7	48	51	0.25
South America	40 (n=50)	33 (n=51)	0.7	10	8	0.38	22	19	0.3
Europe	34 (n=68)	13 (n=86)	3.1**	4	6	0.4	47	59	1.52
Western Europe	30 (n=33)	11 (n=43)	1.99*	3	5	0.37	66	84	1.71
Asia	52 (n=50)	17 (n=48)	3.98**	6	10	0.68	30	60	3.17**
Africa	57 (n=14)	33 (n=18)	1.38	21	33	0.76	21	28	0.42
Bands/Tribes	47 (n=87)	25 (n=105)	3.28**	8	17	1.94	29	29	0.03
Preindustrial States	45 (n=112)	16 (n=125)	5**	7	8	0.25	43	69	4.15**
Male-Edited Collections	44 (n=122)	17 (n=125)	4.9**	9	16	1.84	43	66	3.72**
Female-Edited Collections	44 (n=36)	18 (n=56)	2.73**	6	9	0.6	36	55	1.85
Male Coders	46 (n=37)	19 (n=35)	2.53*	11	22	1.18	34	54	1.72
Female Coders	38 (n=169)	20 (n=208)	3.9**	8	11	1.04	38	50	2.45*

Note: The overall sample size is often larger than the sum of the subgroups. This is because a number of collections could not be efficiently placed in geographic subgroups and because not all collections could be assigned on the basis of editor sex or cultural level.

"n" is number of male and/or female story characters with information on mating preferences.

* indicates $p < .05$.

** indicates $p < .01$.

important *each* quality seemed to be to the character (using a Likert scale), sharper sex differences might have emerged.

However, an interesting thing occurs when antagonists are added to the analysis. Antagonist mate preference profiles form a sharp contrast to those of protagonists. Folktale antagonists seem to powerfully exaggerate stereotypically "shallow" male and female mate preferences. Male and female antagonists place almost no value on the kindness of potential mates, and on this aspect their attractiveness preferences converge. But the interest of male and female antagonists in potential mates' physical attractiveness and wealth/status is sharply polarized. Male antagonists are lechers: two-thirds placed principal weight upon the physical attractiveness of potential mates, versus just 6 percent and 2 percent for wealth/status and kindness, respectively. Female antagonists place overwhelming emphasis on mates who are in possession of wealth or high social status: 56 percent placed principal emphasis on wealth/status, versus 15 percent for physical attractiveness and 2 percent for kindness. In short, sexual dimorphism in the pool of antagonists is much sharper than in the pool of protagonists: overall, male antagonists place 4 times as much emphasis on attractiveness as do female antagonists ($p < .01$; $Z = 6.23$); on the other hand, female antagonists place 9 times as much stress on wealth/status as do male antagonists ($p < .01$; $Z = 7.2$).

The mate preference patterns of antagonists are so dramatic that when males and females are lumped together irrespective of agonistic status, all of the mate preference patterns predicted at the outset of this chapter are in effect at statistically significant levels (see Gottschall, Martin, Rea, and Quish 2004). One possible explanation is that the mate preference profiles of antagonists reflect a widespread moralizing tendency in cross-cultural tales, which functions to stigmatize overt "shallowness" in mate choice.

Level of Physical Attractiveness

Coders were asked of all characters: Is the character portrayed as (1) physically attractive, (2) physically unattractive, (3) average, or (4) is there no information on this topic? They were also asked to provide a count of the number of attractiveness references attached to each character. Coders were instructed to provide attractiveness information only on the basis of the explicit judgments of characters and/or narrators; they were told to avoid providing information based on their individual attractiveness preferences. In practice, codings were overwhelmingly based on explicit applications of synonyms for physical attractiveness or unattractiveness to given characters (e.g., beautiful, handsome, ugly, repulsive).

When information was available regarding the physical appearance of female protagonists, they were almost universally described as attractive. In fact, female protagonists who were explicitly defined as physically *unattractive* were true statistical outliers: just 8 of 1,440 tales included a main female protagonist explicitly defined as unattractive. While male protagonists were also overwhelmingly more likely to be defined as physically attractive, information on this factor was much less likely to be conveyed if the character was male. Overall, 51 percent of tales featuring female protagonists contained explicit information on their level of physical attractiveness versus just 22 percent for male protagonists. Further, when attractiveness information was available, there were approximately 50 percent more references per tale to female physical attractiveness than to male attractiveness (see table 4.5).

It should be stressed that this calculation is based on the number of attractiveness references *only for characters who were described as attractive at least once.* However, it would have also been justifiable to simply calculate the average number of attractiveness references for *every* male and female character in the data set (regardless of whether or not they had been coded as attractive). The latter calculation method produces an even more dramatic difference between the average number of attractiveness references per male and female protagonist. When using this method of calculation, there are about 300 percent more references to the attractiveness of females than to the attractiveness of males in the sample as a whole (.52 attractiveness references per male protagonist versus 1.57 per his female counterpart).

The attractiveness of female protagonists was also emphasized significantly more than that of female antagonists. Overall, in cases where information was conveyed on physical appearance, just 69 percent of female antagonists were defined as physically attractive. Moreover, information on female antagonist physical attractiveness was conveyed less frequently (23 percent of tales) and less repetitively (one-third as many references per tale). There was least emphasis of all placed on the attractiveness of male antagonists.

In short, as a whole and across subsamples, there was intense emphasis on the physical attractiveness of female protagonists relative to other character types. (The issue of sex differences in attractiveness emphasis is the main subject of chapter 6.)

Table 4.5 Physical Attractiveness of Male and Female Protagonists

	Percent with Information on Attractiveness			Percent Attractive			Average References to Attractiveness Per Tale		
	Male	Female	Z-Score	Male	Female	Z-Score	Male	Female	T-Statistic
Overall	22 (n=392)	51 (n=568)	9.83**	96	97	0.23	1.89 (x=149)	3.05 (x=884)	5.47**
North America	7 (n=72)	39 (n=83)	5.16**	100	91	1.82	1.17 (x=7)	3.1 (x=90)	4.97**
South America	13 (n=86)	37 (n=86)	3.85**	85	97	1.21	1.92 (x=22)	2.32 (x=73)	0.64
Europe	37 (n=92)	65 (n=119)	4.16**	100	98	1.01	1.97 (x=63)	2.87 (x=224)	2.42*
Western Europe	37 (n=35)	86 (n=43)	5.03**	100	100	0	1.23 (x=16)	2.87 (x=110)	3.38**
Asia	19 (n=78)	61 (n=122)	6.74**	93	100	1.04	1.86 (x=26)	3.8 (x=228)	3.44**
Africa	24 (n=33)	47 (n=83)	2.46*	100	97	1.01	2.14 (x=15)	3.08 (x=117)	1.44
Bands/Tribes	13 (n=192)	37 (n=297)	6.48**	96	95	0.12	2.09 (x=23)	2.84 (x=111)	1.85
Preindustrial States	29 (n=188)	64 (n=267)	7.85**	98	96	0.98	1.9 (x=52)	3.03 (x=171)	4.39**
Male-edited Collections	23 (n=231)	57 (n=339)	8.59**	96	97	0.2	1.85 (x=89)	3.2 (x=623)	5.16**
Female-edited Collections	23 (n=75)	49 (n=141)	4.10**	100	97	1.44	2 (x=34)	2.76 (x=191)	1.82
Male Coders	34 (n=78)	65 (n=111)	4.3**	96	96	0.65	1.71 (x=41)	3.03 (x=209)	4.93**
Female Coders	17 (n=314)	48 (n=457)	9.65**	96	98	0.68	1.96 (x=108)	3.05 (x=674)	3.92**

Note: The overall sample size is often larger than the sum of the subgroups. This is because a number of collections could not be efficiently placed in geographic subgroups and because not all collections could be assigned on the basis of editor sex or cultural level.

"n" is total number of coded male and/or female protagonists.

"x" is total number of references to attractiveness per subsample.

* indicates *p* < .05.

** indicates *p* < .01.

Ratings of Activity and Heroism

Coders were asked the following questions about all characters: Is the character *more accurately* defined as (1) passive (in the sense that he/she exemplifies patient endurance of hardships/problems, and does not actively pursue goals) or is he/she (2) active (in the sense that he/she actively pursues goals and solutions to hardships/problems), or (3) cannot answer? They were also asked: Does the character accomplish his or her goal(s) through feats of specifically *physical* heroism? Consistent with expectations, the data suggest that female protagonists pursue their goals differently than male protagonists. While 71 percent of male protagonists were defined as actively pursuing their goals, just 51 percent of female protagonists were so defined (see table 4.6).

Female protagonists were also less likely than male protagonists to be defined as engaged in acts of specifically physical heroism. Overall, almost one-third of male protagonists behaved in a physically heroic fashion, versus less than 10 percent of female protagonists. It is important to note that this finding does *not* imply that female protagonists were categorically unheroic; this finding leaves open the possibility that female characters expressed heroism in ways not entailing physical hardihood or risk. It would be interesting to compare male and female characters using different definitions of heroism (e.g., moral heroism) and of activity/passivity.

Patterns of Altruism

Coders were asked: Is the character *primarily* motivated to help (1) him/herself or (2) help others? If the character is primarily motivated to help others, whom does he/she try to help *most:* (1) kin, (2) friends, (3) member(s) of community at large, (4) other? If the character is primarily motivated to aid his/her kin, what kinship category is the character *most interested* in assisting: (1) sibling(s), (2) child and/or children, (3) spouse/mate, (4) parent(s), (5) niece and/or nephew, (6) aunt and/or uncle, (7) cousin(s), (8) grandparent(s), (9) step-relation(s) or in-laws, (10) family as a whole. Across subsamples, female protagonists spent significant amounts of energy on behalf of other people: family, friends, and communities as a whole. In contrast to antagonists who were very rarely motivated to assist persons other than themselves (13 percent female, 5 percent male), 42 percent of female protagonists were so motivated. Most of this energy was expended on behalf of kin (69 percent). Moreover, as predicted, energy

Table 4.6 Personality Descriptors of Male and Female Protagonists

	Active			Heroic		
	Male	Female	Z-Score	Male	Female	Z-Score
Overall	71 (n=381)	51 (n=555)	6.4**	31 (n=392)	9 (n=568)	8.43**
North America	76 (n=71)	49 (n=82)	3.57**	44 (n=72)	11 (n=83)	4.96**
South America	63 (n=84)	45 (n=83)	2.36*	17 (n=86)	6 (n=86)	2.42*
Europe	80 (n=88)	63 (n=117)	2.63*	33 (n=92)	9 (n=119)	4.2**
Western Europe	75 (n=44)	71 (n=58)	0.49	36 (n=44)	7 (n=59)	3.72**
Asia	66 (n=77)	37 (n=119)	4.2**	33 (n=78)	9 (n=122)	4.1**
Africa	77 (n=30)	51 (n=81)	2.74*	18 (n=33)	2 (n=83)	2.28*
Bands/Tribes	69 (n=187)	49 (n=280)	4.44**	40 (n=137)	7 (n=285)	7.24**
Preindustrial States	75 (n=179)	53 (n=253)	4.94**	34 (n=184)	11 (n=269)	6.11**
Male-Edited Collections	76 (n=225)	50 (n=333)	7.54**	38 (n=231)	10 (n=339)	7.74**
Female-Edited Collections	75 (n=72)	54 (n=136)	3.09**	25 (n=75)	8 (n=141)	3.03**
Male Coders	83 (n=76)	50 (n=102)	5.01**	46 (n=78)	13 (n=111)	5.19**
Female Coders	69 (n=305)	51 (n=453)	5.07**	27 (n=314)	8 (n=457)	7.02**

Note: The overall sample size is often larger than the sum of the subgroups. This is because a number of collections could not be efficiently placed in geographic subgroups and because not all collections could be assigned on the basis of editor sex or cultural level.

"n" is number of male and/or female protagonists with information on activity and heroism.

* indicates $p < .05$.

** indicates $p < .01$.

expended on behalf of kin was not disseminated randomly but was directed overwhelming (91 percent) on behalf of family members in the following categories: mates, children, siblings, and parents. Exactly this same pattern of altruism, where aid is primarily extended to mates and to first degree genetic relations, applies to the kin-directed efforts of male protagonists as well as to antagonists of both sexes.

Summary, the Heroine's Face

This composite of the heroine's face obviously does not exhaust its subtleties; it is an effort to lay down, in broad brushstrokes, some main lineaments that consistently apply to female folktale protagonists more than to other character types. It must be strongly emphasized that this composite portrait represents only a rough sketch, with individual storytellers filling in detail, color, and shading in accord with their individual temperaments and sociocultural contexts. Moreover, the following characterization clearly does not apply to every female protagonist in the sample nor can it be argued, since statistically meaningful analyses of individual cultures could not be performed, that it prevails in every tradition; the generalization applies across the 6 large geographical regions, across the 2 levels of cultural complexity, and regardless of the sex of the coders or collection editors (see chapter 5 for further discussion of potential coder/editor bias).

The vast majority of female protagonists are young women at the age of first marriage. When physical descriptions are provided, they are almost universally beautiful, and this beauty is usually stressed repetitively. They are typically unmarried, but they are absorbed with the challenges of finding a mate and usually succeed by tale's end. In comparison to her male counterparts, female protagonists place greater emphasis on a potential mate's kindness and less emphasis on physical attractiveness. They are solicitous of their families' well-being, devoting much energy to promote the welfare of close kin. They achieve their goals through different means than male protagonists: they are less likely to actively pursue their goals and less likely to achieve them in ways requiring conspicuous physical courage. Perhaps not coincidentally, they are far less likely than male protagonists to serve as main characters.

Discussion

These results suggest that evolutionary theory can be a map and legend (though not the only one) for the study of narrative universals—a guide that points the way to likely universals and helps us interpret them. The simplest explanation for the gender patterns revealed in this study—assuming that they are basically valid and can be replicated by others—is that distinct regularities in behavior, psychology, and gender predominate across human populations and are reflected in the world's folk literatures. While this conclusion is out of kilter with a humanities culture that is currently intent on emphasizing the diversity among human groups, it is consistent with the current state of knowledge in the human sciences and with the conclusions of previous generations of scholars who studied regularities in world literature. As Klyde Kluckhohn wrote:

> The mere recurrence of certain motifs in varied areas separated geographically and historically tells us something about the human psyche. It suggests that the interaction of a certain kind of biological apparatus in a certain kind of physical world with some inevitables of the human condition brings about some regularities in the formation of imaginative products, of powerful images. (Kluckhohn 1960, 49)

This is not to deny the established fact of cross-cultural borrowing and sharing of folktales (see Thomson 1932–1936, 1946). It is to stress the equally well-established fact that diffusion cannot account for the many similarities in folktale traditions with little or no cultural contact (see Propp 1968; Thomson 1932–1936, 1946; Tatar 1987). And it is to contend that theories of diffusion tend to overlook an important point: folktales adapt so well to vastly different cultural ecologies because they speak to the common problems and preoccupations of the human condition—problems and preoccupations that are unbounded by culture. Even in the highly unlikely event that the trends reported here result solely from cross-cultural sharing, this explanation could not explain why stories are so "viral" and why, in all cultures, certain story types find human minds to be such susceptible hosts. In other words, even if folktale universals were results of diffusion only, "their persistence cannot be understood except on the hypothesis that these images have a special congeniality for the human mind" (Kluckhohn 1960, 49).

The Politics of Human Universals

In recent decades, literary scholars have aligned searches for human universals, not just narrative universals, with racism, sexism, imperialism, elitism, ethnocentrism, and other ideologies justifying one group's domination of others (Ashcroft et al. 1989, 149; Buck 1991, 30; Bohman 1988, 68; for discussion, see contributors to Mueller 1993). As Dipesh Chakrabarty writes, universal truths are just "[provincial] dialects backed by an army" (2000, 43). For Chakrabarty and many other writers, claims for human universals are—like bombs or bayonets or blankets teeming with small pox bacillus—just one more weapon in the oppressor's arsenal.

This would seem to court an obvious objection: how can claims for human universals, based on the notion that all human beings share the same nature, serve ideologies justifying one group's domination of others? Doesn't this reduce to the absurdity of saying that theories of human equality are too dangerous to entertain lest they promote ideologies of difference and dominance? The answer, as Hogan (1997) and Appiah (1992) cogently explain, is that anti-universalist critics are not objecting to "genuine" universals but to false claims of universality that have sometimes been used to foist the local norms of strong groups onto weaker group. As should be clear, however, the identification of genuine universals (Hogan [1997] calls them "empirical universals"), based on theoretically and methodologically rigorous analyses of culturally diverse samples, cannot serve as a crutch to ideologies of dominance because they posit not difference but sameness. As Hogan writes, no racist has ever possessed the creativity to justify "the enslavement of Africans or colonial rule in India on the basis of a claim that whites and nonwhites share universal human properties. Rather, they based their justifications on presumed differences among Europeans, Africans, and Indians, usually biological differences but cultural differences as well" (1997, 224; see also Hogan 1997, 227).

In fact, the concept of a universal human nature seems like a necessary condition for moral and political action. The structuralist literary analyst Tzvetan Todorov is right when he says, "It is not possible, without inconsistency, to defend human rights with one hand and deconstruct the idea of humanity with the other" (2005, 58; see also Jacoby 2005). Lacking a concept of the universally human, we have no basis for insisting on "human rights," or defining what those rights should be—no basis for advocating emancipation over slavery, for insisting that a sweet-sixteen party is to be preferred as a coming of age ritual to clitorectomy and infibulation, or for believing that Sweden's treatment of women is in any way superior to the Taliban's.

But there is one significant complication in this. The present chapter reveals powerful trends in the ways that male and female characters are portrayed across a broad array of cultures; wherever you go, and whenever you go there, people are people. However, this study also reveals distinct and regular patterns of *difference* in the ways that male characters and female characters are drawn in these traditions. So, based on the moral logic above, should we be concerned that these data could be used (or are—by virtue of their very existence—*being* used) to justify essentialist thinking about gender and thus systems of sexist domination? My response to this question will be given in the next chapter.

Chapter 5

Testing Feminist Fairy Tale Studies*

The defining empirical claim of classic feminist gender theory is that gender is primarily (if not exclusively) a product of nurture not nature. This thinking is distilled in De Beauvoir's pioneering slogan, "One is not born, but rather becomes, a woman" (1949, 267). Behavioral, emotional, psychological, and even physical traits stereotypically associated with males and females have little basis in biology; they are products of the socialization environments particular to given types of societies. This thinking has shaped an immense body of feminist literary criticism and theory over the past several decades.

Nowhere is this truer than in feminist analysis and critique of European fairy tales. While a minority of feminist scholars have touted fairy tales as sources of positive role models for young girls (for example, Lurie 1970, 1971), voices more numerous and loud have charged them with inflicting wanton psychic violence upon the malleable minds of children, especially girls. Beginning with influential analyses by Simone de Beauvoir and Betty Friedan, feminists have argued that European tales are rife with stereotyped male and female ideals: men should be strong, active, and courageous; women should be beautiful, tractable, and passive (De Beauvoir 1949, 126, 128, 163, 167, 178; Friedan 1963, 118, 192). These patterns not only reflect arbitrary cultural norms of the patriarchal West (see Zipes 1986, 3; for overviews see Haase 2000b and De Caro 1983), they also actively perpetuate them: fairy tales enforce "cultural norms that exalt [female] passivity... and perpetuate the patriarchal status quo"; they are manipulative

---

*Some of the material of this chapter was originally published in Chapter Ten of *The Literary Animal*, edited by Jonathan Gottschall and David Sloan Wilson. Evanston, IL: Northwestern University Press (2005).

"parables of feminine socialization"; they "exert awesome imaginative power over the female psyche"; they "prescribe female behavior"; they are "venomous" tools of "a patriarchal plot"; they preserve and "reinforce male hegemony in the civilizing process"; and they train girls to be rape victims.*

While the most prominent feminist work on the fairy tale was conducted in the 1970s and 1980s, its conclusions are still widely credited. Feminist fairy tale research is established in the textbooks (e.g., Tyson 1999, 87–88), and it has strongly influenced recently published tale collections that are designed to correct for gender distortions in the classic European tales (e.g., Ragan 1998a; Yolen and Guevera 2000; Tchana and Schart Hyman 2000). *Marvels and Tales*, a leading journal of fairy tale studies, recently published a sympathetic special issue on feminist approaches to the fairy tale, called *Fairy Tale Liberation—Thirty Years Later* (Haase 2000a; see also DeGraff 1987). To this issue the editor contributes a generally approving critical survey demonstrating that most of the core claims of feminist fairy tale studies continue to enjoy broad support (Haase 2000b).

The claim that European tales reflect and perpetuate the arbitrary gender norms of Western patriarchal societies will be referred to, henceforth, as the social construction hypothesis (SCH). Every reasonable and plausible hypothesis should yield testable, or at least potentially testable, predictions about what patterns a responsible investigator should find if the hypothesis is valid (*if this, then that*). The SCH is no exception. Since gender patterns in European fairy tales are said to reflect socially constructed differences between the sexes, the straightforward prediction of the SCH is that samples of traditional folktales from different world cultures will evince markedly different patterns of female characterization than those identified in European tales. In short, the SCH predicts that an analysis of a culturally diverse sample will reveal diverse gender patterns.

The research described in the previous chapter was designed to gather data for multiple studies, including a test of predictions derived from the SCH. Using this data, we can determine whether specific patterns of gender representation, claimed by feminist fairy tale scholars to be representative of European tales, are also typical of other world regions. If the gender patterns are violated in any subsample, the SCH

---

* See, respectively, Rowe 1986, 209; Kolbenschlag 1981, 3; Rowe 1986, 218; Helms 1987, 3; Daly 1978, 44; Zipes 1986, 9; Brownmiller 1975, 309–310.

is supported; if the patterns are consistent across subsamples, then the SCH is undermined. At the risk of belaboring the findings, I will briefly recap them in light of specific claims in feminist fairy tale scholarship.

Missing Women

A principal feminist claim is that there is a fundamental dearth of main female characters in European folktales relative to main male characters, and that this reflects and perpetuates Western ideals of female subordination and secondariness (e.g., Ragan 1998b, xxii–xxiv). But the findings of this study, and of a follow-up study described in chapter 6, strongly suggest that an underrepresentation of prominent female folktale characters is the rule across cultures (see table 4.1).

Activity and Passivity

The claim that European tales contain disproportionate numbers of passive female protagonists is perhaps the most pervasive and important in feminist fairy tale studies (e.g., Lieberman 1986; Lundell 1986; Stone 1986). In the European tales, the argument goes, only female antagonists are active, communicating the message to girls and women that activity is bad and unfeminine whereas passivity is good, feminine, and worthy of rewards (like marriage and other happy endings). Our results vindicate the claim that active female European folktale protagonists are less commonly encountered than active male protagonists. However, they lend no support to the claim that this is a reflection of arbitrary European norms (see table 4.6). Across all subsamples the percentage of active male protagonists significantly exceeds the percentage of active female protagonists. In fact, while males were always coded as more active, the European and Western European subsamples actually contained the *highest proportions* of active female protagonists in the study. In the European sample, 63 percent of female protagonists were so coded. And the Western European sample was the only one where differences in the levels of activity for male and female characters (75 percent and 71 percent, respectively) were statistically insignificant. In short, these data suggest that, if anything, European tales are socializing young girls to be more—not less—active than girls in other traditions.

Physical Heroism

Closely related to claims about female passivity is the claim that there are fewer physically heroic female protagonists, again reflecting and reinforcing ideals of female weakness, passivity, and disempowerment. Jane Yolen has helped popularize this view: "[Victorian folktale anthologists] regularly subverted and subsumed the stories that starred strong and illustrious female heroes, promoting instead those stories that showed women as weak or witless, or, at the very best, waiting prettily and with infinite patience to be rescued (2000b, *xvii*)." In a different publication, Yolen amplifies: "[Stories with heroic female characters] have always been around, hidden away in the back storeroom of folklore. Disguised. Mutilated. Truncated. Their feet bound as surely as the Chinese bound the feet of young noblewomen even into this century" (2000a, *x*).

Our results show, however, that a dearth of physically heroic female protagonists was not unique to Europe but was the rule across all of the subsamples (see table 4.6).

Emphasis on Female Beauty

The putatively intense emphasis on the beauty of female protagonists deeply concerns feminist fairy tale scholars. European fairy tales are said to teach that "beauty is a girl's most valuable asset" and that "girls win the prize if they are fairest of them all; boys win if they are bold, active, and lucky" (Lieberman 1986, 188). The data support the perception that there is more emphasis on the beauty of female protagonists in European folktales. However, the data also show that this state of affairs is not confined to Europe.

While our findings undercut claims that greater emphasis on female beauty is a product only of European acculturation pressures, emphasis on beauty *was* particularly acute in the European subsamples. For the data-set as a whole, attractiveness information was provided for 51 percent of female protagonists. In Europe, information was provided for 65 percent of female protagonists. By far the greatest amount of emphasis on female attractiveness was found in the sample of Western European tales, where attractiveness information was provided for 86 percent of female protagonists. (See table 4.5; for similar results in a different study see chapter 6). But things are more complex still: While the emphasis on female attractiveness in European tales was especially dramatic, the same patterns applied to the males. For male characters, attractiveness information was markedly more likely to be communicated in the European than non-European samples.

Marriage

Feminist critics contend that "marriage is the fulcrum and major event of nearly every fairy tale; it is the reward for girls" (Lieberman 1986, 189; see also Orenstein 2002, 10; Rowe 1986, 271). According to this line of thought, the tales insidiously suggest that happiness and peace are not to be found within, but must be conferred upon a woman by a man. The data agree with the feminist perception that attracting a suitable romantic partner is a primary challenge for the majority of female protagonists in European folktales. However, while European tales *do* place somewhat greater emphasis on marriage than the tales of other subsamples, marriage is a dominant theme in all of them. Moreover, the data do not support the contention that finding an appropriate mate is somehow more important for female characters than it is for male characters, not in Europe and not anywhere else (see table 4.3).

Stigmatization of Older Women

Finally, feminist critics claim that European fairy tales transmit insidious messages about older women. Older women—more powerful and better able to challenge patriarchal interests—are said to disproportionately inhabit antagonist roles (Bottigheimer 1980; Lieberman 1986, 196). This perception is confirmed by the data. However, once more, the pattern is not unique to Europe but holds true across subsamples. Overall, just 8 percent of female protagonists in the sample were identified as aged forty or over, whereas 42 percent of female antagonists were identified as forty or over. Moreover, the data shows that in every subsample male antagonists were also older than male protagonists: overall, just 10 percent of male protagonists were identified as at least forty whereas 34 percent of male antagonists were identified as forty or older. Thus folktales are a baldly ageist genre: it is not *older women* who are stigmatized, it is *older people* (see table 4.2).

Discussion: Editorial Manipulation, By-Products, and Biological Essentialism

The SCH is anchored in the premise that gender-related patterns long-observed in European fairy tales reflect the arbitrary gender arrangements of specific types of societies. This hypothesis generates the prediction that folktale traditions from different regions of the world, at different levels of cultural complexity, based on different political, religious, and economic systems, should possess substantially different gender-related patterns. That is, we should find regions of the world where female characters are as active as male characters, where male beauty is emphasized as much as, or more than, female beauty, where females are as apt to be the swashbuckling heroes, and so forth. However, while the study revealed significant and important variation across world regions, the broad trends were never violated—not in the regional subsamples, not in the comparisons of band/tribal societies and preindustrial states, and not in samples divided by the sex of editors and coders.

Before the SCH is dismissed, however, one further complication must be addressed. Closely related to the SCH is the claim that the folktale was an originally feminine genre, perhaps originating in matriarchal societies, which was gradually expropriated by males (e.g., Bottigheimer 1980; Gottner-Abendroth 1988; Nitschke 1980; Rowe 1986). In traditional settings the tales passed orally from the lips of mothers to daughters, and on to granddaughters. As the tales were transferred from the oral medium to the printed page, however, women lost control. Feminists note that male editors and anthologists are mainly responsible for constructing the canon of European fairy tales. They tender suggestive evidence that these editors chose tales, suppressed them, or redacted them until collections reflected the conservative patriarchal ideals of late eighteenth- and nineteenth-century bourgeois culture (e.g., Bottigheimer 1982, 1986, 1993; Lurie 1971; Haase 2000b; Helms 1987; Lundell 1986; Ragan 1998b; Rowe 1986; Zipes 1979–1980, 1983a, 1983b, 1986). The end result of this distortion was that the numerous European tales containing strong, active, courageous, and resourceful heroines were suppressed or mangled beyond recognition; they left us only the tales featuring insipid, inert, simpering heroines whose only resources are beauty and tractability, and whose only passion is for finding Prince Charming (Lieberman 1972). In short, the originally "female art" (Rowe 1986, 71) of the fairy tale was turned against women, coming to function as a patriarchal indoctrination vehicle, perfect for grooming girls and boys to assume their respective subordinate and dominant cultural roles.

In theory, this editorial manipulation hypothesis could be modified and extended to undermine confidence in the ability of this research to effectively test the SCH. Since Western males have been responsible for gathering and editing most of the folktale collections that are available in English, the gender patterns revealed in this study could be considered more indicative of consistent patterns of editorial bias than legitimate patterns in the tales.

This possibility seems unlikely for two reasons. First, it would require the assumption that the dozens of male and female folklorists, ethnographers, anthropologists, and other scholars who collected, edited, and translated the tales used in this study—despite their varying national, disciplinary, ideological, and historical backgrounds—made exactly the same type of editorial manipulations and that these manipulations radically altered the nature of the database. Second, the editorial manipulation hypothesis can be indirectly evaluated using the data in this study. Since the hypothesis posits sex-based bias, it predicts that we should find significantly different patterns of characterization in male-edited versus female-edited collections and perhaps even in data collected by males versus females. However, as can be seen in the tables, the variation across these subsamples is not always in the predictable direction, and it is consistent with naturally occurring variation (random or not) across collections and cultures. In no case did results for male or female coders and editors violate the general patterns apparent in the other samples. (The possibility of editorial, and other forms of bias in folktale collections is revisited at length in the coda to chapter 6, "World Folktales' Missing Women.")

*   *   *

In summary, these data do not conflict with the argument that European editors such as Perrault, Lang, and the Grimms made significant alterations to their original source tales (and of course doubt that they did make changes, just as editors of contemporary collections do). Indeed, some trends in the data suggest that gender patterns in European tales have been slanted in the direction feminists have claimed. However, in every case, the European patterns only accentuate trends that are present in other regions. The data do not, therefore, support the bigger feminist claim: but for editorial meddling, the tales would portray significantly (or radically) different gender patterns.

Walls: Adaptations or By-Products?

In response to the initial publication of the material of this chapter in the edited collection *The Literary Animal* (Gottschall and Wilson 2005), a reviewer closely questioned its logic. The reviewer, William Benzon, cites the predictions given at the outset of this chapter ("the SCH predicts that an analysis of a culturally diverse sample will reveal diverse gender patterns") and responds as follows:

> Note that Gottschall is assuming that, since biological mechanisms are the same in all societies, differences and *only* differences are to be accounted for by cultural mechanisms. As my colleague Timothy Perper points out (personal communication), where you find houses, you find walls supporting the roofs on those houses. Does that mean that we are biologically determined to build supporting walls? No, the need for walls is an inescapable consequence of engineering constraints imposed by gravity.
>
> What is at issue is the specific mechanism through which a behavioral result arises. If there is considerable cross-cultural diversity in the relevant fairytale features, then this question does not arise. That diversity is evidence for strong cultural influence. But if there is little cross-cultural diversity, then things are not so clear. (2005–2006; for a critical response to Benzon, see Michelson 2006)

While Benzon is not flying to the rescue of the feminist SCH, he is closely questioning our interpretation of the data. Benzon argues that evidence of a universal behavioral (or psychological or cultural) trait doesn't necessarily represent evidence that the trait is mainly genetically grounded. It could simply be a side effect, in the way that the walls of a home are side effects of their usefulness in holding up the roof.

Leaving aside the ineptness of his analogy (walls are *not* simply for holding up roofs; if you need to hold up a roof, posts are much simpler and cheaper; the walls of homes are functionally designed to hold in warmth while they hold out the elements and intruders), variations on this argument are increasingly common among psychologists and sociologists who would challenge the notion that universal differences between men and women in psychology, behavior, and gender roles strongly imply genetic predisposition (e.g., Eagly and Wood 1999; Wood and Eagly 2002; see also Hogan 2003a).

The argument typically goes something like this: cross-cultural gender differences may be results of universal patterns of social structure that ultimately emerge from the fact that men happen to be bigger and stronger, and women give birth to babies and move around with their food supply. Women can't hunt well (much less fight well) when pregnant or nursing heavily; men can't get pregnant and they can't lactate. In traditional societies, therefore, divisions of labor and social roles by sex just made sense. Therefore studies identifying universal structures of gender may not represent evidence of different default neurobiological settings in men and women; these structures may be emergent properties of the different types of physiologies nature happened to give to men and women (e.g., bigger, stronger men; smaller, physically weaker, childbearing women).

These writers have a point—one that should have been acknowledged in the initial publications of this work. Certain gender patterns revealed in our studies may be explained, at least in part, by the consistently differing social roles of men and women in traditional societies. For example, given that women's lives in such societies are apt to revolve around hearth and home, it is not surprising to find that they are less likely to be portrayed as active or as physically heroic. Similarly, if real men's lives tend to be more diverse in traditional societies, this may help to explain why they are more likely to be the main characters of stories (for further development of this idea, see Coda to chapter 6)

However, while this "social role theory" may explain some portion of the gender divergences described in these chapters, for two principal reasons I think it is vanishingly unlikely to account for the full range of observed gender differences. First, this would require taking seriously the idea that over uncounted generations males and females—and our prehuman ancestors—faced dramatically different challenges in life (for instance, basically everyone agrees that males did most of the hunting, most of the fighting with weapons and fists, most of the public politicking, and most of the competing for multiple mates; females did more of the gathering and most of the child-rearing) and yet the wondrously subtle evolutionary process failed to pay this any heed. Instead, natural selection worked to produce and maintain psychological equipotentiality for men and women in spite of very consistent and very dramatic differences in their survival and reproduction pressures. In other words, the same strong and steady evolutionary pressures that produced sharp differences in male and female bodies—characteristics like muscular strength, body fat percentage, foot speed, cardiovascular capacity, height, and basic body shape—were powerless to effect correlating effects on the brain and the psychology the brain produces.

This scenario, defended by Wood and Eagly (2002, 702–703), seems to me like an argument for creationism from the chin up. Why not apply the same theory to the sex-differentiated behaviors of other social species? For example, what reasons have we, aside from anthropocentric chauvinism, not to invoke social role theory as the ultimate explanation for sex-based behavioral differences in gorillas, chimps or—why not?—chickens? For example, male gorillas/chimps/chickens are on average fiercer than the females not because of evolved behavioral tendencies but because of the social roles they happen to play in their troops/flocks—roles that originate in the unique reproductive roles of females and the fact that male gorillas/chimps/chickens happen to be bigger and stronger.

Second, we don't have to rely only on this strong a priori basis. Some advocates of social role theory tend to downplay the fact that cross-cultural data is not the sum of our evidence. For example, comparative zoology: human patterns of gender are consistent, in many ways, with the most common patterns of sex-stereotyped behavior in other effectively polygynous species, including our closest primate relatives. In addition, there is copious data on hormonal, neurological, and cognitive sex differences (accessible overviews include Hines 2005; Brizendine 2006; Baron Cohen 2003; Geary 1998)—including studies of young infants, and highly illuminating studies of (frequently catastrophic) attempts to surgically "reassign" children with mutilated or ambiguous genitals (see Colapinto 2001). All of these research areas converge in support of the robust a priori basis for crediting the idea that cross-cultural patterns of gender differences reflect deep regularities in evolved biology, and not just regularities in social structure.

Essentialism

But isn't this to slide back into the ooze pit of essentialist thinking when we had finally made progress in clawing our way out? An essentialist position on gender would suggest that there is a constant, unchangeable "essence" (call it "masculinity") that all men possess, and an invariable essence (call it "femininity") that all women possess. Modern biology is almost militantly opposed to essentialist thinking. When biologists look at a given species or variety, they see not essences but continuously variable populations. This "population thinking" is one of the most important concepts in biology, and it is the bottom layer of bedrock in evolutionary theory. Darwin's almost unprecedented ability to think of species not in terms of everlasting platonic types but in terms of populations of diverse and continuously varying individuals was a decisive factor in his theoretical breakthrough (for a brilliant treatment of this issue, see Mayr 1982). So arguing for a substantial genetic component in gender formation is not tantamount to an argument for essentialism.

The findings of the present study join many others in suggesting that there *are* certain statistically reliable gender variances in different *populations* of men and women, but they emphatically do not suggest that all (real) men possess Essence Y and all (real) women possess Essence X. The expectations of the study, which were borne out in the results, were that, across populations, men and women would be more or less likely to possess or express Properties Y or X. We did not expect, or find, essences of maleness and femaleness; we found continuously varying populations. Glancing at the tables will show wide areas of overlap between the "male" and "female" patterns. For example, there are very significant proportions of female characters who are portrayed as active and who are motivated primarily by physical attractiveness in their mating decisions; likewise, there are large numbers of male characters who are portrayed as passive, who don't do anything heroic or courageous, and who are most attracted to romantic partners who are kind. Both sexes are strongly motivated by the desire to marry and to nurture the prospects of their kin.

Furthermore, the present study was specifically designed to *locate cross-culturally stable differences* between male and female characters. In this, our goal was not to resuscitate the fallacy of essentialism or to add our weight to an antifeminist backlash, but to address the specific questions that interested us: (1) In cross-cultural samples, are there universals in the depiction of female protagonists? (2) Are the bold feminist hypotheses about fairy tales (especially the SCH) actually correct? We would fully expect that different investigators, focusing on different questions, would be able to find even wider areas of overlap between the depictions of male and female characters.

* * *

The findings of this research challenge what has been the central dogma of the dominant brand of feminist scholarship in the humanities: that chromosomal sex and socially constructed gender are, at most, distantly related. But no one should be confused: challenging the specific empirical claims of feminist gender theory is not the same thing as challenging the moral and political goals of feminism (see Vandermassen 2005). Equitable treatment of women is a rigid ethical imperative, and it would be a grave mistake to tie this imperative to whatever studies happen to find regarding differences between males and females (see Pinker 2002 for development of this point; see also Campbell 2002). Difference does not logically imply inferiority or justify oppression, regardless of how difference has been treated in the past. If populations of men and women reveal certain standard statistical differences, this does not mean that the differences are "good," inevitable, or immune to social influence. Just lifting one's nose from this book to see all the evidence of shockingly rapid changes in the status of modern women should be enough to dissolve any lingering fears about the inescapable determining power of biology.

Chapter 6

The "Beauty Myth" is no Myth*

Prefatory Note

The study described in this chapter follows up on two of the more dramatic findings from the previously described study: (1) the finding that across regions there are far fewer main female characters, and (2) that sharply more emphasis is placed upon their physical attractiveness. The follow-up study sought to determine if similar patterns would emerge in a content analysis of a different folktale sample using new coders and coding protocol. Moreover, this research, along with the study of romantic love presented in the next chapter, was designed to shore up some of the earlier study's specific methodological limitations. Looking back on this work with the benefit of hindsight, there are at least two main things (along with several smaller things) that should have been done differently. First, a different method of intercoder reliability testing should have been used. For instance, assigning overlapping samples of folktales, so that perhaps 10–15 percent of the entire sample would have been coded by all participants, would have provided a more confident indicator of the reliability of the findings as a whole.

* This research was originally published in the journal *Human Nature* 19 (2008). Kacey Anderson, Chad Burbank, Jasper Burch, Chelsea Byrnes, Christine Callanan, Nicole Casamento, Amy Gardiner, Natalie Gladd, Allison Hartnett, Elisabeth Henry, Eloise Hilarides, Chelsea Lemke, Kristen Manganini, Sara Merrihew, Tonya Milan-Robinson, Patrick O'Connell, Jessica Mott, Kimberly Parker, Karlin Revoir, Nathan Riley, Darcie Robinson, Sheila Rodriguez, Chelsea Sauve, April Spearance, Valerie Stucker, Adam Tapply, Alexa Unser, Christopher Wall, Alexis Webb, and Melinda Zocco contributed to this research.

Second, we should have focused on a smaller number of distinct culture areas—but in more depth. Establishing a sampling pool with closer shores and deeper depths would have mitigated the problem of cultural "lumping." While our grouping of cultures into very broad geographical areas makes a kind of intuitive sense, and while we made an effort to follow anthropological precedents for large-scale cross-cultural studies, the different groupings do clump together disparate cultures. For example, as can be seen in Appendix A, the North American sample awkwardly combines populations that share little with each other beyond their residence upon a common land mass, like the Inuit and the Sioux. Thus there was a significant degree of arbitrariness in our groupings. (It is important to say, however, that we experimented with different groupings in an attempt to devise categories that were both logical and large enough to perform tests for statistical significance. What we found in these experiments is vital: there is no logical way to rearrange these groupings so that the reported trends in male–female characterization evaporate.)

The studies presented in this chapter and the next were designed to improve upon these specific limitations: we employed more powerful methods of intercoder reliability assessment and we made substantial progress in moderating the problem of cultural lumping. These studies also added a significant computerized element to the coding process, which eliminated some of the possible scope for human error.

The main study of this chapter was first published in the scientific journal *Human Nature*—a leading outlet for research on the bio-logical study of human behavior, psychology, and culture. It describes a test of specific scientific hypotheses about the salience of gendered attractiveness emphasis in *Homo sapiens*. This chapter addresses these specific questions: (1) As a rule, are significant female characters sharply underrepresented in world folktales? (2) Is greater cultural emphasis on female attractiveness—long recognized and deplored in Western societies—actually the rule the world over? And, (3) if the answer to either of these questions turns out to be yes, why so? For decades humanists have attributed the marginalization of female lit-erary characters and the valorization of female beauty to historically contingent aspects of Western culture. The former phenomenon is a reflection of women's secondary status in an intensely patriarchal society, and the latter phenomenon is part of a "beauty myth" that functions to maintain women in that secondary status. The research presented in this chapter challenges these views; it therefore has large implications, direct and indirect, to the gender explorations that have been a dominating preoccupation of literary scholars over several decades.

Further, the inclusion of this chapter signals my conviction that a potentially significant role for literary investigators—as original contributors to scientific research programs—is currently going unfulfilled. While this book has emphasized aspects of the sciences that literary scholars can profitably emulate, many scientists are now appreciating that they have a great deal to learn from, and about, the products of a bizarre literary ape. Scientists are beginning to recognize that literature and other art forms represent pristine funds of data and are also sources of vital and compelling questions about humans. To give just one example, the human propensity to produce and consume art is now being counted among the most vexing riddles in human evolutionary study (see Boyd 2005a and Scalise-Sugiyama 2005 for surveys of recent thinking; see also Coe 2003; Dissanayake 1995, 2000). I have elsewhere described the riddle as follows: "In ancestral environments characterized by intense competition for survival and reproduction, how could the evolutionary process 'allow' any animal to spend (waste?) so much time producing, elaborating, and consuming art—time that could be spent pursuing mates and other quarry" (Gottschall and Wilson 2005, 145)?

This scientific attention should remind literary scholars—some of whom seem to have forgotten—that they are not merely the caretakers of frivolous entertainments (though individual works are often, thankfully, both frivolous and entertaining).

Literature scholars are entrusted with, arguably, the most profound and precious repository of information about human nature that exists in the world (the biologist David Sloan Wilson calls world narrative "the natural history of the species" [qt. in Max 2005, 79]).

That literature is a priceless source of information about human nature is, of course, one of the hoarier clichés. Further, scientists have already made efforts to use this information. For instance, in 1923 the psychologist William McDougall wrote, "The wise psychologist will regard literature as a vast storehouse of information about human experience, and will not neglect to draw from it what he can" (9). But these pursuits have always been hampered by what I have elsewhere called "the problem of access" (Gottschall et al. 2004a,

"Sex Differences in Mate Choice Criteria," 109). That is, how does one access literary data in a way that is suitable for a scientific study? Faced with the problem of access, the systematic mining of literary data has rarely been featured in scientific studies of the human behavior and psychology. Of those scientists who have turned to literature, most have relied on the subjective and qualitative methods of literary studies rather than on scientific quantification (for discussion of scattered exceptions, see Laszlo and Cupchick 2003; Schram and Steen 2001).

The case studies in this book suggest the potential of certain scientific methodologies to tame the problem of access and to allow quantitative analysis of the riches of world literature (for other examples, see Singh et al. 2007; Kruger et al. 2005). All of the case studies in this book seek to address specific and pressing literary questions that intersect and overlap with equally important scientific questions.

Some of my readers will now be sputtering, "What the…?! If I wanted to be a scientist I damn well would have become one!" Perhaps. But I would gently remind the reader of some of the arguments in Part I: Literary scholars are already deeply and habitually engaged with issues fully within the scientific purview (or is it the scientists who are meddling inside our purview?), including all of the scientific issues examined in these case studies. And how could it be otherwise? How could literary investigators—even in principal— avoid engaging with fields of behavioral biology, psychology, sociology, gender studies, cognitive science, anthropology and all of the other human-related disciplines? Literature's province is the entire breadth of the human condition; its adequate study cannot be narrower by a mote. Since we cannot avoid engagement with scientific questions about the nature of humans, our cultures, and our products, why not experiment with ways of doing a better job of this than we are currently doing?

The "Beauty Myth" is no Myth: Emphasis on Male–Female Attractiveness in World Folktales

The phenomenon of apparently greater emphasis on women's than on men's physical attractiveness has spawned an array of explanatory responses, but most can be broadly categorized as either evolutionary or social constructivist in nature. Constructivist social scientists and feminists have argued that the pressure women feel to be attractive is a creation of cultural energies. The intense attractiveness pressure endured by Western women is a local and contingent product of specific historical and cultural dynamics. Arguments in this vein can be traced back to the earliest feminists (see Wollstonecraft 1792), but they have received fullest elaboration in Naomi Wolf's *The Beauty Myth* (1991, 2002; see also Brownmiller 1984; Bordo 1993; Cahill 2003; Faludi 1992, Chapter 8; Freedman 1986; Hansen et al. 1986; Travis et al. 2000). In Wolf's highly influential treatment, Western beliefs (or "myths") about women's attractiveness are absolutely untethered to biological reality. Indeed, the idea that anything about beauty can be called "natural" *is* the myth that Wolf sets out to deconstruct. Wolf is aware of biology-based explanations for disproportionate emphasis on women's attractiveness and for certain attractiveness standards, but she dismisses those explanations in no uncertain terms ("none of this is true," 12). Rather, for Wolf, the beauty myth exists to "naturalize" a social construction that serves the interests of patriarchy: "it is the last, best belief system that keeps male dominance intact" (12; for similar arguments, see Baker-Sperry and Grauerholz 2003; Travis et al. 2000; Toerien and Wilkinson 2003).

Apparently, greater emphasis on female than on male attractiveness has also excited sustained interest from evolutionists (for early thinking, see Darwin 1871, especially Chapters 16 and 20; Ellis 1927; Westermarck 1921). The phenomenon represents a challenging evolutionary puzzle because, in most species where there are differences, principal emphasis tends to be placed on male attractiveness. Richard Dawkins neatly described the puzzle in *The Selfish Gene*:

> As we have seen, it is strongly to be expected on evolutionary grounds that, where the sexes differ, it should be the males who advertise and the females who are drab...[B]ut, on average, there can be no doubt that in our society the equivalent of the peacock's tail is exhibited by the female, not by the male...Faced with these facts, a biologist would be forced to suspect that he was looking at a society in which females compete for males, rather than vice versa...Has the male really become the sought-after sex, the one that is in demand, the sex that can afford to be choosy? If so, why? (1976, 64–165; see also Jones 1996, 16–17)

Symons (1979) provided the most influential answer to Dawkins's question, arguing that greater emphasis on female attractiveness— not just in the West but worldwide—reflects the abnormally high variability of human female fertility differences, especially those that are reliably indicated by age (see Buss 1989; see also Sugiyama 2005). Men place great value on female physical attractiveness because it is a trustworthy indicator of relative fertility. Male attractiveness lacks similar salience in women's mating decisions for two principal reasons. First, male fertility is much less variable than female, and those variances are much more difficult to detect (except perhaps in the very old, very young, and very unhealthy). Second, because of the almost uniquely high costs of rearing human young (see Alexander and Noonan 1979), women—unlike most female mammals—must balance preferences for physically attractive mates with preferences for parentally investing mates (for elaboration and extension of these arguments see Gottschall 2007).

This paper describes an attempt to test the constructivist and evolutionary explanations, both of which generate distinct predictions. If, as Wolf and others have argued, greater emphasis on female attractiveness lacks a significant biological foundation and is, instead, a contingent product of specific cultural forces, then an analysis of a culturally diverse sample should reveal marked fluctuation in gendered attractiveness emphasis. If the constructivist explanation is correct, there should be significant numbers of cultures where male and female attractiveness are equally emphasized, and there should be significant numbers of cultures where male attractiveness receives more emphasis. On the other hand, an evolutionary perspective suggests that greater emphasis on female attractiveness will be very broadly encountered. While there may well be variance in the *degree* of overemphasis on female attractiveness across cultures, evolutionary thinking predicts that this overemphasis will be absent, if at all, only in rare and anomalous societies.

A spate of recent studies has strongly challenged one major component of Wolf's beauty myth—the notion that there are no standards of physical attractiveness that transcend local cultural norms (for major meta-analyses, see Feingold 1992; Langlois et al. 2000; for major review articles, see Gangestad and Scheyd 2005; Rhodes 2006; see also contributors to Rhodes and Zebrowitz 2002; Symons 1995; Johnston and Franklin 1993). Evolutionists often proceed as though the other major component of Wolf's thesis—that greater emphasis on women's attractiveness is also socially constructed—has been similarly undercut. Indeed, some compelling evidence does support a general rule of greater emphasis on female physical attractiveness across cultures. For instance, cross-cultural studies find that men consistently express stronger preferences for attractive mates than women do

(Buss 1989; Gottschall et al. 2004a). However, few studies have directly addressed relative emphasis on male–female attractiveness across diverse cultures. Gottschall et al.'s (2005) content analysis of 658 traditional folktale characters from diverse societies (see chapter 4) found that information on physical attractiveness was more than twice as likely to be conveyed, and repeatedly stressed, if the character was female. Similarly, Ford and Beach's landmark study of sexuality in 190 traditional populations noted that "in most societies the physical beauty of the female receives more explicit consideration than does the handsomeness of the male" (1951, 86). Ford and Beach's language, "most societies," implies cultures where "explicit consideration" was equal or male-skewed and therefore offers only ambiguous support to the evolutionary expectation of universality or near-universality. Moreover, Ford and Beach's ubiquitously referenced finding actually consists of a single sentence, and they provide neither a description of their methods for determining relative emphasis nor an identification of the exceptional societies.

In sum, the dearth of systematic cross-cultural investigation means that we do not know whether or not female attractiveness receives more emphasis cross-culturally. To address this issue, we counted references to male versus female attractiveness in a large sample of folktales gathered from 13 diverse cultural areas. The results are consistent with evolutionary predictions and inconsistent with constructivist predictions: Across culture areas, information on physical attractiveness is much more likely to be conveyed for female than for male characters.

Data and Methods

We content-analyzed references to male versus female attractiveness in a sample of 90 collections of world folktales (in all, 16,541 single-spaced pages, 8.17 million words). Within the limits of availability, collections were chosen so as to maximize geographical and cultural variability; the sample included tales from all inhabited continents, from different historical periods, and from societies that varied widely in ecology, geographic location, racial and ethnic composition, political systems, religious beliefs, and levels of cultural complexity (an abbreviated bibliography of all collections is given in table 6.1). Because our method required digitized texts, the bulk of our sample (60 collections) comprised copyright-expired collections that were freely available through an assortment of reputable Internet libraries (e.g., gutenberg.org, sacred-texts.com, various university collections, etc.). We also used a scanner to digitize 30 collections of folktales from areas that were underrepresented online. All collections were of traditional tales, originally transmitted through the oral tradition. All non-English tales had been translated into English, and the sample ran the gamut from polished fairy tales to literal transcriptions of tales told in traditional contexts.

In rare instances where exact copies of given tales appeared in different collections, duplicates were excluded. However, we chose not to exclude tale variants for two reasons. First, we saw no a priori reason to suspect that variants would bias findings toward either of the two hypotheses. Second, folktale variants are just that: variants. We assumed that different treatments of the same tale—frequently tracing to different tellers, in different historical periods, and substantially modified cultural milieus—would often differ significantly in their portrayal of characters' appearances.

We chose folktales as our cross-cultural sample for several reasons. First, folktales are a universal and indigenous narrative form and therefore allow the compilation of samples possessing maximal cultural diversity. Second, they are a "cheap" form of cross-cultural data, available to any researcher with internet access and library privileges. Third, while folktales are not pristine, having suffered potential distortion through poor translation and the whims of collectors and editors, it can be argued that they provide a more direct perspective on life in traditional societies than the heavily mediated accounts of anthropologists and ethnographers. As the folklorist Alan Dundes is fond of saying, folktales can be approached as a form of "autobiographical ethnography" (e.g., 1968, 139, 404). Fifth, most of the 90 collections in our sample date to within a few decades of the year 1900, before many of the represented cultures were saturated by Western influence and—more specifically—by images of attractiveness conveyed by Western mass media.

But using folktales as a source of empirical evidence about human nature is not an uncomplicated matter. Folktales blend factual events with the stuff of fiction, myth, and legend. Many tales are about animals rather than humans, albeit animals endowed with human attributes. This naturally means that it would be naïve to assume that folktales transparently represent given societal features. On the other hand, it would be equally naïve to assume the opposite: that this global repository of cultural information is entirely undependable, as if the stories people tell can tell us nothing about the people who tell them.

For the purposes of this study, we adopted the traditional scholarly assumption that folktales can be sources of valuable social and psychological information about different populations. While the folktales in our sample were mostly compiled, edited, and translated by Westerners (and thus may reflect Western biases), the tales were originally composed in traditional societies and can be cautiously assumed to reflect the traditional attitudes and social patterns of the populations that produced them. More specifically, we can see no reason why a folktale sample would be inappropriate for the question addressed here. If there are important differences in gendered attractiveness emphasis in a given culture, it is reasonable to anticipate that those differences will be reflected in that culture's traditional tales.

With the help of thesauri, we compiled a list of 58 adjectives that are frequently used in English to indicate male and/or female physical attractiveness:

Alluring, Attractive, Beautiful, Brawny, Breathtaking, Broad, Burly, Busty, Buxom, Comely, Coquettish, Curvaceous, Cute, Exquisite, Fair, Feminine, Good Looking, Gorgeous, Handsome, Lovely, Luscious, Maidenly, Manly, Masculine, Muscular, Nubile, Powerful, Pretty, Pulchritudinous, Radiant, Ravishing, Sexy, Shapely, Strapping, Strong, Stunning, Tall, Virile, Voluptuous, Winsome, Womanly

Or physical unattractiveness:

Disfigured, Disgusting, Frightful, Gross, Grotesque, Hideous, Homely, Horrid, Horrible, Loathsome, Monstrous, Repelling, Repugnant, Repulsive, Revolting, Ugly, Unattractive

Then, using Microsoft Word's "find and replace" function, we tagged and highlighted all of the keywords in the collections, and all of their relevant variants (e.g., pretty, prettier, prettiest; ugly, uglier, ugliest). Finally, 30 undergraduates from two St. Lawrence University research methods seminars (6 male, 24 female) coded roughly equal proportions (in page counts, not numbers of collections) of the total sample. Coders were able to move efficiently and precisely through the collections by using Microsoft Word's "find" function to locate the keyword tag (~~). After locating a tagged adjective, coders then used as much of the surrounding context as was required to judge (1) if the adjective was part of a reference to the physical attractiveness of a male, (2) to the physical attractiveness of a female, or (3) to neither (e.g., "a beautiful sunset," "a handsome offer"). Coders also indicated if the adjective positively (e.g., "handsome") or negatively (e.g., "ugly") described the character's appearance. Coders were naïve about specific theory-derived expectations. They were told that our research—whatever we discovered—would help to resolve disagreements about the degree of male–female attractiveness emphasis across cultures. It was repeatedly emphasized that we had no favored outcome: whatever we revealed would represent a valuable contribution. Coding decisions were made independently; coders were told not to discuss judgments with colleagues.

Our shared definition of attractiveness was as follows: Physical Attractiveness is a measure of a person's strictly physical appeal (or lack of appeal) for a romantic, or strictly sexual, relationship. Physically attractive attributes are those which reliably arouse the sexual or romantic interests of members of the opposite sex. Physically unattractive attributes are those which reliably fail to arouse the sexual or romantic interest of the opposite sex. Physically unattractive attributes may, in fact, have precisely the opposite effect. Coders were instructed that our focus was rigorously limited to the appeal of the physical body; they were instructed to disregard other features people tend to find attractive in their mates (e.g., "a beautiful personality"). Finally, coders were told to avoid providing information based on their individual attractiveness preferences. Thus a coder who happened to prefer tall partners would not code a reference to a tall character as an attractiveness reference unless the context clearly indicated physical attractiveness in the specific sense of our definition.

Limitations

This study has several potential limitations. First, there are possible sources of bias in the folktale collections. To concentrate on the most salient, more than half of the collections in our sample were collected, edited, translated, and in some cases, retold, by Westerners, usually males, between 1860 and 1930. It is therefore possible that the sample has been distorted by the biases—male and Western—of ethnographers, collectors, and editors of an imperial era.

This possibility cannot be dismissed. However, concern about this source of bias is mitigated by consistent data trends in the 18 collections edited by mixed gender teams, in the 11 collections produced by women, and in the 31 collections produced after 1960. Moreover, differences in the output of male and female coders were minimal. There is some variance across these comparisons, but it is not always in the obvious direction (e.g., female coders found slightly more references to female beauty than male coders did), and the variance is consistent with random fluctuations across folktale collections (see table 6.1).

A second source of possible distortion is the translation process. However, this source of bias is common to most large-scale cross-cultural studies, and we see no reason to suspect that it would have systematically biased attractiveness emphasis in favor of either of the two hypotheses under test. Indeed, this study's reliance on scores of different translators helps to inoculate it, to some degree, against the possibility of inept or inadequate translation drastically distorting our findings.

Finally, there are potential shortcomings in our method. First, we do not claim that our adjectival list comprehends every word that can be used to indicate physical attractiveness; we sought to produce a list of words that are *commonly used* in a physical attractiveness context, not a comprehensive list of words that *can be used*. We therefore acknowledge that judgment played a significant role in the production of the list. However, the results of our long deliberations about which words to include or exclude (should "scabrous" be included, should "pulchritudinous"?) amounted to very little. This is because 93 percent of the 4479 words coders ultimately identified as attractiveness "hits" ended up being variants of the major adjectives: beautiful, handsome, pretty, lovely, ugly, and fair (comprising 49, 13, 10, 9, 8, and 4 percent of the total "hits," respectively). Just 7 percent of the "hits" (314 in total) were variants of the other 52 adjectives. Folktale language is generally simple, and tellers/translators rarely call on words like "pulchritudinous" or "scabrous" (the former adjective was included in our list but received no "hits"; the latter was excluded) when "beautiful" or "ugly" will suffice. In short, given the very small numbers of "hits" associated with most adjectives on our list, it is not likely that adding more words to the list would have materially altered our primary results. This would only be the case if our list omits *important* adjectives, and we do not believe that it does.

The thick clustering of attractiveness "hits" among a handful of major adjectives is also relevant to another potential criticism. While compiling the list, we discovered a fact that is in itself highly germane to the question at hand: the English language apparently possesses more words that are commonly used to describe female than male physical attractiveness. Our list reflects this linguistic bias; it includes about 50 percent more adjectives that are commonly (though not exclusively) used to describe female attractiveness than are commonly used to describe male attractiveness (17 adjectives are primarily female oriented; 11 are primarily male oriented; 30 are neutral, including—intriguingly—*all* 17 of the words associated with physical unattractiveness). Does this adjectival bias tilt the results in favor of the evolutionary prediction that greater emphasis on female attractiveness will be the rule across human populations?

There are two points to make in response to this question. First, because of the adjectival clustering described above, even if we had been able to identify sufficient additional words to bring "male" and "female" adjectives to parity, it is likely that the final results would have remained very much the same. Again, significant shifts in the final results would only emerge if the list omits *important* "male" adjectives with, say, scores of "hits" between them. We believe that this is not the case. It might still be argued that the number of female-oriented adjectives should have been somehow held down to the male level or that final results should have been adjusted to correct for the adjectival imbalances. But both measures would have distorted the picture of gendered attractiveness salience because they share similarly flawed premises: the premise that adding more adjectives to the list would significantly shift the results, and the premise that the gender bias originates in the adjectival list rather than being a reflection of the available English vocabulary. Is it possible that many of the original languages of the folktales featured a broader vocabulary to describe male attractiveness? Certainly. But it is also likely that, in such cases, English translators simply conveyed those words within the more limited vocabulary available to them.

Finally, and most critically, content analysis depends on the fallible judgments of human coders. Thus conventional measures were taken to maximize coder intersubjectivity by ensuring that coders followed the same protocol. Coding was conducted in one-hour lab sessions to allow for procedural questions, to enable policing of intercoder discussion, and to limit the potential for coder fatigue and/or distraction.

Intercoder reliability was assessed by extracting and compiling a random assortment of tales from 10 diverse collections into a 200 page document (110,538 words) and then having all coders analyze the 126 tagged adjectives in the document. For the two different coding groups, raw intercoder reliability was 88.6 percent and 87.2 percent. The most widely used statistic for computing the reliability of multiple coders is Cohen's Kappa (Cohen 1960;

Fleiss 1971), which seeks to correct for the fact that coders will often arrive at the same result for any given question solely by chance (though some analysts suggest that Cohen's Kappa is an overly conservative measure of reliability, see Potter and Levine-Donnerstein 1999). Chance-corrected agreement for the two groups of coders was similarly strong: 75.8 percent and 72.8 percent. For Cohen's Kappa, "values greater than 75 percent or so may be taken to represent excellent agreement beyond chance, values below 40 percent or so may be taken to represent poor agreement beyond chance, and values between 40 and 75 percent may be taken to represent fair to good agreement beyond chance" (Capozzoli et al. 1999, 6; see also Fleiss 1971; Rourke et al. 2001).

Before reporting our results, one further issue requires clarification. We posit that representations of male and female attractiveness in a culture's folktales can function as an index of relative emphasis on attractiveness in that culture. But it is important to emphasize how imperfect this index is. Variance in numbers of attractiveness references across collections may as often reflect random variance in the contents of collections as real cross-cultural variance. We anticipated that our approach would be most confounded by possible skews in the numbers of prominent male and female characters. For example, in collections of tales that happened to feature many major male characters, it would not be surprising to find more references to male attractiveness than female. Thus a key question we sought to address was not only, "are there more references to male or female attractiveness"?, but, "are attractiveness references *proportional* given the relative prominence of male and female characters"?

A rough estimate of the relative prominence of male and female characters was produced in a computerized count of all male and female personal pronouns (i.e., "he," "he'd," "his," "him," "himself" versus the female equivalents). For two reasons, we opted not to establish relative prominence by a full census, or estimation, of all male and female characters in the sample. First, accurately counting all characters in the sample (or even adequately sampling them) would have meant carefully reading many hundreds of folktales—a task as onerous as the entire study reported here. Second, the vitally important factor is *not* the raw numbers of male and female characters, but their *prominence* in the tales. For instance, one African tale features a central male character, his 3 wives and his 4 daughters. But this female-skewed sex ratio is a misleading indicator of the *prominence* of male and female characters in the story (the females are minor characters and the male hero is more prominent than all 7 females combined). The sex ratio of *main* characters in the tales might therefore provide a somewhat better index to prominence. However, such an index would still be blind to the nonnegligible role played by the African tale's 7 female characters. We therefore judged gendered pronoun counts to potentially be the best indicator of male–female prominence. A full and precise tally of gendered pronouns is easily accomplished with the use of standard computing software, and that tally should roughly reflect the proportion of times that male and female characters (major and minor) were the subjects/objects of sentences.

Male pronouns outnumbered female by 3:1, suggesting that male characters, as a cross-cultural rule, are much more prominent in traditional tales (this is a fascinating result in itself that will be discussed in the coda to this chapter). Some male pronouns were doubtlessly used in the old-fashioned, gender-neutral sense, in which a male pronoun stands for persons of both sexes in the same way that "mankind" usually means "humankind." However, given that there were, on average, 4600 gendered pronouns per collection (over 400,000 in total), it is unlikely that these relatively rare cases could have anything but a negligible influence on the broad results. Moreover, our confidence in this method of estimation was enhanced by results that roughly coincided with those given in chapter 4 (Ragan 2009, forthcoming, using a different method of content analysis, also found strongly male-skewed sex ratios in a study of 30 diverse collections of world folktales).

Results

In 75 of 90 collections there were more references to female than male physical attractiveness. In 30 collections female attractiveness references outnumbered male references by a statistically significant margin; in 4 collections male attractiveness references significantly outnumbered female attractiveness references (see table 6.1; all significance results are based on Z-tests). Collections were grouped into 13 broad culture areas, ranging in size from 4 to 17 collections. Cultural groupings were based on salient geographic, linguistic, and cultural affinities. In every culture area, references to female attractiveness outnumbered references to male attractiveness; female preponderances were statistically significant in all groupings except the Mayan.

Table 6.1 Male–Female Attractiveness Emphasis in World Folk Tales

Left side: Comparison across collections and culture areas of numbers of references to female versus male physical attractiveness.
Right side: Comparison of the numbers of female versus male pronouns and the relative risk, based on pronoun counts, that a character will be referred to as attractive for females versus males. Collections of tales that originated in band and/or tribal societies are italicized. Female-edited collections are underlined.

	Fem. Attract. Refs.	Male Attract. Refs.	Ratio Fem.:Male	Z Score	Fem. Pron.	Male Pron.	Ratio Male: Fem Pron.	Relative Risk Fem.:Male	Z Score
OVERALL (n=90)	2984	1495	2.00	22.25**	103586	311100	3.00	5.99	63.66**
Band and Tribal Societies (n=62)	1648	884	1.86	15.07**	74792	220386	2.95	5.48	45.59**
Preindustrial State Societies (n=28)	1336	611	2.19	16.30**	28794	90714	3.15	6.91	45.12**
Male Coded (n=23)	658	386	1.70	8.42**	27460	85729	3.12	5.32	28.94**
Female Coded (n=67)	2326	1109	2.10	20.76**	76126	225371	2.96	6.21	56.61**
Male Edited (n=61)	1928	896	2.15	19.42**	59368	178404	3.01	6.47	52.50**
Female Edited (n=11)	368	214	1.72	6.38**	10823	25253	2.33	4.01	17.27**
Mixed Edited (n=18)	688	385	1.79	9.25**	33395	107443	3.22	5.75	30.87**
Aboriginal Australia	77	38	2.03	3.64**	1860	7983	4.29	8.70	12.94**
Australian (Parker and Lang, 1897)	3	2	1.50	0.45	455	1009	2.22	3.33	1.39
Australian Legends (Peck, 1925)	23	4	5.75	3.66**	650	2054	3.16	18.17	7.34**
Myths and Legends (Thomas, 1923)	4	2	2.00	0.82	65	649	9.98	19.97	4.77**
Myths and Legends (Smith, 1930)	37	30	1.23	0.86	690	4271	6.19	7.63	9.55**
Africa	60	23	2.61	4.06**	3471	7664	2.21	5.76	8.04**
Kaffir Folklore (Theal, 1886)	14	5	2.80	2.06*	745	1234	1.66	4.64	3.22**
Hausa Folktales (Glew, 1993)	22	13	1.69	1.52	1457	1928	1.32	2.24	2.35*
Hausa Stories (Johnston, 1966)	19	3	6.33	3.41**	571	3544	6.21	39.31	9.70**
Hausa Folk-lore (Shaihua, 1913)	5	2	2.50	1.13	698	958	1.37	3.43	1.56

Continued

Table 6.1 Continued

	Fem. Attract. Refs.	Male Attract. Refs.	Ratio Fem.:Male	Z-Score	Fem. Pron.	Male Pron.	Ratio Male: Fem Pron.	Relative Risk Fem.:Male	Z-Score
Arctic Coast	**51**	**27**	**1.89**	**2.72****	**5842**	**15157**	**2.59**	**4.90**	**7.38****
Chukee Mythology (Bogoras, 1910)	10	1	10.00	2.71	902	2221	2.46	24.62	4.52**
Eskimo of Siberia (Bogoras, 1913)	3	8	0.38	-1.51	172	440	2.56	0.96	-0.06
Tales of the Yukaghir (Bogoras, 1918)	17	12	1.42	0.93	1475	2198	1.49	2.11	2.02*
Eskimo Folk-Tales (Rasmussen, 1921)	15	4	3.75	2.52*	681	2190	3.22	12.06	5.61**
Eskimo Storyteller (Hall, 1988)	6	2	3.00	1.41	2612	8108	3.10	9.31	3.33**
Europe	**499**	**108**	**4.62**	**15.87****	**7638**	**14570**	**1.91**	**8.81**	**24.26****
English Fairy Tales (Jacobs, 1898)	43	7	6.14	5.09**	1268	1832	1.44	8.88	6.42**
Grimm's Fairy Tales (Grimm and Grimm, 1944)	54	8	6.75	5.84**	1512	1757	1.16	7.84	6.38**
Kalevala (Crawford, 1888)	90	13	6.92	7.59**	138	214	1.55	10.74	8.60**
Green Fairy Book (Lang and Gregory, 1948)	196	32	6.13	10.86**	2910	5060	1.74	10.65	15.18**
Hungarian Fairy Tales (Orczy, 1895)	64	18	3.56	5.08**	456	1266	2.78	9.87	10.07**
East O' the Sun (Asbjornsen et al., 1912)	17	14	1.21	0.54	450	1361	3.02	3.67	3.81**
Dutch Fairy Tales (Griffis, 1918)	30	3	10.00	4.70**	614	1099	1.79	17.90	6.49**
Aesop's Fables (Townsend, 1870)	5	13	0.38	-1.89	290	1981	6.83	2.63	1.89**
India	**270**	**155**	**1.74**	**5.58****	**7420**	**16749**	**2.26**	**3.93**	**14.47****
Flowering Tree (Ramanujan et al., 1997)	67	21	3.19	4.90**	2867	4762	1.66	5.30	7.41**
Folk Tales from Kashmir (Sadhu, 1962)	19	7	2.71	2.35*	483	2499	5.17	14.04	7.74**
Indian Fairy Tales (Jacobs, 1892)	46	45	1.02	0.10	971	2865	2.95	3.02	5.43**
Tales of the Punjab (Steel, 1894)	63	38	1.66	2.49*	1209	2734	2.26	3.75	6.78**
Hindu Tales (Mitra, 1919)	41	17	2.41	3.15**	864	2418	2.80	6.75	7.54**
Hindoo Tales (Jacob, 1873)	34	27	1.26	0.90	1026	1471	1.43	1.81	2.29**

Continued

Table 6.1 Continued

	Fem. Attract. Refs.	Male Attract. Refs.	Ratio Fem.: Male	Z-Score	Fem. Pron.	Male Pron.	Ratio Male: Fem Pron.	Relative Risk Fem.:Male	Z-Score
Japan	**207**	**94**	**2.20**	**6.51****	**4131**	**15454**	**3.74**	**8.48**	**20.24****
Folk Tales from Japan (Ashliman, 1996)	20	13	1.54	1.22	232	317	1.37	2.11	2.07*
Japanese Fairy Tales (Ozaki, 1905)	48	12	4.00	4.65**	1161	3415	2.94	11.76	9.57**
Tales of Old Japan (Redesdale, 1871)	43	24	1.79	2.32*	695	3868	5.57	9.97	10.87**
Japanese Tales (Royall, 1897)	55	34	1.62	2.23*	1400	6200	4.43	7.16	10.39**
Folk Legends of Japan (Dorson, 1961)	41	11	3.73	4.16**	643	1654	2.57	9.59	7.98**
Mayan	**72**	**61**	**1.18**	**0.95**	**1654**	**5585**	**3.38**	**3.99**	**8.44****
Mayan Fables (Montejo, 1991)	43	38	1.13	0.56	100	592	5.92	6.70	8.47**
Mayan Folktales (Sexton, 1992)	9	12	0.75	-0.65	530	2376	4.48	3.36	2.90**
Mayan Tales (Laughlin and Karasik, 1988)	18	8	2.25	1.96*	945	2312	2.45	5.50	4.49**
The Ancient Quiche Maya (Goetz et al., 1950.)	2	3	0.67	-0.45	79	305	3.86	2.57	1.06
Middle East	**230**	**176**	**1.31**	**2.68****	**6333**	**34883**	**5.51**	**7.37**	**23.05****
Arabian Nights (Burton, 1850)	66	48	1.38	1.69	2839	10010	3.53	4.85	9.13**
Egyptian Tales (Petrie, 1895)	57	33	1.73	2.53*	125	721	5.77	9.96	11.07**
Legends of the Jews (Ginzberg et al., 1909)	41	47	0.87	-0.64	2756	22101	8.02	7.00	10.54**
Babylonian (Epiphanius and Leonidas, 1901)	66	48	1.38	1.69	613	2051	3.35	4.60	8.49**
Northwest Coastal Indians	**233**	**143**	**1.63**	**4.64****	**12642**	**45950**	**3.63**	**5.92**	**18.90****
Chinook Texts (Boas, 1894)	8	3	2.67	1.51	1223	2979	2.44	6.50	3.18**
Kwakiutl Tales (Boas, 1910)	5	20	0.25	-3.00**	917	4581	5.00	1.25	0.44**
Legends of Vancouver (Johnston, 1966)	5	23	0.22	-3.40**	208	905	4.35	0.95	-0.11
Indian Legends (Carmichael, 1922)	4	12	0.33	-2.00*	98	226	2.31	0.77	-0.45
Tsimshian Texts (Boas, 1902)	6	13	0.46	-1.61	480	2600	5.42	2.50	1.91*
Tlingit Myths (Swanton, 1909)	21	11	1.91	1.77	2465	8737	3.54	6.77	5.94**

Continued

Table 6.1 Continued

	Fem. Attract. Refs.	Male Attract. Refs.	Ratio Fem.:Male	Z-Score	Fem. Pron.	Male Pron.	Ratio Male: Fem Pron.	Relative Risk Fem.:Male	Z-Score
Bella Bella Tales (Boas, 1932)	14	3	4.67	2.67**	1039	3558	**3.42**	15.98	5.86**
Haida Texts (Swanton, 1905)	12	13	0.92	-0.20	2323	12064	**5.19**	4.79	4.32**
Tsimshian I (Cove and McDonald, 1987)	140	45	3.11	6.98**	3070	6826	**2.22**	6.92	12.92**
Tsimshian II (Cove and McDonald, 1987)	18	0	—	4.24	819	3474	**4.24**	—	8.66**
Oceania (minus Australia)	**61**		**4.18**	**10.91**	**7449**	**13274**	**1.78**	**7.45**	**16.40**
Philippine Folklore Stories (Miller, 1904)	7	2	3.50	1.67	148	378	**2.55**	8.94	3.26**
Philippine Folk Tales (Cole, 1916)	42	12	3.50	4.08**	626	2075	**3.31**	11.60	9.27**
Legends of Maui (Westervelt, 1910)	7	0	—	2.65	703	753	**1.07**	—	2.73**
Hawaiian Legends (Westervelt, 1916)	35	6	5.83	4.53**	858	514	**0.60**	3.49	2.99**
Bright Islands (Colum, 1925)	85	23	3.70	5.97**	2168	4864	**2.24**	8.29	10.62**
Kewa Tales (Leroy, 1985)	24	11	2.18	2.20*	2388	3242	**1.36**	2.96	3.12**
Myths of the South Pacific (Gill, 1876)	55	7	7.86	6.10**	558	1448	**2.59**	20.39	10.34**
Southwestern American Indians	**240**	**138**	**1.74**	**5.25**	**7835**	**20306**	**2.59**	**4.51**	**15.28**
Tales of the Cochiti (Benedict, 1931)	6	43	0.14	-5.29**	2660	4272	**1.61**	0.22	-3.75**
Pueblo Folk Stories (Lummis, 1910)	29	23	1.26	0.83	520	1551	**2.98**	3.76	4.99**
The Diné (O'Bryan, 1956)	36	15	2.40	2.94**	895	2807	**3.14**	7.53	7.62**
Myths and Legends of the Pima (Lloyd et al., 1911)	8	5	1.60	0.83	442	1816	**4.11**	6.57	3.78**
Yaqui Myths (Giddings, 1978)	18	2	9.00	3.58	328	1457	**4.44**	39.98	8.09**
Zuni Folk Tales (Cushing, 1901)	108	38	2.84	5.79**	1480	4197	**2.84**	8.06	12.83**
Traditions of the Hopi (Voth, 1905)	35	12	2.92	3.35**	1510	4206	**2.79**	8.12	7.41**

Continued

Table 6.1 Continued

	Fem. Attract. Refs.	Male Attract. Refs.	Ratio Fem.:Male	Z-Score	Fem. Pron.	Male Pron.	Ratio Male:Fem Pron.	Relative Risk Fem.:Male	Z-Score
S. America Indigenous	**508**	**339**	**1.50**	**5.81****	**26869**	**84856**	**3.16**	**4.73**	**24.28****
Yanomamo Indians (Wilbert and Simoneau, 1990)	49	41	1.20	0.84	1914	7591	3.97	4.74	8.03**
Aboriginal Indians of British Guiana (Brett, 1880)	13	4	3.25	2.18*	220	958	4.35	14.15	5.97**
Inca of Peru (Goetz et al., 1950)	16	0	—	4.00	118	131	1.11	—	4.08**
Ayoreo Indians (Wilbert and Simoneau, 1990)	68	31	2.19	3.72**	3685	7434	2.02	4.43	7.46**
Stories from the Amazon (Mindlin, 2002)	49	31	1.58	2.01*	2183	2599	1.19	1.88	2.78**
Cadaveo Indians (Wilbert and Simoneau, 1989)	2	3	0.67	-0.45	308	1324	4.30	2.87	1.20
Chamacoco Indians (Wilbert and Simoneau, 1987)	38	26	1.46	1.50	3159	9197	2.91	4.26	6.17**
Chorote Indians (Wilbert and Simoneau, 1985)	23	21	1.10	0.30	1044	4147	3.97	4.35	5.27**
Cuiva Indians (Wilbert and Simoneau, 1991)	21	4	5.25	3.40**	2620	6879	2.63	13.78	6.29**
Ge Indians (Wilbert and Simoneau, 1978)	28	29	0.97	-0.13	195	6948	35.63	34.40	20.14**
Guajiro Indians (Wilbert and Simoneau, 1986)	53	4	13.25	6.49**	1856	5025	2.71	35.87	11.11**
Makka Indians (Wilbert and Simoneau, 1991)	8	40	0.20	-4.62**	1756	3958	2.25	0.45	-2.11*
Mataco Indians (Wilbert and Simoneau, 1982)	25	20	1.25	0.75	767	4216	5.50	6.87	7.36**
Nivakle Indians (Wilbert and Simoneau, 1987)	29	19	1.53	1.44	2058	9595	4.66	7.12	7.72**
Sikuani Indians (Wilbert and Simoneau, 1992)	17	23	0.74	-0.95	3412	8040	2.36	1.74	1.75

Continued

Table 6.1 Continued

	Fem. Attract. Refs.	Male Attract. Refs.	Ratio Fem.:Male	Z-Score	Fem. Pron.	Male Pron.	Ratio Male:Fem Pron.	Relative Risk Fem.:Male	Z-Score
Suru Indians of Romania (Mindlin, 1995)	16	8	2.00	1.63	458	2016	**4.40**	8.80	5.99**
Toba Indians (Wilbert and Simoneau, 1982)	53	35	1.51	1.92	1116	4798	**4.30**	6.51	9.72**
American Indians (Miscellaneous)	**159**	**89**	**1.79**	**4.45****	**5850**	**19868**	**3.40**	**6.07**	**15.37****
Algonquin New England (Leland, 1884)	38	21	1.81	2.21*	989	4089	**4.13**	7.48	8.58**
Creek Stories (Swanton, 1929)	19	2	9.50	3.71**	422	2308	**5.47**	51.96	9.33**
Legends of the Sioux (McLaughlin, 1990)	21	12	1.75	1.57	633	1712	**2.70**	4.73	4.68**
North Native American Indians (Thompson, 1929)	42	26	1.62	1.94	2127	5924	**2.79**	4.50	6.56**
Blackfoot Tales (Grinnell, 1892)	16	10	1.60	1.18	801	3452	**4.31**	6.90	5.52**
Algonquin Indian Tales (Young, 1903)	23	18	1.28	0.78	878	2383	**2.71**	3.47	4.17**
Miscellaneous Collections									
Folktales of Chile (Saavedra, 1968)	63	17	3.71	5.14**	1618	3473	**2.15**	7.95	8.90**
Ainu Folklore (Batchelor, 1888)	27	5	5.40	3.89	192	270	**1.41**	7.59	4.72**
Tugur Folktales (Sanyshkap et al., 2005)	43	21	2.05	2.75**	2782	5058	**1.82**	3.72	5.27**

* $p < .05$.
** $p < .01$.
n = Number of collections.

The sample was also divided into two broad levels of cultural complexity. The first level consists of tales that circulated primarily in unassimilated band and tribal societies, though the tales may have only been written down after assimilation. The second level consists of tales that circulated mainly in preindustrial state societies. Female preponderances were significant in both samples but more pronounced in the sample from preindustrial state societies. However, much of the disparity between the two levels of cultural complexity reflects the influence of the European sample; as we will see, emphasis on female attractiveness was especially strong in the 8 European collections.

Thus there was a consistent pattern of preponderant emphasis on female attractiveness. While individual collections with preponderantly male references made up 16.6 percent of the sample, preponderant emphasis on females always emerged when more collections from that culture area were considered. Overall, references to female attractiveness outnumbered male references by 2 to 1.

However, it is likely that this figure *significantly and systematically understates* the true disproportion of emphasis on female attractiveness. This is because of the remarkably consistent trend, noted above, whereby narrative emphasis on male characters (as measured by counts of gendered pronouns) was almost invariably greater than narrative emphasis on female characters (in 90 collections of tales there was just one exception: Westervelt's *Hawaiian Legends of Volcanoes*, which focuses tightly on tales about the great fire goddess Pele). These findings suggest that if the collections had proportionate emphasis on male and female characters—while emphasis on attractiveness remained the same—references to female attractiveness would have outnumbered references to male by a much more substantial margin. By dividing the ratio of female to male attractiveness references by the ratio of female to male pronouns, we calculated the likelihood (technically a calculation of "relative risk") that an attractiveness reference would be applied to a female character versus a male character. This analysis suggests that characters in our sample are about 6 times more likely to be described with an attractiveness adjective if they are female than if they are male.

However, even this may understate the disproportion of male–female attractiveness emphasis. The above results lump together positive (e.g., "handsome") and negative (e.g., "ugly") attractiveness attributions. When these attributions are separated, 15 percent of male "hits" are for adjectives associated with *unattractiveness*, compared with just 5 percent of female "hits." Thus, significantly more adjectives indicating physical *unattractiveness* were applied to male than to female characters (for the whole sample $Z = 9.35$; $p < .001$). This general relationship, which was reliably encountered across subsamples, was unexpected, not being an obvious implication of either the constructivist or evolutionary models. Although exploring the causes of this discrepancy is beyond our current scope, this finding does indicate that *positive* emphasis on female beauty is even more intense than the main findings reported here would suggest.

Discussion

These results strongly support the evolutionary prediction that greater emphasis on female physical attractiveness will be the rule across human culture areas; it undercuts the constructivist prediction that different patterns of attractiveness emphasis will be found in different populations, with some emphasizing the attractiveness of males, some emphasizing that of females, and some emphasizing both genders equally. This study, considered alongside recent research demonstrating cross-cultural patterns of physical attractiveness preferences, indicates that the main elements of the beauty myth are not myths: there are large areas of overlap in the attractiveness judgments of diverse populations, and cross-cultural emphasis on physical attractiveness appears to fall primarily, and reliably, upon women.

Of course, this does not imply that everything about human attractiveness is biologically fixed. To rephrase Theodosius Dobzhansky (1973), nothing in physical attractiveness research makes sense except in the light of evolutionary biology *and* culture. While some aspects of physical attractiveness apparently hold steady across societies, evolutionists have long acknowledged the obvious: culture has the power to dramatically shape attractiveness preferences (e.g., Darwin 1871, Chapter 20; Jones 1996). Similarly, the finding of considerable variance across folktale collections and cultural groupings suggests a great boulder of truth in the social constructivist position: there is no reason to believe that the degree of gendered attractiveness emphasis is culturally invariant; in fact, it is likely to vary significantly in different physical and cultural milieus (for empirical evidence in support, see Gangestad and Buss 1993).

In the present study, 5 of 9 Northwestern Indian collections had, *before pronoun imbalances were considered,* more references to male attractiveness.

More germane to the hypotheses tested here, attractiveness references *were* markedly more female-skewed in the European collections than in the other subsamples. This result is intriguingly consistent with a main line of argument in feminist studies of European fairy tales (see chapter 5) and with a more restrained version of the constructivist arguments tested here. In short, while our findings undercut strong constructivist arguments about the ultimate well-springs of disproportionate emphasis on female attractiveness, they are consistent with common claims that these tendencies may be more extreme in the West.

These data may be useful for providing a preliminary indication of the sensitivity of sex-based attractiveness emphasis to cultural shaping, but they must be interpreted very cautiously. While findings indicate a robust cross-cultural trend of greater emphasis on women's attractiveness, much of the variation across cultural samples may reflect idiosyncratic biases in the tellers, collectors, editors, and translators of the tales as much as they reflect real cross-cultural variance. For instance, it cannot be ruled out that the differences between the European and South American samples testify less to genuine cultural differences and more to the fact that the latter sample abounds in mythological tales and the former sample includes more tales focusing on the travails of young lovers. Further study, using different indices of attractiveness emphasis, will be required to gain a more confident estimate of the true magnitude of cross-cultural variance.

Even if there has been exaggeration (several authors have accused Wolf of rampant hyperboles; e.g., Schoemacher 2004; Sommers 1994), Wolf and other constructivists deserve credit for documenting and analyzing some of the high costs to women's psychological and physical health that come with—as Nancy Etcoff puts it—the feeling of being forced into a beauty contest with every other woman (1999, 68). They also offer plausible descriptions of the ways that different actors may profit by exploiting, enhancing, and shaping female attractiveness anxieties. However, the findings reported here suggest that these anxieties are not a *creation* of Western cultural values, or of Madison Avenue, or of a patriarchal conspiracy. They are evolutionary legacies, which are likely experienced across human populations. They reflect the greater importance of beauty to women's mating prospects (Buss 1989; Gottschall 2007)—prospects that, in turn, help to determine socioeconomic status, satisfaction, and ultimately, inclusive fitness.

Coda: World Folktales' Missing Women

For somewhat complicated reasons that we need not go into here, very few biological organisms feature sex ratios that depart significantly from overall parity (Fisher 1958; Hamilton 1967; Trivers and Willard 1973). Humans, with about 105 baby boys born for every 100 baby girls, are at most a mild exception to this rule. No one really knows the exact cause of our mild imbalance—not at the deep evolutionary level, or at the level of immediate physiological causes. But it may well be connected to higher male mortality. At every stage of the life cycle, from conception to the last moments of old age, males (and male conspectuses, embryos, fetuses) perish at higher rates than females do (Kruger and Nesse 2004). Yet in substantial numbers of human societies—past and present—male juveniles have outnumbered female juveniles by far more than 5 percent. This has almost invariably been caused by some combination of sex-selective infanticide, abortion, or parental neglect (see Oster 2005). In recent times these practices have been disturbingly acute in Asian societies (especially China and India), which are currently coping not only with the absence of tens of millions of "missing women" (see Sen 1990; Hudson and Den Boer 2002, 2005; Dickemann 1979; Miller 1981) but also with one of its unforeseen side effects: the dangerously disruptive behaviors of many millions of hopelessly unmarried young men.

If the sex ratio data presented in this chapter, buttressed by similar results given in previous chapters, are roughly on target, then the population of world folktale characters is missing legions of leading female characters. Moreover, if the data are on target, male–female imbalances in folktale traditions are far more extreme than anything that has ever been observed in a human population. The questions surge to mind: Where did the missing women go? What, or who, destroyed them?

As discussed in chapter 5, feminist scholars have long maintained that misogynist editors denuded Western fairy tales of those bold and transgressive heroines whose examples would serve as challenges to patriarchal interests. This proposal can be tried on as an explanation for all of the data patterns so far described in these case studies: perhaps the editors of our volumes, predominantly (though not exclusively) Western and male, consciously or unconsciously selected and edited tales so that an originally large and highly diverse population of female folktale characters was decimated and homogenized. We have already described our reasons for doubting this explanation. Our analysis of gendered trends in male-edited versus female-edited collections gave it little support, and we noted the unlikelihood that all of the editors in our sample—despite their different backgrounds, political leanings, historical contexts, political convictions, nationalities, and sexes—have been unwitting participants in the same conspiracy.

The data presented in this chapter tend to deepen these doubts. In this study we were able to directly compare the degree of gendered attractiveness emphasis in female-edited versus male-edited collections. In the 11 exclusively female-edited collections, 30 percent of the pronoun references were "female" versus 25 percent in the 61 male-edited collections. And this minimal difference emerges entirely from the influence of just 2 collections with far above average narrative emphasis on female characters (Mindlin's *Stories from the Amazon* and Benedict's *Tales of the Cochiti*); in the other 9 female-edited collections, attention to females was at or below the regional average. Though the small sample size obviously means that further study will be required, this preliminary analysis suggests that male editorial bias in unlikely to account for a large amount of the skew in male–female emphasis.

But what if the roles of female characters were diminished—systematically and across the board—earlier than the editorial stage?* That is, the bias could have been in the interactions among the original collectors and tellers of the tales. For instance, it is possible that, due to widespread cultural constraints limiting women's interaction with strange males, the original collectors of the tales worked principally with male informants. If male tale spinners focus on stories about men and boys, while female spinners tell more stories about women and girls, then we might have an explanation for at least some part of the male–female skew. Consider an analogy with Western literature. In a content analysis of plot and character synopses, coders determined that the canon of Western literature—stretching from the earliest Greek beginnings up until the mid-twentieth century—overwhelmingly

---

* I am grateful to Kathleen Ragan's "What Happened to the heroines in Folktales" (2009, forthcoming) for focusing my attention on this possibility.

focused on the trials and exploits of male characters (see Gottschall et al. 2008, in press, "A Census of the Western Cannon"). However, this randomly selected sample of plot summaries included only 8 percent female authors. In an as yet unpublished follow-up study, my colleagues and I checked character sex ratios in 169 plot summaries of nineteenth-century literary works by women and 239 plot summaries of twentieth-century works by women (data source was Magill 1995). In the nineteenth century sample, there was a small tendency among female authors to favor female main characters (overall there were 76 female main characters versus 64 male; the remaining works were coded as lacking a single main character). However, in the twentieth-century sample of female authors, we found an explosion of emphasis on female main characters (overall there were 138 female main characters versus just 56 male).

If this result is valid, and generalizable to other traditions and a vastly different narrative mode (not a sure thing), then the hypothesis of male bias among tale tellers seems like a much more hopeful explanation for sex ratio skews in world folktales than the possibility of near-universal antifemale bias among editors. Anecdotal accounts from Denmark and Afghanistan do suggest that female tale tellers feature a substantially higher percentage of gynocentric tales than male tellers do (see Holbeck 1987; Mills 1985), and Ragan has identified similar patterns in tales by female tellers, albeit in a small sample (2009, forthcoming).

However, the possibility that female tellers contributed a much smaller percentage of tales to the world's folktale collections (*and* that those tellers pay more attention to female characters) is just that: a possibility. In traditional societies the telling of folktales is nothing like an exclusively male domain—in many societies the folktale is a "hearth" genre dominated by female tellers. We might therefore surmise that the collectors of these tales—many of whom were responsible and serious people—would have often sought out contributions by female informants. Moreover, some of the most famous—and from the point of view of some feminists, infamous—collections of folktales depended heavily on contributions of female informants. For example, the Grimms' informants were principally women, and women also played a major role in France. Jack Zipes writes, "It was not Charles Perrault but other groups of writers, particularly aristocratic women, who gathered in salons during the seventeenth century and created the conditions for the rise of the fairy tale" (1994, 18). And yet the familiar imbalances in sex ratio and other gendered characterization patterns are saliently displayed in the classic European tales. For these reasons, an across the board overrepresentation of males in the total population of tale tellers is unlikely to account for the *full* skew in male–female emphasis.

Unlikely, but not impossible. By gathering collections that include specific information on the sex of the original informants, one can find this out. (We sought to check this possibility in our own data, but very few collections included adequate information on the sex of the original tale tellers.) It would also be important to know if tales submitted by female tellers violate the broad, gendered patterns described in these case studies; our hunch is that some patterns *would* vary according to teller sex, but that the steady cross-cultural patterns of gender identified in these case studies *would not* vanish or flip-flop in tales contributed by women.

In the event that future studies show that tales by male and female tellers differ substantially and systematically in the pertinent patterns, at least one further group of studies—and inventive ones at that—will be required to address a final problem and move toward something like a resolution of the case. For even if samples of tales told by females were shown to differ significantly from those contributed by males, it would *not* confirm that any of the gendered patterns identified in these studies were results of specifically male bias. In this event, how would we know that it was the males, and not the females, who were biasing the results?

*   *   *

A multivariate explanation may ultimately be required to explain the full amount of skew in sex-based emphasis on main characters. We therefore strongly encourage future explorations of the possibility that editor, teller, collector, or other sources of bias may contribute to the scarcity of female characters. But if all of these explanations—even considered together—seem unlikely to account for the full amount of male–female skew, what is left? One possibility, which we first raised in chapter 4, is almost never seriously considered. Perhaps the largest proportion of the missing daughters were not destroyed or otherwise excluded—perhaps they never existed in the first place. In contrast to evolutionary biology, there is no mechanism relentlessly working to keep sex ratios in literary genres in equilibrium. The goal of all tale tellers is—first and foremost—to rivet the attention of audiences (see Boyd 2005a). In traditional societies, with clear and often rigid divisions between normative spheres of activity for males and females, it is possible that the normative activities of male characters are simply better at riveting audience attention. The lives of a traditional culture's males—of its warriors, shamans, chieftains, thugs, murderers, political usurpers, wooers, and hunters—may simply possess more dramatic wallop, *on average,* than can typically be generated from the more domestic activities of that culture's females. Disproportions in character sex ratios would, in this view, be interpreted as epiphenomena of standard cross-cultural gender patterns in traditional societies, which, in turn, are based on deep biological structures—structures of gross physical biology, like the necessity in natural fertility societies of keeping lactating mothers and their infants in close proximity, and larger factors of sexual selection acting differently and relentlessly on males and females throughout deep time (see Andersson 1994; Darwin 1871; Miller 1998, 2001).

This possibility can be given in the form of a testable prediction. The proportion of female characters in the literatures, folk or otherwise, of given societies will track with the type and number of "active" roles real women play in those societies. As women move out of traditional roles, character sex ratios should move toward parity. This is nothing like a theory of ironclad determinism. Rather, the theory predicts that as cultures morph and sex roles moderate, so too will the depictions of male and female characters in literary narratives. The dramatic differences in main character sex ratios in nineteenth- and twentieth-century women's writing, noted above, would seem to represent evidence that this transition is well under way in Western societies.

*   *   *

In summary, this chapter presents independent data that staunchly buttress two results from the previous folktale content analysis: across strikingly diverse populations there is apparently vastly less emphasis on female characters in world folktales, but vastly more emphasis on their physical attractiveness. It is possible that these data are fundamentally off base; it is also possible that the data are accurate but the explanation of the trends is not. In any event, the advantage of empirical study is that all reasonable doubts can be systematically addressed—all forms of bias can be exposed—in a process that doggedly, patiently narrows the space of possible explanation. This work marks a beginning of this process. We hope that others will join the effort, and if our findings are ultimately discredited, we will be strongly consoled by two facts. First, our stumbles will have provided the impetus for the development of truer understanding. Second, our failures cannot be demonstrated decisively by anything but careful scientific study. Thus we find ourselves in the rare position where all outcomes count as success.

Chapter 7

Romantic Love: A Literary Universal?*

To love someone romantically is—at least according to innumerable literary works, much received wisdom, and even a gradually coalescing academic consensus—to experience a strong desire for union with someone who is deemed entirely unique. It is to idealize this person, to think constantly about him or her, and to discover that one's own priorities in life have changed dramatically. It is to care deeply for that person's well-being and to feel pain or emptiness when he or she is absent.

But is this intense emotional experience universal, something that is characteristically and quintessentially human, or is it merely a sociocultural construct that belongs to a particular time and place? On this point there is less agreement, both within and between different academic disciplines. The audacious question we want to raise in the pages that follow is whether literature—or more specifically, a large-scale, multiple-coder content analysis of thousands of folktales drawn from diverse corners of the planet—can contribute something to this difficult question about love, culture, and human nature.

*   *   *

Let us first look briefly at the theoretical problem that we aim to address. A widespread view among literary scholars and social scientists over the past decades has been that romantic love is a social construction specific to Western culture. This is part of a relentless

*This research was originally published in *Philosophy and Literature* 30 (2006): 450–470. Marcus Nordlund, Göteborg University, coauthored this chapter. Liana Boop, Lance Branch, Daniel DeLorme, Mackenzie Ewing, John Forrette, Jared Fostveit, Erica Guralnick, Julia Jones, Sarah MacFarland, Maia Moyer, Kevin O'Connor, Spencer Paige, Ann Sargent, Linnea Smolentzov, Michael Stafford, Adam Tapply, Lindsey Taylor, and Sammie-Jo Therrien contributed to this research.

skepticism toward the notion that important categories of human psychology and emotion—romantic and parental love, gender, sexual orientation, and so on—are "natural" rather than constructed. And this position is often, if not always, linked to an ideological concern to de-essentialize (or at least problematize) what is perceived as a fundamentally destructive or oppressive emotion or belief. Taking her cue from Simone de Beauvoir, Marilyn Friedman gives no less than ten reasons why it may be problematic for women to fall in love with men (Friedman 1998).

Of course, no argument of any kind can be strictly ideological in nature since it always involves empirical assumptions—either explicit or implicit—about the nature of things. For example, the psychoanalyst E. S. Person opines that the "best evidence that romantic love is not hardwired into the emotional repertoire of humanity but is a cultural construct is the fact that there are so many cultures in which it is virtually absent" (1992, 383). Another frequent argument for love's constructed-ness has been that "there is no definition that describes love throughout the ages or across cultures" (Beal and Sternberg 1995, 433).

In some literary-critical accounts, it is even argued that romantic love is a cultural invention that can be traced back with precision to the courtly *troubadour* culture of twelfth-century France (e.g., De Rougemont 1939; Bloch 1991). According to yet another school, represented by the influential literary theorist Jonathan Culler, "the notion of romantic love (and its centrality to the lives of individuals) is arguably a massive literary creation" (Culler 1997, 68).

Whereas the social constructivist position on romantic love typically involves a strong commitment to cultural specificity, a weaker version is held even by some cognitive theorists who grant more to biology and panhuman traits. From the perspective of their communicative theory of emotion, Philip Johnson-Laird and Keith Oatley argue that the "components [of romantic love] exist separately in different societies, but their integration into a recognizable complex is a cultural accomplishment [by the West]" (2000, 462).

At the other end of the romantic love continuum we find those who argue that this emotion belongs to a universal human nature, or, more specifically, that it can be attributed to specialized neural circuits whose ultimate purpose is to enhance reproductive success. Not surprisingly, this has been a favorite position among evolutionary psychologists, and it has recently received some support from neuroscience.

For example, the neuroscientists Andreas Bartels and Samir Zeki claim to have uncovered a "functionally specialized system" that lights up in fMRI (functional magnetic resonance imaging) scans of the brains of individuals who claim to be enamored (2000, 3833). Among other things, these studies lend unexpected support to the proverbial idea that "love is blind," since the experience of romantic love can be correlated with the deactivation of brain regions concerned with critically assessing other people's intentions and making moral judgments (2004). Another research team (Helen Fisher and associates) has drawn extensively on similar neuroscientific evidence in support of the hypothesis that human beings come equipped with a tripartite system of attraction, attachment, and sexuality (Fisher et al. 2002; Fisher et al. 2005).

The neuroscientific perspective certainly promises strong support for love's universality. If our emotional experience can be correlated with distinct neural circuits that, in turn, are continuous with our mammalian heritage, then it seems likely that this experience is also somehow part of an evolved human nature. However, given the considerable environmental plasticity of the human brain, pointing to specialized circuits in the brains of Western subjects will hardly persuade anyone who believes that romantic love itself is a Western innovation. At least in principle, a neurophysiological trait can be genotypically *continuous* with other species and still be heavily modulated by environmental factors.

For this reason, a successful case for love's universality would also seem to require solid cross-cultural studies that disproved the standard social constructivist argument that romantic love is absent in a large number of cultures. The matter can only be resolved by integrating cross-cultural analyses with neuroscientific evidence.

Some cross-cultural arguments to this effect have already been put forward. In 1992, the anthropologists Jankowiak and Fischer scrutinized the ethnographic record and uncovered instances of romantic love in almost 90 percent of the cultures studied. Three years after the study, Jankowiak published a collection of essays that fleshes out the argument and adds more empirical material in the form of case studies, but its title still ends with a question mark: *Romantic Passion: A Universal Experience?* (1995).

* * *

The lead authors of this study (Gottschall and Nordlund) are committed to the view that romantic love must be understood with reference to an evolved human nature. This is not to say that emotion can necessarily be *reduced* to a hardwired instinct, impervious to cultural influence, but rather that any satisfying explanation of its nature—including the rather improbable view that it arose in twelfth-century France, alongside the game of tennis—would need to be *anchored* in evolved psychological dispositions that are common to *Homo sapiens*.

Nevertheless, more precise questions about love's nature and origin can be bracketed here since they do not impinge directly on the empirical question of its prevalence. Our precise objective has been to further test the hypothesis of romantic love's universality, and thus to attempt to reproduce the findings of Jankowiak and Fischer in a different cultural medium, through a systematic content analysis of dozens of collections of folktales drawn from diverse world populations.

While using folktales as empirical evidence about human nature involves complications, it is our view that folktales can give valuable information about the ideas, beliefs, dreams, wishes, and fears of people around the world. As long as we respect the complexities involved, there is an important role for literature departments to play in the scientific study of human nature.

Indeed, this study is not the first empirical exploration of romantic love in world literature. In *The Mind and its Stories*, Patrick Colm Hogan surveys a large swathe of world literature and suggests that "romantic union" may be a universal generic prototype (2003b). Strictly speaking, our study is not an attempt to replicate Hogan's findings since we are not in search of a literary subgenre but representations of a human emotion. We also hope to contribute a somewhat more systematic and transparent methodology. But in spite of these differences we think of both studies as joint contributions to the larger question of love's literary universality.

To suggest that romantic love may be universal naturally requires a definition of the emotion itself. In their ethnological study, cited above, Jankowiak and Fischer understood romantic love as "any intense attraction that involves the idealization of the other, within an erotic context, with the expectation of enduring for some time into the future" (1992, 62). This is a practical definition that covers three important aspects of romantic love (idealization, desire, commitment), but it also appears to leave out as much as it includes. A more complete account is offered in Helen Harris's (1995, 102–103) synthesis of previous academic definitions:

1. Desire for union or merger, both physical and emotional
2. Idealization of the beloved
3. Exclusivity (reciprocal)
4. Intrusive thinking about the love object

5. Emotional dependency
6. Reordering of motivational hierarchies or life priorities
7. Powerful empathy and concern for the beloved

In our view this is an impeccable description, but for the benefit of our content analysts we also produced a more concrete and accessible version that would not require additional definitions of the key components. Romantic love is *a feeling expressed in a romantic context between two people; it has a dimension of sexual attraction, even lust, but it is not limited to that; it is an emotion that is typically reserved for only one person (though romantic love is not necessarily inconsistent with sexual promiscuity); it carries the expectation of lasting duration; it involves intense attraction to the beloved's whole person and is not just about attraction to the body.*

The qualifier about sexual promiscuity was intended to detach the emotional content of romantic love from its moral implications and evaluations. Since recent neuroscientific research lends support to the view of romantic passion as an intensely goal-oriented state whose initial phase may even be at cross-purposes with empathy, we also decided to remove this dimension as a necessary defining criterion (Bartels and Zeki 2004). While empathy and concern typically play an important part in romantic love—to love someone romantically is also to care for that person—extreme states of infatuation may not be conducive toward it.

Perhaps less obviously, a study of this kind also presupposes a concept of universality, and we have used the word in accordance with two basic distinctions. The first distinction is that between *cultural* and *human* universals, where a cultural universal is one that can be found in all cultures whereas a human universal characterizes all humans. The second necessary distinction is that between *absolute universals* (that admit no exceptions) and *statistical* universals (that admit exceptions and hence constitute broad patterns rather than absolute rules). Even though we suspect hypothetically that romantic love may be a *statistical human universal* (more specifically, a biological potential in almost every human being)—and therefore most likely an *absolute cultural universal* (that exists in all cultures)—a study of this scope and nature can only produce evidence that is indicative of *statistical cultural universals.*

Data and Methods

Our sample is based upon a sample of 75 collections of folktales from diverse cultures, most of which were identical to those used for the study described in the previous chapter. The main difference is that the present study encompasses far fewer collections from South American indigenous populations. This is because the study of romantic love reached its conclusion before those collections arrived through interlibrary loan (see Appendix B for a list of the collections used in each study). Coding procedures were also similar to those described in the previous chapter. First, with the help of thesauri, we generated a list of 43 words that, in English, are often associated with romantic love:

> Adore, Affection, Ardor, Beloved, Bridal, Bride, Bridegroom, Cherish, Concubine, Consort, Court, Courtesan, Darling, Dear, Desire, Groom, Helpmeet, Honeymoon, Husband, Longing, Love, Make Love, Man and Wife, Marital, Marriage, Mate, Matrimony, Mistress, Newlywed, Nuptials, Paramour, Partner, Passion, Pine, Romance, Sex, Sleep With, Spouse, Wedding, Wedlock, Wife, Woo, Yearn.

As with the list of attractiveness adjectives given in the previous chapter, we do not claim that this list comprehends every word that can be associated with a romantic love context. However, it is important to emphasize that any omissions in this list introduce a bias *against*, not for, the hypothesis of romantic love's universality.

Next, using our word processor's standard "find and replace" function, we "tagged" all of the keywords in the collections, and all of their relevant variants (e.g., love, loved, lover, loving, etc). Finally, 18 undergraduate members of a St. Lawrence University seminar in research methods coded roughly equal proportions (in page counts, not numbers of collections) of the total sample. Coders used our word processor's "find" function to locate the keyword tag (>>). After locating a tagged keyword, coders then used as much of the surrounding context as was necessary to judge (1) whether the reference met our definition of romantic love, (2) whether it did not, or (3) whether the reference was ambiguous.

As in the previously described studies, coders were kept "naïve": they were not appraised of the theoretical controversies about romantic love or about its relationship to larger debates about human nature, and they were not privy to the expectations of the lead authors. They were only told that our investigations—whatever we discovered—would help to resolve questions about the prevalence of romantic love across cultures. It was emphasized that there was no favored outcome: whatever we revealed would represent a valuable contribution. Coding decisions were made independently; coders were told not to discuss judgments with colleagues. Coding was conducted in one-hour lab sessions to allow for procedural questions, to minimize intercoder discussion, and to limit coder fatigue and distraction.

Coders were repeatedly reminded to hew closely to our shared definition of romantic love and to avoid the tendency to respond based on personal intuitions. But the possibility remains that the judgments of individual coders were compromised through subjectivity bias or simple errors. To guard against this possibility, all 536 potential references to romantic love identified in the first stage of coding were subjected to additional scrutiny.

In the second phase of coding, all potential references (including the key words and all relevant context) were cut and pasted into three documents of roughly equal length. Then 3 teams (two with 6 members, one with 5) considered all potential references and simply indicated whether they believed that the reference was clearly consistent with our definition of romantic love or not. We applied a strict standard: no reference to romantic love was accepted as authentic unless coders were unanimous or if there was only one dissenter.

All of these steps were designed to minimize various kinds of bias. The coding task was performed by a team of naïve coders, rather than by the lead authors, to minimize the likelihood that the results would be shaped—consciously or not—by the biases of interested professional researchers (in other words, for the same reason that psychologists do not fill out their own surveys). We formalized our definition of romantic love and included the second coding phase to ensure that our results were based not on the potentially idiosyncratic responses of individual coders but on a rigorous standard of intersubjectivity.

Potential biases remain in our results, some of which will be discussed in more detail below. We hope, however, that the principal bias in this study is a conservative bias purposefully introduced by the researchers. In seeking to shield against the possibility of false positives (accepting a false reference to romantic love), we have heightened our vulnerabilities to false negatives (overlooking legitimate references).

Results

For the purposes of data analysis, collections were grouped into 7 major cultural areas, ranging in size from 5 to 24 collections and 11 subgroupings (variance in sample sizes are a result of availability of collections, not of a methodological choice). Collections were placed into subgroupings only if there were at least 3 collections from that cultural area. Cultural groupings were based on salient geographic, linguistic, and cultural affinities and were guided by anthropological convention (Murdock 1957, 1981).

In the 75 collections, coders identified 263 references that met our shared definition of romantic love: 55 collections had at least one reference to romantic love; 39 of the collections included multiple references. On average, there were 3.51 references to romantic love per collection (see table 7.1). Two-thirds of the accepted references enjoyed unanimous coder agreement; for the other third there was one dissenter.

References to romantic love were not limited to European tales but were found across highly diverse and isolated culture areas. In fact, while not every collection included an unambiguous reference to romantic love, every culture area represented by at least 3 collections of tales did, except for the Philippines. The European total of 3.75 references per collection was only negligibly higher than the sample average, and several cultural areas included more references on

Table 7.1   Results by Broad Cultural Groupings and Subgroupings

	References to Romantic Love	Average References per Collection
Overall (n=75)	263	3.51
Asia (n=15)	94	6.27
India (n=6)	28	4.67
Japan (n=5)	37	7.4
Africa (n=5)	8	1.60
Hausa (n=3)	6	2.00
Europe (n=8)	31	3.75
Middle East (n=6)	23	3.83
Oceania (n=10)	19	1.90
Aboriginal Australia (n=4)	7	1.75
Hawaii (n=3)	6	2.00
Philippines (n=3)	0	0
North Amer. Indian (n=24)	75	3.25
Arctic Coast (n=5)	4	0.80
Northwest Coast (n=10)	68	6.8
Pueblo (n=3)	3	1.00
South America (n=7)	13	1.86
Maya (n=4)	8	2.00

Note: The sample size for the broad cultural grouping is often larger than the sum of the subgroups. This is because many collections could not be efficiently placed in subgroups.
n = Number of collections per grouping.

average. By far the highest averages were not found in Europe but in large samples of tales from Japan, from North West Coastal Indian populations, and from India. Among the collections that could not be efficiently placed into cultural subgroups, the single Ainu collection (with 10 references to romantic love) and the single Western Yugur collection (with 5) stand out.

* * *

This study therefore offers staunch support to the existing evidence that romantic love is a statistical cultural universal. It would also seem to increase the probability that romantic love may be an absolute cultural universal. While the coders found no clear romantic love references in the 3 collections from the Philippines, it would be rash to conclude, on this basis, that romantic love did not exist in this culture at the time the tales were collected or was of minimal importance. Obviously, not every collection of folktales will convey information about every aspect of a given culture. It could be that if we had considered more Philippine collections we would have discovered unambiguous examples. After all, Japan had the most romantic love references per collection; but if we had only considered three Japanese collections (as in the Philippine case) we might have found no love references at all. Every one of the Japanese examples accepted by coders was found in just 3 of our 6 collections.

In a similar vein, while we have taken the trouble to produce statistics on the number of references per cultural grouping, it would be unwise to assume, based on these numbers, that romantic love is, for instance, 3 times as central to Japanese culture as it is to Hawaiian. Folktales can be used as one source of data to see if romantic love is represented in a culture, but they are an imperfect index of cultural importance. Variance in the numbers of love references across culture areas may reflect cultural importance, but it is also likely to reflect random variance in the contents of collections, nonrandom variance (e.g., collections happening to focus on tales of young lovers versus those focusing on myths of cosmology and origins), and variances among individual coders during the first coding stage.

The Many Languages of Love

The fact that we have used English translations raises some questions, one of which concerns the quality of the translations used. Due to the extent of our material and its sheer variety of original languages, we have simply been at the mercy of our translators. A second and perhaps more interesting issue is that of potential linguistic incommensurability. Is it even possible in principle to translate successfully from one language to another if the languages in question differ markedly in their terms for love and affection?

As we saw above, different cultural definitions of love have been used as a central argument for love's status as a social construction. In our view, the important grain of truth in this position—that the way a culture talks about love can reveal important things about how the emotion is understood, conceptualized, and even experienced—is too often buried under a mound of overstated inferences. To posit anything like a direct link between love and linguistics, between what people say and what they feel, is to suggest that (1) human thought and emotion are solely or mainly determined by language and that (2) cultures are unlimited in their capacity to regulate and define individual experience and behavior by linguistic means. Although precisely these notions have been widely propounded by humanists, they enjoy little in the way of empirical support or scientific credence (see Pinker 2000, 2007). A culture may prescribe strict "feeling rules" for its members, but life will always be lived in tension with prescription (Stearns 2000, 20).

According to William Jankowiak, cultural attitudes toward romantic love are indeed highly diverse, with some cultures simply rejecting romantic love "as an evil and frighteningly emotional experience. In others it is tolerated but not celebrated or asserted, and in still others romantic passion is praised as an important and cherished cultural ideal" (Jankowiak 1995, 20). The important point here is that even someone who does not concede Jankowiak's *empirical* argument will be hard pressed to refute its *logical* consequences for the translation problem under scrutiny here.

If Jankowiak is right, then we can certainly expect notable differences between the languages of love in different cultures, particularly as concerns love's moral status and implications. But for the very same reasons it will also be extremely hazardous to extrapolate emotional realities from linguistic realities. *If* it is the case that different cultural attitudes generate different vocabularies for the same emotion, then focusing on language is just as likely to *obscure* as to *clarify* the question of love's universality. Linguistic diversity is simply an insufficient argument for love's supposed constructedness.

On a purely *practical* level, however, the problem of translation still remains, and this is the case regardless of whether we ascribe it to faulty translations, cultural bias, or linguistic incompatibility. Since our study is based on keyword-in-context analyses of short passages rather than summarized accounts of entire texts, it follows that the precise meaning of individual words becomes all the more important. It matters, for example, when a Chinook storyteller informs us that a man has married several women but "loved only the youngest one," and our coders interpret this passage as an instance of romantic love (albeit with reference to a broader textual context than the quotation reproduced here) (Cultee 1894). If the original Chinook word was closer to "like" than "love," this would drastically change the significance of the passage. One way to assess how serious this translation problem has been is to move from statistical analysis to closer, more qualitative consideration of a few examples.

Romantic Love: a Literary Universal?

Considered as a whole, our material covers all attributes of Harris's description of romantic love. "Falling in love" is described as a distinct and recognizable process in tales from regions as diverse as West Africa, Japan, North and South America, the Middle East, Polynesia, China, and Europe. Our instances of *intrusive thinking* come from cultures so diverse as Hawaii (where a young woman professes to love the King so much that she thinks of him day and night, and even in her dreams, and another woman weeps bitterly because the thought of her absent lover never leaves her); Punjab in northern India (where an enamored youth cannot eat or sleep for love of a beautiful maiden); and the Western Yugur steppe of China (where a boy suffers from "lovesickness" and is eventually cured). Wherever lovers are separated for long, intrusive thinking is attended by pain or even despair. This *emotional dependence* takes on cosmic proportions in a Maori tale of creation where the Sun weeps so hard over his separation from his mistress Earth that his tears eventually turn into oceans.

We have also found examples of *emotional commitment, empathy,* and *exclusivity* so strong that lovers are either prepared to sacrifice their own lives for their loved ones (as in a Japanese tale) or continue their relationship beyond death (in a tale from the Heiltsuk Nation of British Columbia, two lovers swear that the one who dies first will return to bring the other to the kingdom of the dead). Other examples are more complex. One tale from the Middle East provides a particularly unpleasant example of how strong love can coexist, without apparent contradiction, with moral judgments that seem diametrically opposed to it. A husband loves his wife so much that he is "ready to sacrifice his life to satisfy her whim." He is, however, also prepared—on the advice of none other than his trusty dog, who has 10 wives and controls them all perfectly—to take a heavy stick and give her a good beating across the back because she is too curious about his secrets (Ginzberg 1909).

In most cases, at least two or more of the defining characteristics of romantic love can be found in a given passage. But an important limitation of this study has been that our coders were provided with a multifactor definition of romantic love but were not given detailed instructions about which, or how many, factors had to be present in order for a particular emotional representation to qualify as "romantic."

On one hand, it seems unreasonable to expect that a single passage must exhibit all 7 factors in the full definition (desire for union, etc.) in order to qualify as fully "romantic." On the other hand, our investigation may have benefited from a formalized multifactor approach of the kind employed, for example, in clinical psychology: that is, if a person's emotional experience meets a *specified* number of criteria associated with romantic love, then that person can be said to be experiencing romantic love. Perhaps future studies will want to explore this approach in order to increase the precision of their findings.

What are the consequences of this methodological limitation? At first sight, it would seem that our findings can still be explained in terms of the moderate constructivist hypothesis espoused by Johnson-Laird and Oatley above: that while the *components* of romantic love exist across the planet, the *integration* of these components into a complex whole is a distinctive Western achievement. When we proceed to examine individual passages, however, the case for the "Western integration" hypothesis becomes shakier and the case for universality stronger. Consider, as an example, this charming story from a collection of Australian Aboriginal stories, originally documented by the anthropologist W. Ramsay Smith. Since the original story is several pages long we give a condensed version of its plot here:

> A male peewee (a species of small magpie) returns to his nest after a long day of food gathering and is surprised to find a beautiful female peewee sitting there. She is lost and very tired, so he invites her to take a nap in his nest. As he watches her sleep he falls in love with her. When she wakes up she is first distraught at finding herself alone with a stranger and starts to cry. He comforts her with kind words and then helps her find her way back to her parents in the south before returning back home.

Three months go by, and all this time the male yearns for his loved one as he watches other animals mate in his surroundings. One night he thinks he hears her voice in a dream and finally decides to fly south again to woo her with his song. When she doesn't appear he worries that she may have been claimed by another peewee, but then he reassures himself. Her eyes spoke clearly of love for him when they first met, so how could she possibly forget him and marry someone she did not love?

Finally, to his great joy, the female appears again, and they sing a hymn to the Sun Goddess before spending the night together in silent communion. In the end they become husband and wife and raise a large family whose grown-up members migrate to other parts of the country. (1930, 41–44)

In this story about bird love—which is well worth reading in its entirety—not one of Harris's 7 key ingredients of romantic love is missing. The male peewee finds the female beautiful and desires her, but his feelings clearly go beyond mere physical attraction. He is concerned for her well-being, he depends on her for his own happiness, and her absence is accompanied by intense feelings of loneliness. He thinks constantly about her for 3 months, and since his feelings appear to be requited he is also convinced that she cannot love anyone else. How appropriate, then, that after this *idealization, exclusivity, intrusive thinking, emotional dependency, powerful empathy, and desire for union,* these avian-Australian lovers should also *rearrange their life priorities* by consummating their love in marriage!

What we have here, then, is a near-perfect example of romantic love from a Native Australian tribe. The anthropologist who collected it at the beginning of the twentieth century claims to have made only "few and slight" alterations to it, and these were deemed necessary "to make clear the meaning, or to give some degree of grammatical correctness to the text without changing the 'aroma' of the story when using equivalent English terms or phrases" (1930, 7–8). In spite of these precautions, it is of course impossible to control fully for the manifold cultural influences and biases that may have crept into its contents.

But such doubts—like any proposed certainties or probabilities—must also be put into perspective. Science, including literary science of the kind we have practiced here, is not a method for providing metaphysical certainty. It is a systematic and probabilistic way of determining where the preponderance of evidence lies. The best that science can do is provide evidence that exceeds all reasonable doubts—as in the cases of evolution, heliocentricity, and continental drift. At the conclusion to this study, however, reasonable people may still doubt that romantic love is an emotion that has emerged independently in all human populations. For instance, while it is for many reasons unlikely that cross-cultural diffusion of folktales or Western sociopolitical hegemony can explain the full breadth of our findings, we cannot absolutely rule out these possibilities. What we *can* assert is that a clear preponderance of evidence derived from systematic studies of ethnography, neuroscience, ethology and, now, world folktales, converges in support of romantic love's universality.

Conclusion: FOTA

So devastating in theory has been the epistemological critique of poststructuralism that one wonders how the movement has survived as long as it has.

(Frederick Crews 2006, 299; italics in original)

In working on this book and developing a better appreciation of literary academics' low morale and their dissatisfactions with "business as usual," I have often had occasion to ponder a question: If the dominant paradigm in literary analysis is weak, if it is manifestly vulnerable on many fronts, if it has failed in providing us all that we believed it promised, how does it persist? That is, despite sagging morale and genres of cruelly whetted polemics (e.g., contributors to Patai and Corral 2005a), recantations (e.g., Lentricchia 1996; Evans 2005), and howls of black despair (e.g., contributors to Mitchell 2004), a serious, radical alternative to the orthodoxies of the liberationist establishment has not materialized (for all of the irony, I agree with Joseph Carroll [1995] that "establishment" is now the appropriate word; or perhaps "hegemony" is better, see Hilfer 2003).

I believe that there are two primary reasons for this. The first is almost vulgar: economics. A profoundly depressed professorial job market—where over 50 percent of jobs are filled by adjuncts and about two-thirds of PhDs never achieve tenure at all (Stanton et al. 2007, 4, 15)—has nurtured a situation where the young scholars (advanced graduate students, recent PhDs, and junior professors) who should be questioning the yellowing scripts of their seniors dare not do so. In a savagely competitive professional marketplace, where there can be *hundreds* of CVs submitted for humble junior professorships, the desire for an office, a classroom, a vocation, and a paycheck garrotes dissent. Young scholars know that to challenge the field's deep theoretical and moralistic verities is to hold their careers cheap: they risk having their manuscripts summarily rejected by journals and presses (in an environment where the motto should be switched from "publish or perish" to "publish [a lot] or forget about coming into existence at all"), they risk alienating the patronage of powerful senior professors, and they court a long stretch in the limbo of adjuncthood. For this last cohort, the adjunct working poor—with adult financial responsibilities and without even the protections of a graduate teaching assistantship (like a multiyear contract and health care insurance)— the pressure not to rock the boat is perhaps greatest of all (see Bousquet 2008). These harsh economic realities have helped produce several PhD-generations of young conformists (see Menand 2005 for similar arguments). In such a punishing competitive environment, those who would offer fundamental challenges to the deeply held beliefs and career accomplishments of the professors staffing the hiring committees and editorial boards are at a distinct survival disadvantage.

This situation contrasts quite sharply with most scientific fields. In the sciences too, established investigators exert conforming pressure on the unestablished. After all, Max Planck was not in jest when he remarked that scientific progress occurs death by death (1949, 33–34).* But he was exaggerating (Planck's "principle" is testable and empirical studies have cast doubt on its validity, see Hull, Tessner, and Diamond 1978, Messeri 1988; see also Blackmore 1978). In general, science succeeds by fomenting a controlled but permanent revolution— its heroes and icons are iconoclasts and overturners. The ethic of revolution is sustained not because scientists are nobler than humanists, but because no matter how powerful a senior scientist becomes, he or she must yield to the neophyte's superior data or be ridiculous (if not pitiable). Moreover, intellectual dissent in the sciences is not *usually* tied up in such intricate ideological knots. As we have seen, it is difficult for humanists to question dominant liberationist tenets without being darkly suspected of championing (through bold activity or craven passivity) political positions that are simply off limits to respectable workers in the field.

The second reason for the paradigm's endurance is bigger than market pressure. For whatever flaws it possesses, the liberationist paradigm has never wanted in the grandeur of its ambitions. If, as Derrida contended, the whole world is text, if all discourse is story,

---

*And Darwin was only half in jest when he wrote in his autobiography, "What a good thing it would be, if every scientific man was to die when sixty years old, as afterwards he would be sure to oppose all new doctrines" (1877a, 100–101).

if there is no extralinguistic reality, if we are all imprisoned by language, then the world's premier intellectuals will not be the specialists in this narrow discipline or that, they will be the mavens of language: the linguist, the critic, the rhetorician, the theorist. The liberationist paradigm encourages its workers to view themselves as a special order of virtuosi, as superordinate intellectuals with authority to decipher and judge all forms of human discourse. At the same time, the liberationists would build on the antifoundation of post-structuralism to challenge virtually everything we had cozened ourselves into *thinking* we knew; in this way, they would expose evil and hasten the meek's inheritance of their fair share of earth.

In short, the liberationist paradigm produced a sharply delineated *narrative of intellectual and moral heroism* in which literary intellectuals play the questing knights. The heroic praxis of the liberationists could only be captured with bold verbs. Radical intellectuals would "question," "transgress," "demystify," "trespass," "transcend," "destabilize," "transform," "liberate," "resist," and so on. The liberationist scholar would give assertive voice to the silenced, bravely expose the hidden agendas behind all received pieties, and always have the guts to oppose power—and damn the consequences. In short, the tenacity of the liberationist paradigm is no wonder. Those who have challenged it have offered nothing to rival its potential for heroism.

I would therefore argue that the current paradigm owes its longevity primarily to the absence of a comparably ambitious and attractive alternative, to the fact that almost *any* proposed alternative would massively diminish the field's self-regard. In foreign policy circles, there is an acronym that describes one of the reasons why the United States props up some oppressive and dictatorial regimes: FOTA (fear of the alternative). *If the House of Saud falls will the Wahabis come to power?* Literary scholars face similar fears of the potential alternatives to the liberationist regime: Should the paradigm collapse, what will there be left for us to do? How will we define and describe ourselves, and how should we go about our work? Are we, who were to be transformers and transcenders, to go back to frivolous, circular, interminable debates about this poem or that? Daniel O'Hara's response to Knapp and Michaels' early anti-Theory polemic, "Against Theory," expresses precisely this anxiety: "[Knapp and Michaels would] return us [to the world] of our grandfathers, the world of the New Critics and the gentlemen-scholars of literary history" (1983, 732).

So while this book represents something like a total challenge to dominant literary modes, it is not primarily intended as another polemic. Rather, it seeks to introduce, defend, and concretely illustrate a constructive alternative. The model proposed here peels away from previous modes and stresses the necessity of elementary reform. While I understand that calls for drastic change are certain to be met with skeptical resistance (if they are not simply ignored as the ravings of a heretic), I believe this proposal has a major strength in its favor: Like the dominant paradigm, it is animated by an ambitious, idealistic vision of what a scholar of literature can accomplish.

*   *   *

Indulge me by considering a dangerous question, one that has been my constant preoccupation as I research and write this book: "What reason have we been given to believe that the Big Ideas in modern critical theory meaningfully and adequately model reality?" For the reader who wishes to address this question most efficiently, it may help to consult representative compilations like Norton's monumental anthology of criticism and theory (Leitch 2001), able primers like Tyson's *Critical Theory* (1999), or serviceable references like David Macey's *Critical Theory* (2001) or Lentricchia and McLaughlin's *Critical Terms for Literary Study* (1995). Read through the anthologized writings. Scan the text books and the dictionary entries.

Now, which ideas are likely to be true? (true, that is, in the specific sense of monopolizing a preponderance of available evidence, withstanding the most searching challenges that can be made, and more adequately accounting for the available data than competing theories). Is it the still influential psychoanalytic claims for the awesome consequences of the depraved, parricidal sexuality of human infants? Is it Lacan's less phantasmagoric theory of the mirror stage? Is it the Marxist concept of class strife at the root of everything? Or is it Foucault's amorphous power at the root, or the feminists' patriarchy? Or is it *différance*, textuality, logocentrism, heteronormativity, the phallus, or the name-of-the-father? Is it the Sapir-Whorfian hypothesis that nuances of languages rigidly channel our thought? Is it the claim that what we might conceivably call "true" is hopelessly and irretrievably contaminated by power? Is it the sharp segregation of biological sex from socially constructed gender and sexual orientation that serves as the foundation for most feminist and queer theory? Or, more specifically, is it the theory of Performativity in the process of "girling" and "boying"? Is it the driving claim of the "linguistic revolution," that language utterly produces, rather than describes, our reality? Is it the hard constructivist assertion that the suite of behaviors, predispositions, and norms that we call "human nature" was effectively invented in recent centuries?

The list of possibilities could be extended, but the point is clear. If any of these Big Ideas are, in their essentials, valid, then why have their proponents given so little in the way of genuine positive evidence for them? Why have they seemed to assiduously avoid the negative? Why does the warrant for these antiauthoritarian conceptions rest so ponderously upon the charismatic authority of their proposers? Why do these Big Ideas lack any currency in fields of political theory, economics, linguistics, psychology, cognitive science, neuroscience, and biology? Why, in fact, have these fields rejected most of these hypotheses for their failures—relative to competitor hypotheses—to account for our best currently available data?

Read through anthologies, text books, and dictionaries like those described above, and the editors and authors will often say (typically in the course of an argument from authority): "Derrida [or Freud or Lacan or Butler or Althusser or Kristeva] demonstrated X." But usually they didn't. Most of the big, seminal ideas in modern critical theory do not consist of *demonstrations*, they consist of *statements* and logical long jumping from little premises to big conclusions. The statements are not, as a rule, backed by evidence that would lead a responsibly skeptical interrogator to concede that a preponderance of evidence has been produced; on the contrary, many of the statements amount to little more than what Robert de Beaugrande has called "sheer magisterial assertion" (1989, 10).

In fact, while it is painful to write this, I cannot believe that it will be very controversial: in no other academic discipline are such extravagant and far-reaching fact claims routinely harnessed to such paltry evidence. In saying this, I do not claim that the varying obsessions of modern critical theory lack validity (economics *is* important, culture and language *are* powerful, oppression *is* real); I claim that the theories and concepts we deploy to understand them have demonstrated little.

What I am describing, in short, is the failure of modern literary studies to significantly narrow our allotted sector of the space of possible explanation. This is not because we have asked the wrong questions or devised uncreative answers and it is not the result of some fundamental intractability of humanities questions. Nor are the causes of the failure ineffable or elusive. On the contrary, they can be succinctly described and decisively confronted. To review, the first problem is theoretical: literary theory is deeply rooted in theories of human nature that are defunct (and flawed theory cannot propagate good and fruitful hypotheses). The second reason is methodological. We lack methods for deciding which of our theory-generated hypotheses is closer to the truth. The third is attitudinal. Many literary scholars have more or less dismissed the possibility of generating reliable knowledge, and the shape of hypotheses is determined at least as much by their political desirability as by their correspondence to what we intersubjectively define as "reality."

The result is the runaway expansion of the space of possible explanation—a permanent inflationary period. In literary studies, our store of hypotheses expands year by year as many thousands of new hypotheses are—in conference papers, journals, and books— balanced atop the existing stock. Since no one can agree on a way to show that an idea in literary studies is wrong, no one can be right. Books, papers, and words keep piling up but, more often than not, genuine advances in knowledge do not.

The argument of this book is that an opportunity exists to blaze a radically different course. Nothing in this argument is mushy or arcane: it is a call to establish a new humanities on surer foundations— foundations of consilient theory, a more diverse and sophisticated methodological toolkit, and the pursuit of disinterested inquiry. It is a call to move closer to the sciences in theory, method, and ethos. If these steps are taken, literary studies can once again have consequence outside the narrow, shrinking preserve of its own societies, conferences, and journals. We can make more reliable and durable contributions to the study of literature and we can participate more fully in revealing the ultimate subject of the humanities: humans. By reimagining our approach to knowledge generation, humanities scholars can rejoin the oldest, and still the premier, quest of all the disciplines: to better understand human nature and its place in the universe.

It is a good time to be a literary scholar after all.

Author's Previous Works

The Rape of Troy: Evolution, Violence, and the World of Homer (2008)
The Literary Animal: Evolution and the Nature of Narrative (coedited with
David Sloan Wilson, 2005)

Appendix A

Folktale Collections and Cultural Groupings for Chapters 4 and 5

Collections

Abjornsen, Peter Christen. 1960. *Norwegian Folktales.* New York: Viking Press.

Abrahams, Roger D. 1985. *Afro American Folktales.* New York: Pantheon Books.

Allen, Louis A. 1975. *Time Before Morning.* New York: Crowell.

Allen, Philippa, and Washington Matthews. 1930. *Whispering Wind: Folktales of the Navaho Indians.* Chicago, IL: Thomas S. Rockwell.

Alpers, A. 1964. *Maori Myths and Tribal Legends.* Auckland: Paul Longman.

Ausubel, Nathan. 1948. *A Treasury of Jewish Folklore.* New York: Crown Publishers.

Bakare, Gbadamosi, and Ulli Beier. 1968. *Not Even God is Ripe Enough.* London and New York: Heinemann Educational.

Bender, Mark, and Huana Su. 1984. *Daur Folktales.* Beijing, China: New World Press.

Berard Haile. 1938. *Origin Legend of the Navaho Enemy Way.* London and New York: Oxford University Press.

Biesele, Megan. 1993. *Women Like Meat.* Bloomington, IN: Indiana University Press.

Bruchac, Joseph, and Daniel Burgevin. 1985. *Iroquois Stories.* Trumansburg, NY: Crossing Press.

Bull, Jeffrey. 1966. *Tibetan Tales.* London: Hodder and Stoughton.

Canfield, William Walker. 1971. *The Legends of the Iroquois.* Port Washington, NY: D. J. Friedman.

Carpenter, Frances. 1947. *Tales of a Korean Grandmother.* New York: Junior Literary Guild.

Colum, Padraic. 1925. *The Bright Islands*. New Haven: Yale University Press.

———. 1925. *Tales and Legends of Hawaii: At the Gateway of the Day*. New Haven: Yale University Press.

Courlander, Harold. 1987. *The Fourth World of the Hopis*. Albuquerque, NM: University of New Mexico Press.

Curtin, Jeremiah. 1975. *Myths and Folktales of Ireland*. New York: Dover.

Daejiell, Elphinstone. 1969. *Folk Stories from Southern Nigeria*. New York: Negro Universities Press.

De Laguna, Frederica, Norman Reynolds, and Dale De Armond. 1995. *Tales From the Dena*. Seattle, WA: University of Washington Press.

Deng, Francis Mading. 1974. *Dinka Folktales*. New York: Africana Publishing Company.

Dobsinský, Pavol. 2001. *Traditional Slovakian Tales*. Armonk, NY: M. E. Sharp.

Drower, E. S. 1931. *Folktales of Iraq*. Oxford: Oxford University Press.

Fillmore, Parker. 1921. *The Laughing Prince*. New York: Harcourt, Brace, and Company.

Frankel, Ellen. 1989. *The Classic Tales: 4000 Years of Jewish Lore*. Northvale, NJ: J. Aronson.

Giray, Eren. 1986. *Nsiirin! Nsiirin!: Jula Folktales from West Africa*. East Lansing, MI: Michigan State University Press.

Grimm, Jacob, and Wilhelm Grimm. 1944. *Grimm's Fairy Tales*. New York: Pantheon Books.

Grinnell, George Bird. 1962. *Blackfoot Lodge Tales*. Lincoln, NE: University of Nebraska Press.

Grottanelli, Vinigi L. 1988. *The Python Killer: Stories of Nzema Life*. Chicago, IL: University of Chicago Press.

Guo, Xu, Lucien Miller, and Kun Xu. 1994. *South of the Clouds*. Seattle, WA: University of Washington Press.

Han, Carolyn, and Ji Li. 1997. *Tales from Within the Clouds*. Honolulu, HI: University of Hawaii Press.

Haney, Jack V. 2001. *Russian Wondertales*. Armonk, NY: M. E. Sharpe.

Hangin, John. 1998. *Mongolian Folklore: A Representative Collection from the Oral Literary Tradition*. Bloomington, IN: The Mongolia Society.

Hensman, Bertha. 1971. *More Hong Kong Tale Spinners*. Hong Kong: Chinese University.

Himmelheber, Hans, and Ann Fienup-Riordan. 2000. *Where the Echo Began*. Fairbanks, AK: University of Alaska Press.

Hindes Groome, Francis. 1977. *Gypsy Folk-Tales*. New York: Arno Press.

Hower, E. 1991. *Pomegranate Princess*. Detroit, MI: Wayne State University Press.

Kennedy, Patrick. 1976. *Irish Fireside Folktales*. Dublin: Mercier Press.

Langloh Parker, K., Henrietta Drake-Brockman, and Elizabeth Durack. 1966. *Australian Legendary Tales*. New York: Viking Press.

LeRoy, John D. 1985. *Kewa Tales*. Vancouver, BC: University of British Columbia Press.

Levy, Reuben. 1923. *Three Dervishes and Other Persian Tales*. Oxford: Oxford University Press.

Lewis-Williams, David. 2000. *Stories That Float from Afar*. Cape Town, TX: Texas A&M University Press.

Mayer, Mercer. 1980. *East of the Sun and West of the Moon*. New York: Four Winds Press.

McAlpine, Helen, William McAlpine, and Joan Kiddell-Monroe. 1997. *Japanese Tales and Legends*. Oxford: Oxford University Press.

McLaughlin, Marie L. 1990. *Myths and Legends of the Sioux*. Lincoln, NE: University of Nebraska Press.

Métayer, Maurice. 1977. *Tales from The Igloo*. New York: St. Martin's Press.

Morris, Cora. 1931. *The Gypsy Story Teller*. New York: Macmillan.

Muhawi, Ibrahim, and Sharif Kana'nah. 1989. *Speak Bird, Speak Again*. Berkeley, CA: University of California Press.

Palkó, Zsuzsanna, and Linda Dégh. 1996. *Hungarian Folktales*. Jackson, MI: University Press of Mississippi.

Petrovitch, Woislav. 1915. *Tales and Legends of the Serbians*. New York: Frederick Stokes.

Philip, Neil. 1995. *The Penguin Book of Scottish Folktales*. London: Penguin Books.

Ramanujan, A. K., Stuart H. Blackburn, and Alan Dundes. 1997. *A Flowering Tree and Other Oral Tales from India*. Berkeley, CA: University of California Press.

Riordan, James. 1990. *The Sun Maiden and the Crescent Moon*. New York: Interlink Books.

Saavedra, Yolando Pino. 1967. *Folktales of Chile*. Chicago, IL: University of Chicago Press.

Sexton, James D. 1992. *Mayan Folktales*. New York: Anchor Books.

Sharp Carter, Dorothy, and Trina Schart Hyman. 1974. *Greedy Mariani and Other Folktales of the Antilles*. New York: Atheneum.

Smith, W. R. 1970. *Myths and Legends of the Australian Aboriginals*. New York: Johnson Reprint Corporation.

Sun, Ruth, and Thanh Duc Ho. 1967. *Land of Seagull and Fox*. Rutland, VT: C. E. Tuttle.

Totten, Eugene C. and Mary Lou Totten. 1987. *Tales of Ticasuk*. Fairbanks, AK: University of Alaska Press.

Undset, Sigrid. 1948. *True and Untrue, and Other Norse Tales*. New York: A. A. Knopf.

Van Deusen, Kira. 1999. *The Raven and the Rock*. Seattle, WA: University of Washington Press.

von Löwis, August. 1971. *Russian Folktales*. London: Bell.

Wang, Chi-Chen. 1968. *Traditional Chinese Tales*. New York: Greenwood Press.

Werner, Alice. 1968. *Myths and Legends of the Bantu*. London: Cass.

Wheeler, Post, and Harold Gould Henderson. 1976. *Tales from Japanese Storytellers*. Rutland, VT: C. E. Tuttle.

Wilbert, Johannes, Karin Simoneau, Michel Perrin, and Cesáreo de Armellada. 1986. *Folk Literature of the Guajiro Indians*. Los Angeles, CA: UCLA Latin American Center Publications.

Wolkstein, Diane, and Elsa Henriquez. 1980. *The Magic Orange Tree and Other Haitian Folktales*. New York: Schocken Books.

Zenani, Nongenile Masithathu, and Harold Scheub. 1992. *The World and the Word*. Madison, WI: University of Wisconsin Press.

Cultural Groupings

1. Overall (n = 658 tales): Aboriginal Australian, African American, Blackfoot, Chamacoco, Dena, East African Tribes, Gê, Germany, Guajiro, Gypsy (Roma), Haiti, Hawaii, Hopi, Hungary, India, Inuit, Iraq, Ireland, Iroquois, Japan, Israel, Korea, !Kung San, Maya, Navaho, New Guinea, Nigerian Tribes, Nivkalé, China, Norway, Palestine, Persia, Mongolia, Russia, Scotland, Siberian Indians, Sikuani, Sioux, Slovakia, Southern African Tribes, Tibet, Tlingit, Vietnam, West African Tribes (excluding Nigeria), Yamana, Yanomami, Yugoslavia.

2. North America (n = 101 tales): Blackfoot, Dena, Hopi, Inuit, Iroquois, Maya, Navaho, Sioux, Tlingit.

3. South America (n = 109 tales): Chamacoco, Gê, Guajiro, Nivkalé, Sikuani, Yamana, Yanomami.

4. Europe (n = 135 tales): Germany, Gypsy (Roma), Hungary, Ireland, Norway, Scotland, Slovakia, Yugoslavia.

5. Western Europe (n = 72 tales): Germany, Ireland, Norway, Scotland.

6. Africa (and diaspora) (n = 91 tales): African American, East African Tribes, Haiti, !Kung San, Nigerian Tribes, Southern African Tribes, West African Tribes (excluding Nigeria).

7. Asia (n = 136 tales): China, Japan, Korea, India, Mongolia, Russia, Siberia, Tibet, Vietnam.

8. Bands and tribes (n = 337 tales): Aboriginal Australia, Blackfoot, Dena, East African Tribes, Hawaii, Hopi, Inuit, Iroquois, !Kung San, Navaho, New Guinea, Nigerian Tribes, Siberian Indians, Sioux, Southern African Tribes, Tlingit, West African Tribes.

9. Preindustrial states (n = 291 tales): Germany, Gypsy (Roma), Hungary, India, Iraq, Ireland, Japan, Israeli, Korea, China, Norway, Palestine, Persia, Mongolia, Russia, Scotland, Slovakia, Tibet, Vietnam, Yugoslav.

10. Male-analyzed tales (n = 141).
11. Female-analyzed tales (n = 517).
12. Tales from male-edited collections (n = 390).
13. Tales from female-edited collections (n = 158).

n=number of tales per culture.

Appendix B

Folktale Collections for Chapters 6 and 7

Indicates collections that were included in the "Beauty Myth" study, but not in the study of Romantic Love
Indicates collections that were included in the study of Romantic Love, but not in the study of the "Beauty Myth"

Anonymous. 1901. *Moorish Literature*. New York: Colonial Press.**
Asbjørnsen, P. C., J. E. Moe, G. Thorne-Thomsen. 1912. *East o' the Sun and West o' the Moon: With other Norwegian Folktales*. Chicago: Row, Peterson.
Ashliman, D. L. *Folktales from Japan and Japanese Legends of Supernatural Sweethearts*. http://www.pitt.edu/~dash/japan.html (accessed February 2005).
Batchelor, J. 1888. *Specimens of Ainu Folklore. Transactions of the Asiatic Society of Japan* 16:111–150, 18:25–86, 20:216–277.
Benedict, R. 1931. *Tales of the Cochiti Indians*. Washington, DC: U.S. Government Printing Office.
Boas, F. 1894. *Chinook Texts*. Washington, DC: U.S. Government Printing Office.
———. 1902. *Tsimshian Texts*. Washington, DC: U.S. Government Printing Office.
———. 1910. *Kwakiutl Tales*. New York: Columbia University Press.
———. 1932. *Bella Bella Tales*. New York: American Folk-lore Society.
Bogoras, W. 1910. *Chuckchee Mythology*. New York: G. E. Stechert.
———. 1913. *The Eskimo of Siberia*. New York: G. E. Stechert.
———. 1918. *Tales of Yukaghir, Lamut and Russianized Natives of Eastern Siberia*. New York: Anthropological Papers of The American Museum of Natural History Vol. XX, Part 1.
Brett, W. H. 1880. *Legends and Myths of the Aboriginal Indians of British Guiana*. London: W. W. Gardner.

Burton, R. F. 1850. *The Arabian nights.* http://www.sacred texts.com/neu/burt1k1/ (accessed February 2005).

Carmichael, A. 1922. *Indian Legends of Vancouver Island.* Toronto, Canada: Musson Books.

Carpenter, F. 1947. *Tales of a Korean Grandmother.* New York: Junior Literary Guild.**

Cole, M. C. 1916. *Philippine Folk Tales.* Chicago: A. C. McClurg.

Colum, P. 1925. *The Bright Islands.* New Haven: Yale University Press.

Cove, J. J. and G. F. MacDonald. 1987. *Tsimshian Narratives I: Tricksters, Shamans and Heroes.* Ottawa: Canadian Museum of Civilization.

———. 1987. *Tsimshian Narratives II: Trade and Warfare.* Ottawa: Canadian Museum of Civilization.

Crawford, J. M. 1888. *The Kalevala: The Epic Poem of Finland.* New York: J. B. Alden.

Cushing, F. H. 1901. *Zuñi Folk Tales.* New York: G. P. Putnam's Sons.*

Dorson, R. M. 1961. *Folk Legends of Japan.* Rutland, VT: C. E. Tuttle.

Downing, C. 1964. *Tales of the Hodja.* London: Oxford University Press.**

Epiphanius, H. and L. Leonidas. 1901. *Babylonian and Assyrian Literature Comprising the Epic of Izdubar: Hymns, Tablets, and Cuneiform Inscriptions.* New York: Colonial Press.

Giddings, R. W. 1978. *Yaqui Myths and Legends.* Tuscon: University of Arizona Press.*

Gill, W. W. 1876. *Myths and Songs of the South Pacific.* London: Henry S. King and Co.

Ginzberg, L., H. Szold, P. Radin, and B. Cohen. 1909. *The Legends of the Jews.* Philadelphia: The Jewish Publication Society of America.

Glew, R. S. and C. Babalé. 1993. *Hausa Folktales from Niger.* Athens, OH: Ohio University Center for International Studies.

Goetz, D., S. G. Morley, and A. Recinos. 1950. *Popol Vuh: The Sacred Book of the Ancient Quiché Maya.* Norman, OK: University of Oklahoma Press.

Griffis, W. E. 1918. *Dutch Fairy Tales for Young Folks.* New York: Thomas Y. Crowell.

Grimm, J. and W. Grimm. 1944. *Grimm's Fairy Tales.* New York: Pantheon Books.

Grinnell, G. B. 1892. *Blackfoot Lodge Tales: The Story of a Prairie People.* New York: Scribner.

Hall, E. S. 1998. *The Eskimo Storyteller: Folktales from Noatak, Alaska.* Fairbanks, AK: University of Alaska Press.

Honey, J. A. 1910. *South African Folk Tales.* New York: Baker & Taylor.**

Jacob, P. W. 1873. *Hindoo Tales or the Adventures of Ten Princes.* London: Strathan and Co.

Jacobs, J. 1892. *Indian Fairy Tales.* New York: G. P. Putnam.

———. 1898. *English Fairy Tales.* New York: G. P. Putnam.

Johnson, P. E. 1926. *Legends of Vancouver.* Toronto, Canada: McClelland and Stewart.

Johnston, H. A. S. 1966. *A Selection of Hausa stories.* Oxford: Clarendon Press.

Lang, A., and D. L. Gregory. 1948. *The Green Fairy Book.* New York: Longmans, Green.

Laughlin, R. M., and C. Karasik. 1988. *The People of the Bat: Mayan Tales and Dreams from Zinacantfin.* Washington, DC: Smithsonian Institute Press.

Leland, C. 1884. *The Algonquin Legends of New England.* Cambridge: The Riverside Press.

LeRoy, J. 1985. *Kewa Tales.* Vancouver, BC: University of British Columbia Press.

Lloyd, J. W., A. Comalk-Hawk-Kih, and E. H. Wood. 1911. *Aw-aw-tam Indian Nights: The Myths and Legends of the Pimas of Arizona.* Westfield, NJ: The Lloyd Group.*

Lummis, C. F. 1910. *Pueblo Indian Folk-Stories.* New York: Century.

Markham, C., and A. Valdez. 1910. *Apu Ollantay: A Drama of the Time of the Incas Sovereigns of Peru About A. D. 1470.* In *Incas of Peru*, edited by C. R. Markham. New York: Dutton.*

McLaughlin, M. 1990. *Myths and Legends of the Sioux.* Lincoln: University of Nebraska Press.

Miller, J. M. 1904. *Philippine Folklore Stories.* Boston, MA: Ginn.

Mindlin, B. 2002. *Barbecued Husbands and Other Stories From the Amazon.* New York: Verso.*

———. 1995. *Unwritten Stories of the Suruí Indians of Rondônia.* Austin, TX: University of Texas.*

Mitra, S. M. 1919. *Hindu Tales from the Sanskrit.* London: Macmillan.

Montejo, V. 1991. *The Bird Who Cleans the World and Other Mayan fables.* Willimantic, CT: Curbstone Press.

O'Bryan, A. 1956. *The Diné: Origin Myths of the Navaho Indians.* Washington, DC: U.S. Government Printing Office.*

Orczy, E. 1969. *Old Hungarian Fairy Tales.* New York: Dover Publications.

Ozaki, Y. T. 1905. *Japanese Fairy Tales.* New York: A. L. Burt.

Parker, K. L. and A. Lang. 1897. *Australian Legendary Tales: Folklore of the Noongahburrahs as Told to the Piccaninnies.* London: D. Nutt.

Peck, C. W. 1925. *Australian Legends: Tales Handed Down from the Remotest Times by the Autocthonous Inhabitants of our Land.* Sydney, Australia: Stafford.

Petrie, W. M. 1895. *Egyptian Tales.* London: Methuen.

Pino Saavedra, Y. 1967. *Folktales of Chile.* Chicago: University of Chicago Press.*

Ramanujan, A. K., S. H. Blackburn, and A. Dundes. 1997. *A Flowering Tree and Other Oral Tales from India.* Berkeley, CA: University of California Press.

Rasmussen, K. 1921. *Eskimo Folk-Tales.* London.

Redesdale, L. 1871. *Tales of Old Japan.* London: Macmillan.

Royall, T. 1987. *Japanese Tales.* New York: Pantheon.

Sadhu, S. L. 1962. *Folk Tales from Kashmir.* New York: Asia Publishing House.

Sanyshkap, A., X. Khunjis, Z. Yùméi, A. Serin, et al. 2005. *Western Yugur Folktales.* http://home.arcor.de/marcmarti/yugur/folktale/folktale.htm (accessed February 2005).

Sexton, J. D. 1992. *Mayan Folktales: Folklore from Lake Atitlán, Guatemala.* New York: Doubleday.

Shaihua, M. 1913. *Hausa Folk-Lore.* Oxford: Clarendon Press.

Shedlock, M. L. 1920. *Eastern Stories and Legends.* New York: E. P. Dutton.**

Smith, W. R. 1930. *Myths and Legends of the Australian Aboriginals.* New York: Johnson Reprint.

Steel, F. A., J. L. Kipling, and R. C. Temple. 1894. *Tales of the Punjab Told by the People.* London: Macmillan.

Swanton, J. R. 1905. *Haida Texts and Myths.* Washington, DC: U.S. Government Printing Office.

———. 1909. *Tlingit Myths and Texts.* Washington, DC: U.S. Government Printing Office.

———. 1929. *Myths and Stories of the Southeastern Indians.* Washington, DC: U.S. Government Printing Office.

Theal, G. M. 1886. *Kaffir Folklore: A Selection From the Traditional Tales Current Among the People Living on the Eastern Border of the Cape Colony.* London: S. Sonnenschein, Le Bas, and Lowrey.

Thomas, W. J. 1923. *Some Myths and Legends of the Australian Aborigines.* Melbourne, Australia: Whitcombe and Tombs.

Thompson, S. 1929. *Tales of the North Native American Indians.* Cambridge, MA: Harvard University Press.

Townsend, G. F. 1882. *Aesop's Fables.* Chicago: Belford, Clarke, and Co.

Voth, H. R. 1905. *The Traditions of the Hopi.* Chicago: Field Columbian Museum.*

Westervelt, W. D. 1910. *Legends of Ma-ui, a Demi-God of Polynesia and of his Mother Hina.* Honolulu, HI: Hawaiian Gazette.

———. 1916. *Hawaiian Legends of Volcanoes: Collected and Translated from the Hawaiian.* Boston: Ellis Press.

Wilbert, J. and K. Simoneau. 1978. *Folk Literature of the Gê Indians.* Los Angeles: University of California Latin American Center Publications.*

———. 1982. *Folk Literature of the Mataco Indians.* Los Angeles: University of California Latin American Center Publications.*

———. 1985. *Folk Literature of the Chorote Indians.* Los Angeles: University of California Latin American Center Publications.*

———. 1986. *Folk Literature of the Guajiro Indians.* Los Angeles: University of California Latin American Center Publications.*

————. 1987. *Folk Literature of the Chamacoco Indians.* Los Angeles: University of California Latin American Center Publications.*

————. 1987. *Folk Literature of the Nivakle Indians.* Los Angeles: University of California Latin American Center Publications.*

————. 1989. *Folk Literature of the Caduveo Indians.* Los Angeles: University of California Latin American Center Publications.*

————. 1991. *Folk Literature of the Cuiva Indians.* Los Angeles: University of California Latin American Center Publications.*

————. 1991. *Folk Literature of the Makka Indians.* Los Angeles: University of California Latin American Center Publications.*

————. 1990. *Folk Literature of the Yanomami Indians.* Los Angeles: University of California Latin American Center Publications.

————. 1992. *Folk Literature of the Sikuani Indians.* Los Angeles: University of California Latin American Center Publications.*

————. 1982. *Folk Literature of the Toba Indians.* Los Angeles: University of California Latin American Center Publications.*

Young, E. R. 1903. *Algonquin Indian Tales.* Cincinnati, OH: Jennings and Pye.

Works Cited

Alcock, J. 2001. *The Triumph of Sociobiology*. Oxford: Oxford University Press.

Alexander, R. 1987. *The Biology of Moral Systems*. New York: Aldine de Gruyter.

Alexander, R. D. and K. M. Noonan. 1979. "Concealment of Ovulation, Parental Care, and Human Social Evolution." In *Evolutionary Biology and Human Social Behavior: An Anthropological Perspective*, edited by N. A. Chagnon and W. Irons, 402–435. North Scituate, MA: Duxbury Press.

Andersson, M. 1994. *Sexual Selection*. Princeton: Princeton University Press.

Appiah, K. 1992. *In My Father's House: Africa in the Philosophy of Culture*. New York: Oxford University Press.

———. 2005. "The Battle of the Bien-Pensant." In *Theory's Empire: An Anthology of Dissent*, edited by D. Patai and W. Corral, 441–448. New York: Columbia University Press.

Arleo, A. 1997. "Counting-Out and the Search for Universals." *Journal of American Folklore* 110:391–407.

Arnold, M. 1864 [2001]. "The Function of Criticism at the Present Time." In *The Norton Anthology of Theory and Criticism*, edited by B. Leitch, 806–825. New York: Norton.

Ashcroft, B., G. Griffiths, and H. Tiffin. 1989. *The Empire Writes Back: Theory and Practice in Post-Colonial Literatures*. New York: Routledge.

Bacon, F. 1620 [2002]. *Novum Organum*. Cambridge: Cambridge University Press.

Baker-Sperry, L. and L. Grauerholz. 2003. "The Pervasiveness and Persistence of the Feminine Beauty Ideal in Children's Fairy Tales." *Gender and Society* 17:711–726.

Barash, D. and N. Barash. 2005. *Madame Bovary's Ovaries: A Darwinian Look at Literature*. New York: Delacorte Press.

Barbrook, A., C. Howe, N. Blake, and P. Robinson. 1998. "The Phylogeny of the Canterbury Tales." *Nature* 394:839.

Barkow, J., L. Cosmides, and J. Tooby, eds. 1992. *The Adapted Mind*. Oxford: Oxford University Press.

Baron Cohen, S. 2003. *The Essential Difference: The Truth About the Male and Female Brain.* New York: Penguin.

Barrett, L., R. Dunbar, and J. Lycett. 2003. *Human Evolutionary Psychology.* Princeton: Princeton University Press.

Barrett, P., P. Gautrey, S. Herbert, D. Kohn, and S. Smith. 1989. *Charles Darwin's Notebooks, 1836–1844: Geology, Transmutation of Species, Metaphysical Enquiries.* Ithaca, NY: Cornell University Press.

Barry, J. M. 2004. *The Great Influenza: The Epic Story of the Deadliest Plague in History.* New York: Penguin.

Bartels, A. and S. Zeki. 2000. "The Neural Basis of Romantic Love." *Neuroreport* 11:3829–3834.

———. 2004. "The Neural Correlates of Maternal and Romantic Love." *Neuroimage* 21:1155–1166.

Barthes, R. 1971. "Réponses." *Tel Quel* 47:89–107.

———. 1972. *Mythologies.* New York: Hill and Wang.

Beall, A. and R. Sternberg. 1995. "The Social Construction of Love." *Journal of Social and Personal Relationships* 12:417–438.

Benzon, W. 2005/2006. "Signposts for a Naturalist Criticism." *Entelechy* 6 (Fall/Winter). http://www.entelechyjournal.com/billbenzon.html. Accessed April 21, 2008.

Bernstein, M. 2007. "Experimental Philosophy Meets Experimental Design: 23 Questions." Paper presented at the annual convention of the Mid-South Philosophical Society.

Blackmore, J. 1978. "Is Planck's 'Principle' True?" *The British Journal for the Philosophy of Science* 29:347–349.

Blake, W. 1988. "Annotations to Sir Joshua Reynolds's Discourses, c. 1798–1809." In *The Complete Poetry and Prose of William Blake,* edited by David Erdman, 635–662. New York: Anchor Press.

Bloch, H. 1991. *Medieval Misogyny and the Invention of Western Romantic Love.* Chicago: University of Chicago Press.

Bloom, H. 1995. *The Western Canon: The Books and School of the Ages.* London: Macmillan.

Boas, F. 1911. *The Mind of Primitive Man.* New York: Macmillan.

Boghossian, P. 1996. "What the Sokal Hoax Ought to Teach Us: The Pernicious Consequences and Internal Contradictions of 'Postmodern' Relativism." *Times Literary Supplement,* December 13. 14–15

Bohman, J. 1988. "Introduction to Jean-Francois Lyotard." In *After Philosophy: End or Transformation?* edited by K. Baynes, J. Bohman, and T. McCarthy, 67–71. Cambridge, MA: MIT Press.

Booth, W. 1979. *Critical Understanding: The Power and Limits of Pluralism.* Chicago: University of Chicago Press.

———. 2004. "To: All Who Care About the Future of Criticism." *Critical Inquiry* 30:350–354.

Bordo, S. 1993. *Unbearable Weight: Feminism, Western Culture, and the Body.* Berkeley: University of California Press.

Bottigheimer, R. 1980. "The Transformed Queen: A Search for the Origins of Negative Female Archetypes in Grimms' Fairy Tales." *Amsterdamer Beitrage zur neueren Germanistik* 10:1–12.

———. 1982. "Tale Spinners: Submerged Voices in Grimms' Fairy Tales." *New German Critique* 27:141–150.

———. 1986. "Silenced Women in the Grimms' Tales: The Fit Between Fairy Tales and Society in Their Historical Context." In *Fairy Tales and Society: Illusion, Allusion, and Paradigm*, edited by Ruth Bottigheimer, 115–131. Philadelphia: University of Pennsylvania Press.

———. 1993. "Luckless, Witless, and Filthy-Footed: A Sociocultural Study and Publishing History Analysis of 'The Lazy Boy.'" *Journal of American Folklore* 106:259–284.

Bousquet, M. 2008. *How the University Works: Higher Education and the Low Wage Nation*. New York: New York University Press.

Boyd, B. 2003. "Review of *Shakespeare, Co-Author: A Historical Study of Five Collaborative Plays*." *Shakespeare Quarterly* 54:458–461.

———. 2005a. "Evolutionary Theories of the Arts." In *The Literary Animal*, edited by Jonathan Gottschall and David Sloan Wilson, 147–176. Evanston, IL: Northwestern University Press.

———. 2005b. "Literature and Evolution: A Bio-Cultural Approach." *Philosophy and Literature* 29:1–23.

———. 2006. "Getting it All Wrong." *American Scholar* 75:18–30.

Brizendine, L. 2006. *The Female Brain*. New York: Morgan Road Books.

Bromwich, D. 1997. "Scholarship as Social Action." In *What's Happened to the Humanities?* edited by Alvin Kernan, 220–244. Princeton, NJ: Princeton University Press.

Brooks, C. 1942 [1975]. *The Well Wrought Urn: Studies in the Structure of Poetry*. New York: Macmillan.

Brownmiller, S. 1975. *Against Our Will*. New York: Fawcett Columbine.

———. 1984. *Femininity*. New York: Linden Press.

Buck, D. 1991. "Forum on Universalism and Relativism in Asian Studies: Editor's Introduction." *The Journal of Asian Studies* 50:29–34.

Buss, D. M. 1989. "Sex Differences in Human Mate Preferences: Evolutionary Hypotheses Tested in 37 Cultures." *Behavioral and Brain Sciences* 12:1–49.

———. 2003. *The Evolution of Desire: Strategies in Human Mating*. New York: Basic Books.

———, ed. 2005. *The Handbook of Evolutionary Psychology*. New York: Wiley.

Buss, D. M. and D. Schmitt. 1993. "Sexual Strategies Theory: An Evolutionary Perspective on Human Mating." *Psychological Review* 100:204–232.

Butler, C. 2002. *Postmodernism: A Very Short Introduction*. Oxford: Oxford University Press.

Cahill, A. 2003. "Feminist Pleasure and Feminine Beautification." *Hypathia* 18:42–64.

Campbell, A. 2002. *A Mind of Her Own: The Evolutionary Psychology of Women*. Oxford: Oxford University Press.

Campbell, J. 1936 [1968]. *The Hero with a Thousand Faces*, 2nd ed. Princeton: Princeton University Press.

Capozzoli, M., L. McSweeney, and D. Sinha. 1999. "Beyond Kappa: A Review of Interrater Agreement Measures." *The Canadian Journal of Statistics* 27:3–23.

Carroll, J. 1995. *Evolution and Literary Theory*. St. Louis, MO: University of Missouri Press.

———. 2003. "Adaptationist Literary Study: An Emerging Research Program." *Style* 36:596–617.

———. 2004a. *Literary Darwinism: Evolution, Human Nature, and Literature*. New York: Routledge.

———. 2004b. "Modern Darwinism and the Pseudo-Revolutions of Stephen Jay Gould." In *Literary Darwinism: Evolution, Human Nature, and Literature*, 227–246. New York: Routledge.

———. 2008 (forthcoming). "An Evolutionary Paradigm for Literary Study." *Style*.

Carroll, J., J. Johnson, J. Gottschall, and D. Kruger (under consideration). *Graphing Jane Austen: Human Nature in British Novels of the Nineteenth Century*.

Cartwright, N. 1999. *The Dappled World: A Study of the Boundaries of Science*. Cambridge: Cambridge University Press.

Cavalli-Sforza, L. 2001. *Genes, Peoples, and Languages*. Berkeley, CA: University of California Press.

Chakrabarty, D. 2000. *Provincializing Europe: Postcolonial Thought and Historical Difference*. Princeton, NJ: Princeton University Press.

Clutton-Brock, T. H. and G. H. Parker. 1992. "Potential Reproductive Rates and the Operation of Sexual Selection." *Quarterly Review of Biology* 67:437–456.

Coe, K. 2003. *The Ancestress Hypothesis: Visual Art as Adaptation*. New Jersey: Rutgers University Press.

Cohen, J. 1960. "A Coefficient of Agreement for Nominal Scales." *Educational and Psychological Measurement* 20:37–46.

Cohen, R., ed. 2005. "Essays in the Humanities." *New Literary History* 36, 1.

Colapinto, J. 2001. *As Nature Made Him: The Boy Who Was Raised as a Girl*. New York: Harper Perennial.

Cook, V. 1976. "Lord Raglan's Hero: A Cross-Cultural Critique." *Florida Anthropologist* 87:147–154.

Cooke, B. 2002. *Human Nature in Utopia: Zamyatin's We*. Evanston, IL: Northwestern University Press.

Crews, F. 2001. *Postmodern Pooh*. New York: Northpoint Press.

———. 2005. "The Grand Academy of Theory." In *Theory's Empire: An Anthology of Dissent*, edited by D. Patai and W. Corral, 218–233. New York: Columbia University Press.

———. 2006. *Follies of the Wise: Dissenting Essays*. Emeryville, CA: Shoemaker and Hoard.

Cronin, H. 1993. *The Ant and the Peacock*. Cambridge: Cambridge University Press.

Culler, J. 1997. *Literary Theory: A Very Short Introduction*. Oxford: Oxford University Press.

Cultee, C. 1894. *Chinook Texts*. Washington, DC: U.S. Government Printing Office.

Cunningham, V. 2005. "Theory What Theory?" In *Theory's Empire: An Anthology of Dissent*, edited by D. Patai and W. Corral, 24–40. New York: Columbia University Press.

Daly, M. 1978. *Gyn/Ecology: The Metaethics of Radical Feminism*. Boston: Beacon.

Darwin, C. 1831–1836 [2001]. *Charles Darwin's Beagle Diary*. Cambridge: Cambridge University Press.

———. 1859 [2003]. *On the Origin of Species by Means of Natural Selection*. Peterborough, Ontario: Broadview Books.

———. 1871 [1998]. *The Descent of Man and Selection in Relation to Sex*. New York: Prometheus Books.

———. 1872 [1998]. *The Expression of the Emotions in Animals and Man*. Oxford: Oxford University Press.

———. 1877a. *The Autobiography of Charles Darwin*. New York: W. W. Norton.

———. 1877b [1993]. "A Biographical Sketch of an Infant." *Mind* 2:285–294.

Darwin, F. and A. C. Seward, eds. 1903. *More Letters of Charles Darwin*. London: John Murray.

Davis, C. 2004. *After Poststructuralism: Reading, Stories, and Theory*. New York: Routledge.

Dawkins, R. 1976 [1989]. *The Selfish Gene*. Oxford: Oxford University Press.

———. 1998. *Unweaving the Rainbow: Science, Delusion, and Appetite for Wonder*. New York: Houghton and Mifflin.

———. 2005. *The Ancestor's Tale*. New York: Houghton Mifflin.

———. 2006. *The God Delusion*. New York: Houghton and Mifflin.

De Beaugrande, R. 1989. "Synoptic Sketch of a New 'Society.'" *Poetics* 18:7–27.

De Beauvoir, S. 1949 [1953]. *The Second Sex*. New York: Knopf.

De Caro, F. 1983. *Women and Folklore: A Bibliographic Study*. Westport, CN: Greenwood Press.

De Rougement, D. 1939 [1983]. *Love in the Western World*. Princeton, NJ: Princeton University Press.

Degler, C. 1991. *In Search of Human Nature: The Decline and Revival of Darwinism in American Social Thought*. Oxford: Oxford University Press.

DeGraff, A. 1987. "The Fairy Tale and Women's Studies: An Annotated Bibliography." *Marvels and Tales* 1:76–82.

Delbanco, A. 1999. "The Decline and Fall of Literature." *New York Review of Books* 46, November 4.

Dennett, D. 1995. *Darwin's Dangerous Idea: Evolution and the Meanings of Life.* New York: Simon and Schuster.

Deresiewicz, W. 2008. "Professing Literature in 2008." *The Nation*, March 11, http://www.thenation.com/doc/20080324/deresiewicz. Accessed April 21, 2008

Diamond, J. 1997. *Guns, Germs, and Steel: The Fates of Human Societies.* New York: W. W. Norton and Company.

Dickemann, M. 1979. "Female Infanticide, Reproductive Strategies, and Social Stratification." In *Evolutionary Biology and Human Social Behavior: An Anthropological perspective*, edited by N. A. Chagnon and W. Irons, 321–367. North Scituate, MA: Duxbury Press.

Dion, K., E. Berscheid, and E. Walster. 1972. "What is Beautiful is Good." *Journal of Personality and Social Psychology* 24:285–290.

———. 1995. *Homo Aestheticus: Where Art Comes From and Why.* Seattle, WA: University of Washington Press.

———. 2000. *Art and Intimacy: How the Arts Began.* Seattle, WA: University of Washington Press.

Dobzhansky, T. 1973. "Nothing in Biology Makes Sense Except in the Light of Evolution." *The American Biology Teacher* 35:125–129.

Donoghue, D. 2005. "Theory, Theories, and Principles." In *Theory's Empire: An Anthology of Dissent*, edited by D. Patai and W. Corral, 109–120. New York: Columbia University Press.

Dunbar, R. and L. Barrett. 2007. *The Oxford Handbook of Evolutionary Psychology.* Oxford: Oxford University Press.

Dundes, A. 1968. *Every Man His Way: Readings in Cultural Anthropology.* Englewood Cliffs, NJ: Prentice Hall.

———. 1980. "The Hero Pattern and the Life of Jesus." In *Interpreting Folklore*, edited by Alan Dundes, 223–261. Bloomington, IN: Indiana University Press.

Dupré, J. 1993. *The Disorder of Things: Metaphysical Foundations of the Disunity of Science.* Cambridge, MA: Harvard University Press.

Durkheim, É. 1895 [1962]. *The Rules of the Sociological Method.* New York: Free Press.

Eagleton, T. 1981. "The Idealism of American Theory." *New Left Review* 125:53–65.

———. 1983 [1996]. *Literary Theory: An Introduction.* Minneapolis, MN: University of Minnesota Press.

———. 2003. *After Theory.* New York: Basic Books.

Eagly, A. and W. Wood. 1999. "The Origins of Sex Differences in Human Behavior: Evolved Dispositions Versus Social Roles." *American Psychologist* 54:408–423.

Eagly, A., R. Ashmore, and M. Makhijani. 1991. "What is Beautiful is Good, But...: A Meta-Analytic Review of Research on the Physical Attractiveness Stereotype." *Psychological Bulletin* 110:109–128.

Ehrenreich, B. and J. McIntosh. 1997. "The New Creationism: Biology Under Attack." *Nation*, June 9.

Ekman, P. 1998. "Universality of Emotional Expression? A Personal History of the Dispute." In *The Expression of the Emotions in Man and Animals,* edited by Paul Ekman, 363–396. Oxford: Oxford University Press.

Eldredge, N. and S. J. Gould. 1972. "Punctuated Equilibria: An Alternative to Phyletic Gradualism." In *Models in Paleobiology,* edited by T. J. M. Schopf, 82–115. San Francisco: Freedman, Cooper and Company.

Ellis, H. 1927. *Studies in the Psychology of Sex, Volume IV.* Philadelphia: F. A. Davis.

Ellis, J. M. 1997. *Literature Lost: Social Agendas and the Corruption of the Humanities.* New Haven: Yale University Press.

Emerson, R. W. 1844 [1990]. "The Poet." In *Essays: First and Second Series.* New York: Vintage. 261–291.

Engell, J. and A. Dangerfield. 1998. "The Market-Model University: Humanities in the Age of Money." *Harvard Magazine* 100:48–55, 111.

Etcoff, N. 1999. *Survival of the Prettiest.* New York: Doubleday.

Evans, D. 2005. "From Lacan to Darwin." In *The Literary Animal: Evolution and the Nature of Narrative,* edited by J. Gottschall and D. S. Wilson, 38–55. Evanston, IL: Northwestern University Press.

Faludi, S. 1992. *Backlash: The Undeclared War Against Women.* New York: Anchor.

Feingold, A. 1992. "Good-Looking People Are Not What We Think." *Psychological Bulletin* 111:304–341.

Feynman, R. 2001. *The Pleasure of Finding Things Out.* New York: Penguin.

Fish, S. 1976. "Interpreting the Variorum." *Critical Inquiry* 3:191–196.

———. 1980. "Interpreting 'Interpreting the Variorum.'" In *Is There a Text in This Class? The Authority of Interpretive Communities,* edited by Stanley Fish, 174–180. Cambridge, MA: Harvard University Press.

———. 1995. *Professional Correctness: Literary Studies and Political Change.* Oxford: Oxford University Press.

———. 2004. "Theory's Hope." *Critical Inquiry* 30:374–378.

———. 2008. *Save the World on Your Own Time.* Oxford: Oxford University Press.

Fisher, H., A. Aron, and L. Brown. 2005. "Romantic Love: An fMRI Study of a Neural Mechanism for Mate Choice." *Journal of Comparative Neurology* 493:58–62.

Fisher, H., A. Aron, D. Mashek, H. Li, and L. Brown. 2002. "Defining the Brain Systems of Lust, Romantic Attraction, and Attachment." *Archives of Sexual Behavior* 31:413–419.

Fisher, R. A. 1958. *The Genetical Theory of Natural Selection*. New York: Dover Publications.

Fleiss, J. L. 1971. "Measuring Nominal Scale Agreement Among Many Raters." *Psychological Bulletin* 76:378–382.

Flesch, W. 2008. *Comeuppance: Costly Signaling, Altruistic Punishment, and Other Biological Components of Fiction*. Cambridge: Harvard University Press.

Fludernik, M. 2005. "Threatening the University—The Liberal Arts and the Economization of Culture." *New Literary History* 36:57–70.

Fontenrose, J. 1959. *Python: A Study of the Delphic Myth and its Origins*. Berkeley, CA: University of California Press.

Ford, C. and F. Beach. 1951. *Patterns of Sexual Behavior*. New York: Harper and Row.

Freedman, R. 1986. *Beauty Bound*. New York: Lexington Books.

Freeman, D. 1983. *Margaret Mead and Samoa: The Making and Unmaking of an Anthropological Myth*. Cambridge, MA: Harvard University Press.

Friedan, B. 1963. *The Feminine Mystique*. New York: Dell.

Friedman, M. 1998. "Romantic Love and Personal Autonomy." In *Philosophy of Emotions*, edited by Peter French and Howard K. Wettstein, 162–181. Notre Dame, IN: University of Notre Dame Press.

Frye, N. 1949 [1969]. *Fearful Symmetry: A Study of William Blake*. Princeton, NJ: Princeton University Press.

Gangestad, S. W. and D. M. Buss. 1993. "Pathogen Prevalence and Human Mate Preferences." *Ethology and Sociobiology* 14:89–96.

Gangestad, S. and G. Scheyd. 2005. "The Evolution of Human Physical Attractiveness." *Annual Review of Anthropology* 34:523–548.

Gazzaniga, M. 2000. *The Mind's Past*. Berkeley, CA: University of California Press.

Geary, D. 1998. *Male, Female: The Evolution of Human Sex Differences*. Washington, DC: American Psychological Association.

Geary, D., J. Vigil, and J. Byrd-Craven. 2004. "Evolution of Human Mate Choice." *Journal of Sex Research* 41:27–42.

Ginzberg, L., ed. 1909. *The Legends of the Jews*. New York: Jewish Publication Society of America.

Gitlin, T. 2005. "The Cant of Identity." In *Theory's Empire: An Anthology of Dissent*, edited by D. Patai and W. Corral, 400–410. New York: Columbia University Press.

Goodheart, E. 1999. *Does Literary Studies Have a Future*. Madison, WI: University of Wisconsin Press.

———. 2005. "Casualties of the Culture Wars." In *Theory's Empire: An Anthology of Dissent*, edited by D. Patai and W. Corral, 508–522. New York: Columbia University Press.

Gottner-Abendroth, H. 1988. *Die Gottin und ihr Heroes: Die Matriarchalen Religionen in Mythos, Marchen und Dichtung*. Munich: Frauoffensive.

Gottschall, J. 2003. "The Tree of Knowledge and Darwinian Literary Studies." *Philosophy and Literature* 27:255–268.

———. 2004. "Literary Universals and the Sciences of the Mind." *Philosophy and Literature* 28:202–217.

———. 2005. "Quantitative Literary Study: A Modest Manifesto and Testing the Hypotheses of Feminist Fairy Tale Studies." In *The Literary Animal: Evolution and the Nature of Narrative*, edited by J. Gottschall and D. S. Wilson, 199–224. Evanston, IL: Northwestern University Press.

———. 2007. "Greater Emphasis on Female Attractiveness in *Homo sapiens*: A Revised Solution to an Old Evolutionary Riddle." *Evolutionary Psychology* 5:347–358.

———. 2008. *The Rape of Troy: Evolution, Violence, and the World of Homer.* Cambridge: Cambridge University Press.

Gottschall, J. and D. S. Wilson, eds. 2005. *The Literary Animal: Evolution and the Nature of Narrative.* Evanston, IL: Northwestern University Press.

Gottschall, J., J. Martin, H. Quish, and J. Rhea. 2004a. "Sex Differences in Mate Choice Criteria are Reflected in Folktales From Around the World and in Historical European Literature." *Evolution and Human Behavior* 25:102–112.

Gottschall, J., R. Berkey, C. Drown, M. Fleischner, M. Glotzbecker, K. Kernan, et al. 2004b. "Patterns of Characterization in Folk Tales Across Geographic Regions and Levels of Cultural Complexity: Literature as a Neglected Source of Quantitative Data." *Human Nature* 15:365–382.

——— 2005. "The Heroine with a Thousand Faces: Universal Trends in the Characterization of Female Folk Tale Protagonists." *Evolutionary Psychology* 3:85–103.

Gottschall, J., C. Callanan, N. Casamento, N. Gladd, K. Manganini, T. Milan-Robertson, et al. 2007. "Are the Beautiful Good in Western Literature? A Simple Illustration of the Necessity of Literary Quantification." *Journal of Literary Studies* 23:41–62.

Gottschall, J., E. Allison, P. Cahill, K. Carpentier, J. DeRosa, C. Drown, et al. 2008 (In press). "A Census of the Western Canon: Literary Studies and Quantification." *Interdisciplinary Literary Studies.*

Gould, S. J. 1991. "Male Nipples and Clitoral Ripples." In *Bully For Brontosaurus*, edited by S. J. Gould. New York: Penguin Books.

———. 1994. *Hens Teeth and Horses Toes.* New York: W. W. Norton.

Graff, G. 1989. *Professing Literature: An Institutional History.* Chicago: University of Chicago Press.

Graff, G. and M. Warner, eds. 1989. *The Origins of Literary Study in America: A Documentary Anthology.* New York: Routledge.

Graunt, J. 1662. *Natural and Political Observations Mentioned in a Following Index and Made upon the Bills of Mortality.* London: Martin, Allestry and Dicas.

Graunt, J. 1665. *London's Dreadful Visitation*. London: E. Cotes.

Greenblatt, S. 2003. " 'Stay, Illusion'—On Receiving Messages from the Dead." *PMLA* 118:417–426.

Greene, B. 2003. *The Elegant Universe: Superstrings, Hidden Dimensions, and the Quest for the Ultimate Theory*. New York: Vintage.

———. 2005. *The Fabric of the Cosmos: Space, Time, and the Texture of Reality*. New York: Vintage.

Haase, D., ed. 2000a. "Fairy Tale Liberation—Thirty Years Later." Special Issue, *Marvels and Tales* 14.

———. 2000b. "Feminist Fairy-Tale Scholarship: A Critical Survey and Bibliography." *Marvels and Tales* 14:15–63.

Hamilton, W. D. 1964. "The Genetical Evolution of Social Behavior, I and II." *Journal of Theoretical Biology* 7:1–52.

———. 1967. "Extraordinary Sex Ratios." *Science* 156:477–448.

Hansen, J., E. Reed, and M. Waters. 1986. *Cosmetics, Fashions, and the Exploitation of Women*. New York: Pathfinder Press.

Harpham, G. 2005a. "The End of Theory, the Rise of the Profession: A Rant in Search of Responses." In *Theory's Empire: An Anthology of Dissent*, edited by D. Patai and W. Corral, 381–394. New York: Columbia University Press.

———. 2005b. "Response." *New Literary History* 36:105–109.

Harris, H. 1995. "Rethinking Polynesian Heterosexual Relationships: A Case Study on Mangaia, Cook Islands." In *Romantic Passion*, edited by W. Jankowiak, 95–127. New York: Columbia University Press.

Haydon, F. H. 1876. *Correspondence and Table Talk*. London: Chatto and Windus.

Headlam Wells, R. 2005. *Shakespeare's Humanism*. Cambridge: Cambridge University Press.

Helms, C. 1987. "Storytelling, Gender and Language in Folk/Fairy Tales: A Selected Annotated Bibliography." *Women and Language* 10:3–11.

Hilfer, T. 2003. *The New Hegemony in Literary Studies: Contradictions in Theory*. Evanston, IL: Northwestern University Press.

Hines, M. 2005. *Brain Gender*. Oxford: Oxford University Press.

Hirsch, E. D. 1967. *Validity in Interpretation*. New Haven: Yale University Press.

Hockey, S. 2000. *Electronic Texts in the Humanities: Principles and Practice*. Oxford: Oxford University Press.

Hogan, P. 1997. "Literary Universals." *Poetics Today* 18:223–249.

———. 2003a. *Cognitive Science, Literature, and the Arts: A Guide for Humanists*. New York: Routledge.

———. 2003b. *The Mind and its Stories: Narrative Universals and Human Emotion*. Cambridge: Cambridge University Press.

Holbek, B. 1987. *Interpretation of Fairy Tales: Danish Folklore in a European Perspective*. Helsinki: Academia Scientiarum Fennica.

Howe, C., A. Barbrook, M. Spenser, P. Robinson, B. Bordalejo, and L. Mooney. 2001. "Manuscript Evolution." *Trends in Genetics* 17:147–152.

Hudson, V. and A. Den Boer. 2002. "A Surplus of Men, a Deficit of Peace: Security and Sex Ratios in Asia's Largest States." *International Security* 26:5–38.

———. 2005. *Bare Branches: The Security Implications of Asia's Surplus Male Population.* Cambridge, MA: MIT.

Hull, D., P. Tessner, and A. Diamond, 1978. "Planck's Principle: Do Younger Scientists Accept New Scientific Ideas with Greater Alacrity than Older Scientists?" *Science* 202:717–723.

Hunt, L. 1997. "Democratization and Decline: The Consequences of Demographic Change in the Humanities." In *What's Happened to the Humanities?* edited by Alvin Kernan, 17–31. Princeton, NJ: Princeton University Press.

Huxley, T. H. 1870 [2005]. "Biogenesis and Abiogenesis." In *Collected Essays of T. H. Huxley: Discourses Biological and Geological, Part Eight,* 229–271. Whitefish, MT: Kessinger Publishing.

Ibsch, E. 1989. " 'Facts' in the Empirical Study of Literature: The United States and Germany—A Comparison." *Poetics* 18:389–404.

Jacoby, R. 2005. "Thick Aestheticism and Thin Nativism." In *Theory's Empire: An Anthology of Dissent,* edited by D. Patai and W. Corral, 490–507. New York: Columbia University Press.

Jameson, F. 1991. *Postmodernism, or, The Cultural Logic of Late Capitalism.* Durham, NC: Duke University Press.

Janko, R. 1982. *Homer, Hesiod and the Hymns.* Cambridge: Cambridge University Press.

Jankowiak, W. ed. 1995. *Romantic Passion: A Universal Experience?* New York: Columbia University Press.

Jankowiak, W. and T. Fischer. 1992 [1998]. "A Cross-Cultural Perspective on Romantic Love." In *Human Emotions: A Reader,* edited by J. Jenkins and K. Oatley, 55–62. Oxford: Blackwell.

Jobling, I. 2001. "The Psychological Foundations of the Hero-Ogre Story: A Cross-Cultural Study." *Human Nature* 12:247–272.

Johnson, N. and S. Kotz. 1997. *Leading Personalities in Statistical Sciences: From the Seventeenth Century to the Present.* New York: John Wiley.

Johnson-Laird, P. and K. Oatley. 2000. "Cognitive and Social Construction in Emotions." In *Handbook of Emotions,* edited by Michael Lewis and Jeannette M. Haviland-Jones, 458–475. New York: Guilford.

Johnston, V. and M. Franklin. 1993. "Is Beauty in the Eye of the Beholder?" *Ethology and Sociobiology* 14:183–199.

Jones, D. 1996. *Physical Attractiveness and the Theory of Sexual Selection.* Ann Arbor, MI: University of Michigan Press.

Kahneman, D. and A. Tversky. 1996. "On the Reality of Cognitive Illusions." *Psychological Review* 103:582–591.

Kant, I. 1790 [1987]. *Critique of Judgment.* Indianapolis, IN: Hackett Publishing Co.

Kenny, A. 1986. *A Stylometric Study of the New Testament*. Oxford: Oxford University Press.

Kermode, Frank. 2005. "Changing Epochs." In *Theory's Empire: An Anthology of Dissent*, edited by D. Patai and W. Corral, 605–620. New York: Columbia University Press.

Kernan, A. 1992. *The Death of Literature*. New Haven: Yale University Press.

———, ed. 1997. *What's Happened to the Humanities?* Princeton, NJ: Princeton University Press.

Kluckhohn, C. 1960. "Recurrent Themes in Myths and Mythmaking." In *Myth and Mythmaking*, edited by H. Murray, 46–60. New York: George Braziller.

Knobe, J. "What is Experimental Philosophy?" (forthcoming). *The Philosopher's Magazine*.

Kolbenschlag, M. 1981. *Kiss Sleeping Beauty Goodbye: Breaking the Spell of Feminine Myths and Models*. Toronto: Bantam.

Koppel, M., S. Argamon, and A. Shimoni. 2002. "Automatically Categorizing Written Texts by Author Gender." *Literary and Linguistic Computing* 17:401–412.

Krippendorff, K. 1980. *Content Analysis: An Introduction to its Methodology*. Beverly Hills: Sage Publications.

Kroeber, A. L. 1910. "The Morals of Uncivilized Peoples." *American Anthropologist* 12:437–447.

———. 1917. "The Superorganic." *American Anthropologist* 19:163–213.

Kruger, D. and R. Nesse. 2004. "Sexual Selection and the Male:Female Mortality Ratio." *Evolutionary Psychology* 2:66–77.

Kruger, D., M. Fisher, and I. Jobling. 2005. "Proper Hero Dads and Dark Hero Cads: Alternate Mating Strategies Exemplified in British Romantic Literature." In *The Literary Animal*, edited by Jonathan Gottschall and David Sloan Wilson, 225–243. Evanston, IL: Northwestern University Press.

Lackman, J. 2006. "The X-Philes." *Slate*, March 2.

Langlois, J., L. Kalakanis, A. Rubenstein, A. Larson, M. Hallam, and M. Smoot. 2000. "Maxims or Myths of Beauty? A Meta-Analytic and Theoretical Review." *Psychological Bulletin* 126:390–423.

Laszlo, J. and C. Cupchick. 2003. "Psychology of Literary Narratives: Studies of Identity and Conflict." *Empirical Studies in the Arts* 23:1–4.

Latour, B. 2004. "Why Has Critique Run Out of Steam? From Matters of Fact to Matters of Concern." *Critical Inquiry* 30:225–248.

Leitch, V., ed. 2001. *The Norton Anthology of Theory and Criticism*. New York: Norton.

Lentricchia, F. 1996. "Last Will and Testament of an Ex-Literary Critic." *Lingua Franca*, September/October.

Lentricchia, F. and T. McLaughlin, eds. 1995. *Critical Terms for Literary Study*. Chicago: University of Chicago Press.

Levin, R. 2003. *Looking for an Argument: Critical Encounters with the New Approaches to the Criticism of Shakespeare and his Contemporaries.* Madison, NJ: Farleigh Dickinson University Press.

Lewontin, R., S. Rose, and L. Kamin. 1984. *Not in Our Genes.* New York: Pantheon.

Lieberman, M. 1972 [1986]. "Some Day My Prince Will Come: Female Acculturation Through the Fairy Tale." In *Don't Bet on the Prince: Contemporary Feminist Fairy Tales in North America and England,* edited by Jack Zipes, 185–200. New York: Methuen.

Lopez, J. and G. Potter. 2005. *After Postmodernism: An Introduction to Critical Realism.* New York: Continuum.

Lowie, R. H. 1917. "The Universalist Fallacy." *New Republic* 13:4–6.

Lundell, T. 1986. "Gender-Related Biases in the Type and Motif Indexes of Aarne and Thompson." In *Fairy Tales and Society: Illusion, Allusion, and Paradigm,* edited by Ruth Bottigheimer, 149–163. Philadelphia: University of Pennsylvania Press.

Lurie, A. 1970. "Fairy Tale Liberation." *New York Review of Books* 17, December. 42–44

———. 1971. "Witches and Fairies: Fitzgerald to Updike." *New York Review of Books* 17, December. 6–11

Lyotard, J. F. 1986 [2001]. "Defining the Postmodern." In *The Norton Anthology of Theory and Criticism,* edited by B. Leitch, 1612–1615. New York: Norton.

Macey, D. 2000. *Dictionary of Critical Theory.* New York: Penguin.

Magill, F. 1995. *Masterplots II: Women's Literature Series.* Pasadena, CA: Salem Press.

Mantzavinos, C. 2005. *Naturalistic Hermeneutics.* Cambridge: Cambridge University Press.

Martindale, C. 1990. *The Clockwork Muse: The Predictability of Artistic Change.* New York: Basic Books.

———. 1996. "Empirical Questions Deserve Empirical Answers." *Philosophy and Literature* 20:347–361.

Marx, K. 1977. "For a Ruthless Criticism of Everything Existing." Letter to Arnold Ruge, 1843. In *Karl Marx: Selected Writings,* edited by David McLellan, 12–15. Oxford: Oxford University Press.

Max, D. 2005. "The Literary Darwinists." *New York Times Magazine,* November 6.

Mayr, E. 1982. *The Growth of Biological Thought: Diversity, Evolution, and Inheritance.* Cambridge, MA: Harvard University Press.

———. 2001. *What Evolution Is.* New York: Basic Books.

McDonald, L. 1993. *The Early Origins of the Social Sciences.* Montreal and Kingston Canada: McGill-Queen's University Press.

McDougall, W. 1923. *An Outline of Psychology.* New York: Scribner.

McQuillan, M., R. Mcdonald, R. Purves, and S. Thompson, eds. 2000. *Post-Theory: New Directions in Critique.* Edinburgh, UK: Edinburgh University Press.

Menand, L. 1997. "The Demise of Disciplinary Authority." In *What's Happened to the Humanities?* edited by Alvin Kernan, 201–219. Princeton, NJ: Princeton University Press.

———. 2001. "The Marketplace of Ideas." *American Council of Learned Societies Occasional Paper*, no. 49. http://www.acls.org/op49.htm. Accessed. April 21, 2008

———. 2005. "Dangers Within and Without." *Profession* 10–17.

Messeri, P. 1988. "Age Differences in the Reception of New Scientific Theories: The Case of Plate Tectonics Theory." *Social Studies of Science* 18:91–112.

Miall, D. 2006. *Literary Reading: Empirical and Theoretical Studies*. New York: Peter Lang.

Michelson, D. 2006. "Re-reading the Signposts: A Response to William Benzon's Book Review 'Signposts for a Naturalist Criticism.'" *Entelechy* 7 (Spring/Summer). http://www.entelechyjournal.com/davidmichelson. htm. Accessed April 21, 2008.

Miller, B. 1981. *The Endangered Sex: Neglect of Female Children in Rural North India*. Ithaca: Cornell University Press.

Miller, G. 1998. "How Mate Choice Shaped Human Nature: A Review of Sexual Selection and Human Evolution." In *Handbook of Evolutionary Psychology: Ideas, Issues, and Applications*, edited by C. Crawford and D. Krebs, 87–130. London: Lawrence Erlbaum Associates.

———. 2001. *The Mating Mind*. New York: Anchor Books.

Mills, M. 1985. "Sex Role Reversals, Sex Changes, and Transvestite Disguise in the Oral Tradition of a Conservative Muslim Community in Afghanistan." In *Women's Folklore, Women's Culture*, edited by R. Jordan and S. Kalicik, 187–213. Philadelphia: University of Pennsylvania Press.

Mitchell, W., ed. 2004. "The Future of Criticism—A Critical Inquiry Symposium." *Critical Inquiry* 30, 2.

Moretti, F. 2005. *Graphs, Maps, and Trees: Abstract Models for a Literary History*. New York: Verso.

Moulton, R. 1888 [1989]. "Shakespeare as Dramatic Artist: A Study of Inductive Literary Criticism." In *The Origins of Literary Studies in America: A Documentary Anthology*, edited by G. Graff and M. Warner, 61–76. New York: Routledge.

Mueller, J., ed. 1993. "Universals/Essentialisms." Special Issue, *Modern Philology* 90.

Murdock, G. P. 1957. "World Ethnographic Sample." *American Anthropologist* 59:664–688.

———. 1981. *Atlas of World Cultures*. Pittsburgh: University of Pittsburgh Press.

Nanda, M. 2005. "Postcolonial Science Studies." In *Theory's Empire: An Anthology of Dissent*, edited by D. Patai and W. Corral, 575–584. New York: Columbia University Press.

Neuendorf, K. 2002. *The Content Analysis Guidebook*. Thousand Oaks, CA: Sage Publications.

Nichols, S. 2004. "Folk Concepts and Intuitions: From Philosophy to Cognitive Science." *Trends in Cognitive Sciences* 8:514–518.

Nitschke, A. 1980. "Aschenputtel aus der Sicht der Historicshen Verhaltensforschung." In *Und Wenn Sie Nicht Gestoben Sind: Perspektiven auf das Marchen*, edited by Helmut Brackert, 71–88. Frankfurt: Suhrkamp.

Nordlund, M. 2002. "Consilient Literary Interpretation." *Philosophy and Literature* 26:312–333.

———. 2007. *Shakespeare and the Nature of Love: Literature, Culture, Evolution*. Evanston, IL: Northwestern University Press.

Oakley, F. 1997. "Ignorant Armies and Nighttime Clashes." In *What's Happened to the Humanities?* edited by Alvin Kernan, 63–83. Princeton, NJ: Princeton University Press.

O'Hara, D. T. 1983. "Revisionary Madness: The Prospects of American Literary Theory at the Present Time." *Critical Inquiry* 9:725–742.

Olson, S. 2002. *Mapping Human History: Discovering the Past Through Our Genes*. Boston: Houghton Mifflin.

Orenstein, C. 2002. *Little Red Riding Hood Uncloaked: Sex, Morality and the Evolution of a Fairy Tale*. New York: Basic Books.

Oster, E. 2005. "Hepatitis B and the Case of the Missing Women." *Journal of Political Economy* 113:1163–1216.

Patai, D. and W. Corral, eds. 2005a. *Theory's Empire: An Anthology of Dissent*. New York: Columbia University Press.

———. 2005b. Introduction to *Theory's Empire: An Anthology of Dissent*, edited by D. Patai and W. Corral, 1–17. New York: Columbia University Press.

Perloff, M. 2005. "Crisis in the Humanities? Reconfiguring Literary Study for the Twenty-First Century." In *Theory's Empire: An Anthology of Dissent*, edited by D. Patai and W. Corral, 668–684. New York: Columbia University Press.

Person, E. S. 1992. "Romantic Love: At the Intersection of the Psyche and the Cultural Unconscious." In *Affect: Psychoanalytic Perspectives*, edited by Theodore Shapiro and Robert N. Emde, 383–412. Madison, CT: International Universities Press.

Pinker, S. 1995. *How The Mind Works*. New York: Norton.

———. 2000. *The Language Instinct*. New York: Perennial Press.

———. 2002. *The Blank Slate*. New York: Viking.

———. 2007. *The Stuff of Thought: Language as a Window into Human Nature*. New York: Viking.

Planck, M. 1949. *Scientific Autobiography and Other Papers*. New York: Philosophical Library.

Poovey, M. 2004. "For What it's Worth..." *Critical Inquiry* 30:429–433.

Popping, R. 2000. *Computer-Assisted Text Analysis*. London: Sage Publications.

Porter, T. 1986. *The Rise of Statistical Thinking, 1820–1900*. Princeton, NJ: Princeton University Press.

Potter, W. and D. Levine-Donnerstein. 1999. "Rethinking Validity and Reliability in Content Analysis." *Journal of Applied Communication Research* 27:258–284.

Propp, V. 1968. *Morphology of the Folktale*. Austin, TX: University of Texas Press.

Quasthoff, U. 1996. "Narrative Universals? Some Considerations and Perspectives." In *Contrastative Sociolinguistics*, edited by Marlis Hellinger and Ulrich Ammon, 475–495. Berlin: Mouton de Gruyter.

Rabkin, E. 2004. "Science Fiction and the Future of Criticism." *PMLA* 119:457–473.

Ragan, K. 1998a. *Fearless Girls, Wise Women, and Beloved Sisters: Heroines in Folktales From Around the World*. New York: Norton.

———. 1998b. Introduction to *Fearless Girls, Wise Women, and Beloved Sisters: Heroines in Folktales from Around the World*, edited by Kathleen Ragan, xxi–xxvii. New York: Norton.

———. Unpublished Manuscript. "What Happened to the Heroines in Folktales: A Statistical Analysis of the Cultural Filters Between Oral and Published Folktales." To be published in the Fall 2009 issue of the journal *Marvels and Tales*.

Raglan, F. R. S. 1936 [1990]. *The Hero: A Study in Tradition, Myth, and Drama*. Princeton, NJ: Princeton University Press.

Ramsay Smith, W. 1930 [1970]. *Myths and Legends of the Australian Aboriginals*. New York: Johnson.

Rank, O. 1909. *The Myth of the Birth of the Hero*. New York: Journal of Nervous and Mental Disease Publishing.

Rhodes, G. 2006. "The Evolutionary Psychology of Facial Beauty." *Annual Reviews of Psychology* 57:199–226.

Rhodes, G. and L. Zebrowitz, eds. 2002. *Facial Attractiveness: Evolutionary, Cognitive and Social Perspectives*. Westport, CT: Ablex Publishing.

Richardson, A. 2000. "Rethinking Romantic Incest: Human Universals, Literary Representation, and the Biology of the Mind." *New Literary History* 31:553–572.

Richardson, P. and R. Boyd. 2005. *Not by Genes Alone: How Culture Transformed Human Evolution*. Chicago: University of Chicago Press.

Ridley, M. 1995. *The Red Queen*. New York: Penguin Books.

———. 2003. *Nature Via Nurture*. New York: Harper Collins.

Robinson, H. C. 1869. *Diary, Reminiscences, and Correspondences of Henry Crabb Robinson*. London: Macmillan.

Rose, H. and S. Rose, eds. 2000. *Alas, Poor Darwin: Arguments Against Evolutionary Psychology*. New York: Harmony.

Ross, J. 2006. "Review of *The Literary Animal: Evolution and the Nature of Narrative*, edited by J. Gottschall and D. S. Wilson." *Journal of the American Medical Association* 295:1457.

Rourke, L., T. Anderson, D. Garrison, and D. Archer. 2001. "Methodological Issues in the Content Analysis of Computer Conference Transcripts." *International Journal of Artificial Intelligence in Education* 12:8–22.

Rowe, K. 1986. "Feminism and Fairy Tales." In *Don't Bet on the Prince: Contemporary Feminist Fairy Tales in North America and England*, edited by Jack Zipes, 209–226. New York: Methuen.

Ryle, G. 1949. *The Concept of the Mind*. Chicago, IL: University of Chicago.

Sabin, M. 1997. "Evolution and Revolution: Change in the Literary Humanities, 1968–1995." In *What's Happened to the Humanities?* edited by Alvin Kernan, 84–106. Princeton, NJ: Princeton University Press.

Sagan, C. 1997. *The Demon Haunted World*. New York: Ballantine Books.

Sarup, M. 1993. *An Introductory Guide to Post-Structuralism and Postmodernism*. Harlow, England: Longman.

Scalise Sugiyama, M. 2005. "Reverse Engineering Narrative: Evidence of Special Design." In *The Literary Animal*, edited by Jonathan Gottschall and David Sloan Wilson, 177–198. Evanston, IL: Northwestern University Press.

Schmidt, S. 1982. *Foundations of an Empirical Study of Literature: Components of Basic Theory*. Hamburg, Germany: Helmut, Buske, Verlag.

———. 1992. "Looking Back–Looking Ahead. Literary Studies: Trends in the Nineties." *Poetics* 21:1–4.

Schoemacher, C. 2004. "A Critical Appraisal of the Anorexia Statistics in *The Beauty Myth*: Introducing Wolf's Overdo and Lie Factor (WOLF)." *Eating Disorders: The Journal of Treatment and Prevention* 12:97–102.

Scholes, R. 1999. *The Rise and Fall of English*. New Haven: Yale University Press.

———. 2005. "Whither, or Wither, the Humanities?" *Profession* 7–9.

———. 2006. "Response to Hoff and Fromm." *PMLA* 121:297–298.

Schram, D. and G. Steen, eds. 2001. *The Psychology and Sociology of Literature: In Honor of Elrud Ibsch*. Amsterdam: John Benjamins.

Schreibman, S., R. Siemens, and J. Unsworth, eds. 2004. *A Companion to the Digital Humanities*. Oxford: Blackwell.

Segestrale, U. 2000. *Defenders of the Truth*. Oxford: Oxford University Press.

Sen, A. 1990. "More than 100 Million Women Are Missing." *New York Review of Books* 37, December 20. 61–66

Shermer, M. 2006. *Why Darwin Matters: The Case Against Intelligent Design*. New York: Owl Books.

Sidanius, J. and F. Pratto. 2004. *Social Dominance: An Intergroup Theory of Social Hierarchy and Oppression*. Cambridge: Cambridge University Press.

Siegel, L. 2005. "Queer Theory, Literature, and the Sexualization of Everything: The Gay Science." In *Theory's Empire: An Anthology of*

Dissent, edited by D. Patai and W. Corral, 424–440. New York: Columbia University Press.

Siemens, R. and S. Schreibman, eds. 2008. *A Companion to Digital Literary Studies*. Oxford: Blackwell.

Singer, P. 1999. *A Darwinian Left: Politics, Evolution, and Cooperation*. New Haven: Yale.

Singh, D., P. Renn, and A. Singh. 2007. "Did the Perils of Abdominal Obesity Affect Depiction of Feminine Beauty in the Sixteenth to Eighteenth Century British Literature? Exploring the Health and Beauty Link." *Proceedings of The Royal Society London, Series B* 274:891–894.

Slingerland, E. 2008. *What Science Offers the Humanities: Integrating Body and Culture*. Cambridge: Cambridge University Press.

Smith, J. 1995. "Genes, Memes, and Minds." *New York Review of Books* 42, November 30.

Smolin, L. 2006. *The Trouble with Physics*. New York: Houghton Mifflin.

Sommers, C. 1994. *Who Stole Feminism?* New York: Simon and Schuster.

Spivak, G. 2005. *Death of a Discipline*. New York: Columbia University Press.

Stanton, D., M. Bérubé, L. Cassuto, M. Eaves, J. Guillory, and D. Hall. 2007. "Report of the MLA Taskforce on Evaluating Scholarship for Tenure and Promotion." http://www.mla.org/tenure_promotion. Accessed April 21, 2008

St. Clair, W. 2007. *The Reading Nation in the Romantic Period*. Cambridge: Cambridge University Press.

Stearns, P. 2000. "History of Emotions: Issues of Change and Impact." In *Handbook of Emotions*, edited by Michael Lewis and Jeannette Haviland-Jones, 16–29. New York: Guilford Press.

Sternberg, M. 2003a. "Universals of Narrative and Their Cognitivist Fortunes (I)." *Poetics Today* 24:297–396.

———. 2003b. "Universals of Narrative and Their Cognitivist Fortunes (II)." *Poetics Today* 24:517–639.

Stigler, S. 1986. *The History of Statistics: The Measurement of Uncertainty Before 1900*. Cambridge, MA: Harvard University Press.

———. 1999. *Statistics on the Table: The History of Statistical Concepts and Methods*. Cambridge, MA: Harvard University Press.

Stone, K. 1986. "Feminist Approaches to the Interpretation of Fairy Tales." In *Fairy Tales and Society: Illusion, Allusion, and Paradigm*, edited by Ruth Bottigheimer, 229–235. Philadelphia: University of Pennsylvania Press.

Storey, R. 1996. *Mimesis and the Human Animal*. Evanston, Illinois: Northwestern University Press.

Sugiyama, L. 2005. "Physical Attractiveness in Adaptationist Perspective." In *The Handbook of Evolutionary Psychology*, edited by David Buss, 292–333. New York: Wiley.

Sulloway, F. 1996. *Born to Rebel: Birth Order, Family Dynamics, and Creative Lives*. New York: Pantheon.

Symons, D. 1979. *The Evolution of Human Sexuality.* Oxford: Oxford University Press.

———. 1995. "Beauty is in the Adaptations of the Beholder: The Evolutionary Psychology of Human Female Sexual Attractiveness." In *Sexual Nature/Sexual Culture* edited by P. Abramson and S. Pinkerton, 80–118. Chicago: University of Chicago Press.

Tatar, M. 1987. *The Hard Facts of the Grimms' Fairy Tales.* Princeton, NJ: Princeton University Press.

Tchana, K. and T. Hyman. 2000. *The Serpent Slayer and Other Stories of Strong Women.* Boston: Little, Brown.

Tetlock, P. 1995. "Complex Answers to a Simple Question: Is Integrative Complexity 'Politically Correct?'" In *The Social Psychologists: Research Adventures,* edited by Gary Brannigan and Matthew Merrens, 139–153. New York: The McGraw-Hill.

Thompson, S. 1932–1936. *Motif-Index of Folk-Literature.* Bloomington, IN: Indiana University Press.

———. 1946. *The Folktale.* New York: The Dryden Press.

———. 2005. "Traveling Through American Criticism." In *Theory's Empire: An Anthology of Dissent,* edited by D. Patai and W. Corral, 52–59. New York: Columbia University Press.

Toerien, M. and S. Wilkinson. 2003. "Gender and Body Hair: Constructing the Feminine Woman." *Woman's Studies International Forum* 26:333–344.

Tooby, J. and L. Cosmides. 1992. "The Psychological Foundations of Culture." In *The Adapted Mind,* edited by Jerome Barkow, Leda Cosmides, and John Tooby, 19–136. Oxford: Oxford University Press.

Travis, C., K. Meginnis, and K. Bardari. 2000. "Beauty, Sexuality, and Identity: The Social Control of Women." In *Sexuality, Society, and Feminism: Psychological Perspectives on Women,* edited by C. Travis and J. White, 237–272. Washington, DC: American Psychological Association.

Trilling, L. 1939. *Matthew Arnold.* New York: Norton.

Trivers, R. 1971. "The Evolution of Reciprocal Altruism." *The Quarterly Review of Biology* 46:35–57.

———. 1972. "Parental Investment and Sexual Selection." In *Sexual Selection and the Descent of Man 1871–1971,* edited by B. Campbell, 136–179. Chicago, IL: Aldine Publishing.

———. 1974. "Parent-Offspring Conflict." *American Zoologist* 14:249–264.

Trivers, R. and D. Willard. 1973. "Natural Selection of Parent Ability to Vary the Sex Ratios of Offspring." *Science* 179:90–92.

Turchin, P. 2003. *Historical Dynamics: Why States Rise and Fall.* Princeton, NJ: Princeton University Press.

———. 2005. *War and Peace and War: The Life Cycles of Imperial Nations.* New York: Plume.

Tylor, E. 1871. *Primitive Culture.* London: J. Murray.

Tyson, L. 1999. *Critical Theory Today.* New York: Garland.

Vandermassen, G. 2005. *Who's Afraid of Charles Darwin: Debating Feminism and Evolutionary Theory.* New York: Rowman and Littlefield Publishers.

Van Peer, W., J. Hakemulder, and S. Zyngier. 2007. *Muses and Measures. Empirical Research Methods for the Humanities.* Cambridge: Cambridge Scholars Publishing.

Vickers, B. 2002. *Shakespeare, Co-Author: A Historical Study of Five Collaborative Plays.* Oxford: Oxford University Press.

———. 2005. "Masters and Demons." In *Theory's Empire: An Anthology of Dissent,* edited by D. Patai and W. Corral, 247–270. New York: Columbia University Press.

Von Hahn, J. 1876. *Sagwissenschaftliche Studien.* Jena: Mauke.

Wallace, A. R. 1867. *Westminster Review.* July.

Warner, J. 1998. *Against the Spirit of System: The French Impulse in Nineteenth Century American Medicine.* Princeton, NJ: Princeton University Press.

Weber, R. 1990. *Basic Content Analysis.* Newbury Park, California: Sage Publications.

Weinberg, S. 1992. *Dreams of a Final Theory.* New York: Pantheon Books.

Weisbuch, R. 1999. "Six Proposals to Revive the Humanities." *Chronicle of Higher Education,* March 26.

Wells, S. 2004. *The Journey of Man: A Genetic Odyssey.* New York: Random House.

Westermarck, E. 1921. *The History of Human Marriage, Volume I.* London: Macmillan.

Whitfield, J. 2006. "Textual Selection." *Nature* 439:388–389.

Wilde, O. 1888 [1908]. "The Critic as Artist." In *The First Collected Edition of the Works of Oscar Wilde,* edited by Robert Ross. London: Methuen and Co.

Williams, G. 1966. *Adaptation and Natural Selection.* Princeton: Princeton University Press.

Wilson, D. S. 2007. *Evolution for Everyone.* New York: Delacorte.

Wilson, D. S. and E. O. Wilson. 2007. "Rethinking the Theoretical Foundation of Sociobiology." *The Quarterly Review of Biology* 82: 327–348.

Wilson, E. O. 1975. *Sociobiology: The New Synthesis.* Cambridge: Harvard University Press.

———. 1998. *Consilience: The Unity of Knowledge.* New York: Knopf.

Wilson, W. 1893 [1989]. "Mere Literature." In *The Origins of Literary Studies in America: A Documentary Anthology,* edited by G. Graff and M. Warner, 82–89. New York: Routledge.

Windram, H., C. Howe, and M. Spencer. 2005. "The Identification of Exemplar Change in the *Wife of Bath's Prologue* Using the Maximum Chi-Square Method." *Literary and Linguistic Computing* 20:189–204.

Woit, P. 2006. *Not Even Wrong.* New York: Basic Books.

Wolf, N. 1991. *The Beauty Myth: How Images of Female Beauty are Used Against Women.* New York: William Morrow.

———. 2002. New Introduction to *The Beauty Myth: How Images of Female Beauty are Used Against Women,* 1–6. New York: William Morrow.

Wollstonecraft, M. 1792. *A Vindication of the Rights of Woman.* Boston: Peter Edes.

Wood, W. and A. Eagly. 2002. "A Cross-Cultural Analysis of the Behavior of Women and Men: Implications for the Origins of Sex Differences." *Psychological Bulletin* 128:699–727.

Woodring, C. 1999. *Literature: An Embattled Profession.* New York: Columbia University Press.

Wright, R. 1995. *The Moral Animal.* New York: Vintage Books.

Yolen, J. 2000a. Foreword to *Fearless Girls, Wise Women, and Beloved Sisters: Heroines in Folktales From Around the World,* edited by Kathleen Ragan, xvii–xx. New York: W. W. Norton.

———. 2000b. Introduction to *Not One Damsel in Distress.* New York: Harcourt.

Yolen, J. and S. Guevera. 2000. *Not One Damsel in Distress: World Folktales for Strong Girls.* San Diego, CA: Harcourt.

Zipes, J. 1979–1980. "Who's Afraid of the Brother's Grimm? Socialization and Politi[ci]zation Through Fairy Tales." *The Lion and the Unicorn* 32:4–56.

———. 1983a. *Fairy Tales and the Art of Subversion: The Classical Genre for Children and the Process of Civilization.* New York: Wildman.

———. 1983b. *The Trials and Tribulations of Little Red Riding Hood.* New York: Bergin and Garvey Publishers.

———. 1986. Introduction to *Don't Bet on the Prince: Contemporary Feminist Fairy Tales in North America and England,* edited by Jack Zipes, 1–38. New York: Methuen.

———. 1994. *Fairy Tale as Myth; Myth as Fairy Tale.* Lexington, KT: University of Kentucky Press.

Index

disinterestedness, 67–8, 71–2,
  74–5, 176
Dobzhansky, Theodosius, 148
Durkheim, Émile, 18, 31

Eagleton, Terry, 7, 72, 81
Eagly, Alice, 122–4
Emerson, Ralph Waldo, 57
essentialism, 5, 6, 113, 119
  as un-biological, 124–5
  versus "population thinking,"
    124–5
Etcoff, Nancy, 149
evolutionary psychology, 22–7, 41,
  93–4
  as biosocial, 33
  evidence sources, 25–6
  humanities attitudes toward,
    22–3
  hypothesis testing, 24–5
  ideological ramifications, 27–32,
    33–4, 81
  and just-so stories, 23–4
  and racial differences, 31
  scientific controversy, 22–7
evolutionary theory, 13, 21
  adaptation versus by-product,
    122–4
  kin selection theory, 93–4
  and Naziism, 31
  and population thinking, 124–5
  and secular creationism, 21–2,
    122–4
  sexual selection, 94
  slow acceptance of, 30

female protagonists
  activity versus passivity, 94,
    108
  ages of, 100
  altruism of, 110
  emphasis on beauty, 105–6,
    127–9
  heroism of, 108
  marriage patterns, 100–5
  mating preferences of, 100–5

similarities to male protagonists,
    125
  summary of traits, 110
  see also female protagonists,
    underrepresentation of;
    feminist fairy tale studies
female protagonists,
  underrepresentation of, 94,
    98–9, 117, 127–9, 139–50,
    147, 150–5
  editorial bias as explanation,
    150–1
  as reflecting life in traditional
    societies, 153–4
  storyteller bias as explanation,
    151–3
feminism, 74, 125–6
feminist fairy tale studies, 115–16
  and activity/passivity of female
    characters, 117
  and beauty of female characters,
    118
  and heroic female characters, 118
  influence of, 116
  and male editorial dominance,
    97, 120–1, 150–1
  and marriage, 119
  and social constructivism, 111,
    115–16, 119–20
  and stigmatization of older
    females, 119
  and underrepresentation of
    female characters, 117
  see also female folktale
    protagonists; female
    protagonists,
    underrepresentation of
Feynman, Richard, 56
Fish, Stanley, ix, 63, 77
folktale case studies
  coding procedures, 95–6, 135–6,
    162–3
  intercoder reliability, 97–8,
    127–8, 138–9
  limitations of, 97–8, 127–8,
    136–8, 163, 165–7, 168